W9-AOG-858

THE PHILOSOPHICAL VISION
OF JOHN DUNS SCOTUS

THE PHILOSOPHICAL VISION
OF JOHN DUNS SCOTUS

AN INTRODUCTION

MARY BETH INGHAM AND
MECHTHILD DREYER

THE CATHOLIC UNIVERSITY OF AMERICA PRESS
WASHINGTON, D.C.

The paper used in this publication meets the minimum requirements of American National Standards for Information Science—Permanence of Paper for Printed Library materials, ANSI Z39.48-1984.

∞

LIBRARY OF CONGRESS

CATALOGING-IN-PUBLICATION DATA

Ingham, Mary Beth, 1951–

The philosophical vision of John Duns Scotus : an introduction /

Mary Beth Ingham and Mechthild Dreyer.

p. cm.

Includes bibliographical references.

ISBN 0-8132-1369-X (alk. paper) — ISBN 0-8132-1370-3 (pbk. : alk. paper)

1. Duns Scotus, John, ca. 1266–1308.   I. Dreyer, Mechthild, 1955–   II. Title.

B765.D74I54 2004

189′.4—dc21

2003010173

CONTENTS

PREFACE & ACKNOWLEDGMENTS

Over the past thirty years, renewed attention has turned to John Duns Scotus, a Franciscan philosopher-theologian of the last decades of the thirteenth century. Ever an important figure (both as a theologian and philosopher) for Franciscans, Scotus is once again attracting the attention of contemporary scholars, due in part to his ethical positions on freedom and moral goodness. But it is not merely his ethics that is attracting current attention. His epistemological, logical, and theological positions have been the focus of recent international congresses and monographs.[1] Renewed interest in issues belonging to the philosophy of religion has resulted in his rediscovery by a larger group of scholars, beyond those who share his

1. In addition to the regular meetings of scholars working on Scotus since 1965 (The International Scotistic Commission), in 1994 a conference on his Metaphysics and Ethics took place at the University of Bonn, Germany. The papers from that conference were published in *John Duns Scotus: Metaphysics and Ethics,* ed. L. Honnefelder, R. Wood, M. Dreyer (Leiden: Brill, 1996). Richard Cross has recently published several monographs on Scotus's thought: *The Physics of Duns Scotus* (Oxford: Clarendon Press, 1998) and *John Duns Scotus* (Oxford: Great Medieval Thinkers Series, 1999). Most recently, *The Cambridge Companion to Duns Scotus,* ed. Thomas Williams (New York: Cambridge University Press, 2003), offers a collection of essays on various philosophical aspects of Scotist thought.

spiritual or theological tradition. For the benefit of those not necessarily familiar with the medieval approach to philosophical questions, nor with the way theologians and religious of the High Middle Ages understand the relationship of philosophical speculation to their theological positions, we offer this present study. Its purpose is to introduce the reader to Scotus's philosophical vision. It is our intent that such a volume could serve as a first step to further study of the philosophy of the man known as the Subtle Doctor. To that end, we set forth in what follows the main positions and offer the most recent secondary literature on key philosophical points, inviting the interested reader or scholar to move into the more intricate dimensions of this Franciscan's thinking.

In order to understand Scotus's philosophical vision, it is important to have a basic awareness of the historical moment that served as context for his philosophical and theological reflection as well as an awareness of his life and works. Indeed, a central historical assumption grounds the present work. This assumption involves both the importance of the philosophical discussion of the late thirteenth century, to which Scotus was heir, and the place of the Franciscan tradition within the larger context of academic discourse. The fact that Scotus was himself a Franciscan friar teaching and writing at the end of the thirteenth century is an important element to any adequate understanding of his contribution to the history of philosophy. Such is the case for two reasons. First, the intellectual development and spiritual formation of someone like Scotus has a marked effect on the manner by which he proceeds. The influence of Patristic sources and biblical commentaries on his formation should not be overlooked, nor should one ignore the spiritual backdrop against which such sources cast philosophical questions. Scotus uses Augustine, Anselm, and Richard of St. Victor as particular philosophical authorities; these thinkers were also spiritual masters. Second, the precise historical moment of the last quarter of the thirteenth centu-

ry requires us to take seriously the questions posed by Scotus's predecessors, and how he received them for his own teaching. We no
longer see Bonaventure, Scotus, and Aquinas as the only philosophical masters of the thirteenth century. We cannot simply assume that
Scotus's text matches up easily with a text of Thomas Aquinas. Nor
can we assume that a question of contemporary philosophical import meant for Scotus what it means for philosophers today. We
must approach Scotist thought with as much historical sensitivity as
possible, better to recognize what is at work in the texts themselves.

In the first chapter, we lay out the historical context within
which to understand Scotist thought. We recognize the significance
of men like Henry of Ghent (d. 1293), Godfrey of Fontaines (d.
1306/09), and Giles of Rome (d. 1316). We consider the careful re-
framing of Aristotelian thought that was the focus of these thinkers,
in light of the significance of a reflection upon freedom and upon
theology as a scientific discipline. This is the scholarly world in
which Scotus was educated and trained for a higher, more significant academic role. It is the world in which he lived and taught for a
brief time. We also present the sparse biographical information
available and an indication of the present state of his works.

Following this, we take up the philosophical vision according to
standard categories: epistemology, metaphysics, and ethics. We look
first at the question of cognition and how, for Scotus, the act of
knowing is intimately connected to what can be known. Chapter 2
presents abstractive and intuitive cognition, the formal distinction,
and the univocity of being. The nature of metaphysics as a science
and the demonstration of God's existence are the focus of chapter 3.
The importance of the contingent order, the nature of possibility,
and the primacy of the individual are presented in chapter 4. Chapter 5 deals with the science of ethics and its foundation in the will.
Chapter 6 develops the will's foundational rationality and freedom
in greater depth. Chapter 7 presents moral goodness, wisdom and

virtue as the fulfillment of practical perfection. Since it is Scotus's focus on the rationality of loving and, consequently, on the rational will that has attracted the most attention in recent years, these three chapters will engage in a more careful exposition and discussion of current scholarly positions on these issues. Chapter 8 completes the entire study as we consider the significance of Scotus's philosophical vision in light of the development of Western thought, as the late Middle Ages gives rise to Modern Philosophy.

This volume is the result of a collaborative effort on the part of the authors. A much simpler introduction to Scotist metaphysics and ethics in German appeared in 2003 as *Johannes Duns Scotus zur Einführung*. Chapters 3 and 4 of this present volume are the work of Mechthild Dreyer and appear with permission of Junius Verlag, Hamburg, Germany. Jeffrey Wilson provided us with an English translation, which was then rendered more harmonious with the rest of the book. We are grateful to Loyola Marymount University for providing a subvention for this portion of the work. Finally, special thanks to Susan Needham and Elizabeth Kerr of CUA Press for their assistance in the production of this work.

November 8, 2003
Los Angeles, California

THE PHILOSOPHICAL VISION
OF JOHN DUNS SCOTUS

1. THE HISTORICAL MOMENT

F ROM THE EARLIEST DECADES of the thirteenth century, Latin scholars[1] enjoyed a rich textual renaissance that was
to have a profound impact on the disciplines of philosophy
and theology. While in the twelfth century, philosophy had been understood to be a propadeutic discipline, preparatory for further
study in law, medicine, or theology, the thirteenth century witnessed its birth as an independent field of academic study, largely
due to the arrival of the complete Aristotelian *corpus*. The growth of
the universities that also took place during this time was aided by
the entrance of texts both from the Arab and Greek traditions. The
introduction of texts from the Arab tradition was made possible
through the team of translators in the School of Toledo; texts from
the Greek tradition were direct translations into Latin. By the end of
the century, members of the Faculty of Arts (comparable to a philosophy faculty) had their own body of textual material from which to

---

1. That is, those whose language of discourse was Latin.

lecture. This material included Aristotle's *Physics, Metaphysics, Nico-machean Ethics, De anima* and *Politics.* These texts enabled the masters to offer courses that could consider questions independently of any theological dimension. While Aristotle's *Organon* or logical works had been part of early medieval culture from the sixth century, making up the *trivium* (the study of grammar, dialectic, and rhetoric), these other, more substantive philosophical texts only began to enter the intellectual west in the middle of the twelfth century and were not completely received until the early decades of the fourteenth century.[2]

Aristotle's thought brought a new way of understanding and explaining reality, according to a different scientific model independent of any obvious religious tradition. Aristotle's entrance introduced a fully developed scientific theory, including the canons for a well-founded scientific argument (in his *Posterior analytics*), with the substantive content of natural science, cognitive psychology, metaphysics, ethics, and politics. Since all university education depended entirely upon texts for commentary (such as the Bible and *Book of Sentences*), the existence of purely philosophical texts enabled the members of the Faculty of Arts to move beyond the *trivium* (grammar, dialectic, and rhetoric) and *quadrivium* (mathematics, geometry, music, and astronomy). Now, like the theologians, they had their own content and sources. Their curriculum could be autonomous.

Latin scholars did not encounter an Aristotelian text as a whole work (that is, as a single, complete philosophical text) nor did Aristotle (the Philosopher) enter the Latin culture unaided. Texts were

---

2. On the reception of Aristotle, see B. G. Dod, "Aristotles latinus," in *The Cambridge History of Later Medieval Philosophy,* ed. A. Kenny, N. Kretzmann, J. Pinborg (Cambridge: Cambridge University Press, 1982), 45–79; on the specific impact of Aristotle's *Ethics,* see G. Wieland, "The Reception and Interpretation of Aristotle's *Ethics,*" in *The Cambridge History,* 657–72.

transmitted in sections at a time (as if in periodical installments) from the Spanish School of Toledo. These translators worked with texts received from Arabic schools of philosophy, such as the important School of Baghdad. This received textual legacy included not merely the primary text of Aristotle, but also commentaries on his texts by the important Arab philosophers such as Ibn Sina (Avicenna) and Ibn Rushd (Averroes), as well as earlier Christian neoPlatonist commentators such as Eustratius. While the Latins knew they were seeing commentaries with the original texts, it was not at all clear to them what belonged to Aristotle's original intent and what had been transformed by the interpretation of a commentator.[3] In addition, there were texts falsely attributed to Aristotle. The *Liber de causis* is the most famous example of an influential yet spurious text that had enormous impact on how the Philosopher was understood. Thomas Aquinas was the first to have doubts about the authenticity of this text and noted the strong similarity to Proclus's *Elements of Theology*. Few of his contemporaries, however, agreed. Indeed, until the nineteenth century the *Liber de causis* was held by philosophers to be an Aristotelian text.

Scholars eagerly received the Aristotelian texts as they came from Spain. The work of sorting, digesting, and understanding the implications of this new scientific way of seeing the world was stimulating throughout the century. As the educational system moved from its monastic origins, through cathedral schools to the university centers, the important link between the Church and the growing universities made such intellectual novelty a flashpoint for ecclesiastical authority in the great centers of learning, most notably Paris and

3. Avicenna's *Metaphysics* is an important example of how an Arab thinker aided Western understanding of the difficult Aristotelian text. However, Avicenna does bring his own platonizing approach to the Aristotelian text, thereby reframing the text for the Latins. His approach was influential on Scotus. See E. Gilson, "Avicenne et le point de départ de Duns Scot," in *Archives d'histoire doctrinale et littéraire du Moyen Age* (1927), 89–150.

Oxford. As early as 1231, a committee was formed by Pope Gregory IX to purge the Aristotelian texts of error. As one moves beyond the mid-point of the century, benign approaches such as that of Albert the Great (who wished only to "make Aristotle available to the Latins") gave way to those of men like Bonaventure, Henry of Ghent, and Etienne Tempier, who both criticized and condemned some of Aristotle's conclusions, in light of truths affirmed by faith.

1.1 Philosophy in the Late Thirteenth Century

By 1270, three positions attributed to Aristotle were understood to form a constellation that challenged traditional positions and pointed to a view of reality that was secular, rationalist, and naturalist. These positions involved the eternity of the world, monopsychism, and astral determinism. Monopsychism (a theory that there is only one Mind for all humanity) and astral determinism (that the stars determine human behavior) explained human behavior in such a way that moral responsibility could be reduced, if not dismissed altogether. The eternity of the world removed the need for any creator God, and undermined the authority of Scripture. In his series of lectures, the *Collationes in Hexameron (1273)*, Bonaventure excoriated Aristotelian philosophy as a most serious form of error. He much preferred the more Christian-friendly Platonic vision with its Ideal world, the creation myth in the *Timaeus* and the defense of individual knowing as recollection. Indeed, Augustine's philosophical journey in the *Confessions* had shown that Platonic thought was a prelude to Christianity.

Because of the perceived threat of these new texts, the life at the universities of Paris and Oxford (the most prominent in Europe) was peppered by several prohibitions of Aristotle. While the prohibitions, begun as early as 1215, only meant that the texts could not be read and lectured on in a public forum, they could be (and were) read privately. The various censures appear not to have had great effect, since the University of Paris decreed in 1255 that all texts of Aristotle should be studied in the Faculty of Arts. The situation reached a crescendo with the condemnations of 1270 and 1277.

By the final quarter of the century, the Aristotelian-inspired philosophical position framed an intellectual portrait of human excellence.[4] According to this approach, human perfection involves no more than personal meditation or speculation on the eternal, separated substances. Ultimate human fulfillment becomes the work of each person individually. In other words, this approach offered all the benefits of a religion without God (or at least without the need for a personal God) to the educated intellectual. One could dispense with the Bible or any revealed text as superfluous. All that mattered for salvation was commitment to the way of philosophical speculation: the eternal and perfect world of immaterial substances. Each person was responsible for his own salvation and, as Boethius of Dacia claimed: "There is no life superior to that of the philosopher." According to this approach, Aristotle had correctly outlined the journey toward human fulfillment: it was intellectual transcendence, whether or not this involved any survival after death.

As the 1260s gave way to the 1270s the concern for the growing autonomy of the Faculty of Arts and for the type of philosophical ideal they appeared to advocate led to a decisive ecclesiastical move. Etienne Tempier, Bishop of Paris, established a commission in 1277 to examine what was being taught and to enumerate and correct the "errors of the philosophers" once and for all. This commission worked with a speed unlike the others: in three months, its mem-

---

4. An excellent presentation of the situation during the last quarter of the thirteenth century can be found in Alain de Libera, *Penser au Moyen Age* (Paris: Seuil, 1991), Luca Bianchi/Eugenio Randi, *Vérités Dissonantes: Aristote à la fin du Moyen Age* (Fribourg: Cerf, 1993) and F. Van Steenberghen, "La philosophie à la veille de l'entrée en scène de Jean Duns Scot," in *De doctrina I. Duns Scoti,* ed. C. Bérubé (Rome: Cura Commissionis Scotisticae, 1968), I:65–74.

bers had compiled 219 propositions that they claimed were either held or taught by Arts Masters teaching in Paris. These Masters held and taught the truth of such propositions on the authority of Aristotle. On March 7, 1277, the list was promulgated.[5] The propositions were taken from all domains of philosophical inquiry, including such positions as:

(1) some maintaining that this world is the only possible world

(2) some describing the necessity of divine action and creation

(3) those affirming the dependence of the will on the intellect and denying it any freedom to choose counter to the dictates of right reasoning

(4) those upholding the influence of the movement of the heavens upon human behavior (astral determinism)

(5) those defending the superiority of the life of philosophy and the study of philosophy to the study of scripture

(6) those affirming the possibility of true happiness in this life.

The Condemnation of 1277 was unlike any other of that century, both in scope and influence. It set the next generation of scholars in a more critical relationship to the texts of Aristotle and other philosophers. It also turned their reflection to the areas of freedom, contingency and the nature of scientific knowledge. If the thirteenth century began with an optimistic and open attitude toward the Stagirite, it ended with a more distanced, critical assessment of the limits of philosophical reasoning and with a reflection upon the conditions for human knowing, *pro statu isto* (in this present life). The perspective of revelation, and specifically Christian revelation, served as a critical tool in the examination of philosophical conclusions about the extent of scientific knowledge, the contours of human per-

5. For a listing of the condemned articles see R. Hissette, *Enquête sur les 219 articles condamnés à Paris le 7 mars 1277* (Louvain-Paris, 1977), and D. Piché, *La Condamnation Parisienne de 1277* (Paris: Vrin, 1999).

fection and fulfillment, and the nature of free choice and freedom for rational beings. By the close of the century, for reasons not completely reducible to the fact of the condemnation, the scholarly community was not as willing to accept the Arab-Aristotelian model of a single, necessary universe whose creator acts necessarily. The importance of the contingency of the created order became the starting point for reflection upon divine action in history, the nature and scope of scientific knowledge, possibilities beyond what is actual, and the nature of freedom.

Scotus's thought can only be correctly understood as part of this second critique of Aristotelian philosophy. His own philosophical re-working of key philosophical elements is best understood against the background of the overly intellectualized, philosophical model, especially as it had emerged from the 1250s and as it appeared in the constellation formed by several propositions condemned in 1277.[6] Taken together, these propositions offer a distinct portrait for human salvation that equates the intellectual life of the philosopher with that of the divinity. This life can appear as a valid and viable alternative to a Christian life. It offers all the elements of spiritual development: asceticism, reflection, self-knowledge, meditation, good works. The keystone of this life is the intellect, and how intellectual activity defines human dignity. This sort of ideal is most clearly set forth by Aristotle in Book X, 6–9 of the *Nicomachean Ethics* as the *telos teleotaton*, or ultimate goal of human fulfillment. It is the contemplative, speculative ideal of the philosopher.

Scotus seeks to correct this perspective, with the help of none other than Aristotle himself. The philosophers are wrong, he argues; ordered love, not knowledge, defines and perfects human rationality. Human dignity has its foundation in rational freedom. In contrast to the philosophical, intellectualist model of human nature and

6. See M. B. Ingham, "The Condemnation of 1277: Another Light on Scotist Ethics," *Freiburger Zeitschrift für Philosophie und Theologie* 37 (1990): 91–103.

destiny, the Franciscan offers and strengthens the Christian alternative, centered not merely on knowledge but on rational love.
Throughout his brief career, Scotus works to put together a more
overtly Christian perspective on the world, the person, and salvation
that might stand up to this philosophical intellectual/speculative
model and, by using the best of its resources, transcend it. The Franciscan consistently defends a position wherein the fullest perfection
of the human person as rational involves loving in the way God
loves, rather than knowing in the way God knows. His position in
this overall project can best be understood within Franciscan spiritu-
ality, which emphasizes the will and its attraction to beauty, love,
and simplicity.[7] The project itself can best be approached when we
take care to see how it fits into the larger framework that informed
his entire life, not simply his teaching and intellectual reflection.

In this way, it is a type of "faith seeking understanding" à la
Anselm, insofar as Scotus tries to lay out the deeper structure of a
reality based upon divine rational love, a reality that is entirely consistent with Scripture, especially the scriptural depiction of God as
the personal God of the Exodus, the Incarnation, and the Resurrec-
tion, a Trinity of persons who long to reveal themselves to us and, in
that self-revelation, establish a covenant relationship.

In order to reframe the philosophical project in Christian terms,
Scotus makes good use of Aristotelian logical and metaphysical categories. The logically possible becomes his methodical tool of choice
as he considers, not what actually exists, but what might exist in
light of human experience. The category of "what might exist" is,
for Scotus, a better frame for understanding divine choices than that
of "what actually exists". Scotus uses modal categories to open up
the domain of reflection on divine options and creative opportuni-
ties, bringing the God of revelation (a personal God who faces

7. See F. X. Putallaz, *Figures Franciscains: De Bonaventure à Duns Scot* (Paris:
Cerf, 1997), 81–140.

choices) into a closer relationship with the created order. Scotus also uses the Aristotelian categories of being to refocus the questions of cognition and the object of metaphysics. For Scotus, the transcendentals being *(ens),* true *(verum),* and good *(bonum)* are not a subset of the study of metaphysics. They are themselves the object of this important philosophical inquiry.

Scotus's response to the Condemnation of 1277 involves not the rejection of Aristotle, but the re-tooling of the philosophical domain against the background of the central revelation: God is Love. The Franciscan's re-configuration begins with a critique of Aristotle's theory of abstractive cognition as the complete explanation of human powers of knowing. It moves from there to a reflection upon the nature of metaphysics as a science of being. It concludes with a study of the will as rational and free.

1.2 Scotus's Life and Works

John Duns Scotus was born in Duns, Scotland, most likely in spring 1266.[8] At an early age, possibly as young as fourteen, he entered the newly founded Franciscan mendicant order (c. 1280). His teachers quickly recognized the youth's intellectual ability and took him to Oxford where he could study with the masters of the Franciscan order. During that time, the major religious orders studied philosophy and natural sciences in their own houses of study, rather than with the regent master of the Faculty of Arts. This regimen of study, known as the *lectorate,* involved a formation track internal to the religious order and not specifically tied to the student's later aca-

8. This date is determined on the basis of ecclesiastical records for his ordination in March 1291. Since canon law required the age of twenty-five for ordination, and since there had been an ordination in December 1290 for which Scotus was, apparently, not eligible, scholars conclude that his twenty-fifth birthday occurred between December 1290 and March 1291. If true, this would put his birth between December 1265 and March 1266.

demic career. Within this track, each province could send two or three men to the major centers of learning, especially the University of Paris. There is no record of anyone sent to Paris to complete his education who had not studied there earlier as part of the *lectorate* program. Recent historical research of William Courtenay points to the possibility that Scotus himself was chosen for such an academic honor.[9] If this conjecture proves true, then it would place Scotus in Paris during the important period from 1285 to 1288, when Henry of Ghent was teaching there. This would account for references in his works to debates that took place during that decade.

These early years of *lectorate* study would have introduced the young man to both Aristotelian logic and natural philosophy, along with the theology required for ordination to the priesthood, which took place on March 17, 1291. There is no doubt that Scotus began his theological studies in Oxford in 1288, most probably as a student of William of Ware. After the six years during which time he held the status of *auditor*, as a bachelor, Scotus lectured on Peter Lombard's *Book of Sentences*. Peter Lombard's *Sentences* was the standard text for theological education, since it represents a synthesis of the teachings of the Fathers of the Church on all matters of doctrinal importance. Scotus's earliest (and incomplete) commentary, the *Lectura*, records lectures given possibly between 1298 and 1300. In summer 1300, Scotus began the formal revision of this text while still at Oxford, as he himself notes in the *Prologue*.[10] This revised (yet also incomplete) commentary is called the *Ordinatio*. This term is a technical one: it refers to the more formal, revised, and personally re-

9. On the *lectorate* track and the possibility for Scotus's own intellectual formation, see William Courtenay, "The Instructional Programme of the Mendicant Convents at Paris in the Early Fourteenth Century," in *The Medieval Church: Universities, Heresy and the Religious Life (Essays in Honour of Gordon Leff)*, ed. P. Biller, B. Dobson (The Boydell Press, 1999), 77–92. See also Bert Roest, *A History of Franciscan Education (c. 1210–1517)* (Leiden: Brill, 2000).

10. *Ordinatio Prologue* II, q. un., n. 112 (ed. Vat. 1:77).

viewed manuscript of the *Sentences*, for which Scotus would have taken up and corrected some material from his earlier teaching. It is the sort of text that an author prepares for final edition. It is possible that this more formal revision was begun in light of the move to Paris, to take place in autumn 1302, for which Scotus may have been given a year's advance notice. We do know that he continued revising this major text while in Paris. His move to the French university would have come at the request of the Minister General, who, upon the recommendation of the General Chapter, appointed select men to complete their studies at this prestigious university. Once in Paris, Scotus would begin again with his third commentary on the *Sentences* (known as the *Reportatio Parisiensis*) for another set of students. A *Reportatio* refers to student notes of university lectures. In his first year, he may also have participated in the disputation between the Franciscan Regent Master, Gonsalves of Spain, and the Dominican Master, Meister Eckhart.[11]

The years of his intellectual development in Paris, however, were not peaceful. This was the period of political and ecclesiastical hostility between King Philip the Fair of France and Pope Boniface VIII. In June 1303, Scotus's teaching was interrupted when he and other Franciscans were forced into exile for their failure to support the King in his attempts to depose the Pope.[12] During the following year, he may have gone back to Oxford or Cambridge, where he continued to lecture and work on the *Ordinatio*. It may also have been the period when Scotus disputed his Oxford *Collationes*.[13] He

11. See A.B. Wolter "Reflections on the Life and Works of Scotus," *American Catholic Philosophical Quarterly* 67 (1993), 11.

12. William Courtenay documents Scotus as a member of the Franciscan Parisian convent in June 1303. See his "The Parisian Franciscan Community in 1303," *Franciscan Studies* 53 (1993): 155–73.

13. Stephen Dumont argues for this in "William of Ware, Richard of Conington and the *Collationes Oxonienses* of John Duns Scotus," in *John Duns Scotus: Metaphysics and Ethics*, 84–5.

was not to return to Paris until sometime after April 8, 1304, when Pope Benedict XI lifted the ban placed on the University of Paris and the King allowed the exiles to return. Records show that Scotus incepted as Master in Paris in 1305, and engaged in only one set of disputed questions.[14] The important appointment as Regent Master ordinarily lasted two years at the most and, in 1307, Gonsalvus of Spain (Minister General and possibly the man with whom Scotus had studied)[15] sent him to Cologne to oversee the teaching of Theology. There is some suggestion that the move to Cologne was precipitated by the "formidable enemies" he had in Paris, due to his controversial positions on the rationale for the Incarnation and his defense of the Immaculate Conception.[16] In November 1308, Scotus died quite unexpectedly, at the age of forty-two. He is buried in the Franciscan church *(Minoritenkirche)* not far from the Cologne cathedral.

Scotus's travels during his years of study and teaching, along with his early death, account for the enormous quantity of textual material in various states of completion. This textual situation has given rise to the variety of scholarly opinions on Scotus's positions on important questions, such as the nature of freedom and the way in which God relates to the created order. Let us just note that a serious debate continues to engage the scholarly community about the real positions Scotus held and taught.

Most of the famous medieval teachers, like Thomas Aquinas and Bonaventure, authored other, more systematic works as well as their

14. Either in Advent 1306 or Lent 1307.

15. Once elevated to the position of Minister General, Gonsalvus may have sent Scotus to Cologne because of the way the young bachelor performed in his disputation with Meister Eckhart. See W. Frank and A. B. Wolter, *Duns Scotus, Metaphysician* (West Lafayette: Purdue University Press, 1995), 4–5.

16. Both Scotus's position that the Incarnation was not the result of original sin and therefore his rejection of Anselm's standard *Cur Deus homo?* argument as well as his teaching on the sinless conception of Mary challenged traditional theological positions.

commentaries on the *Sentences*. Composed later in their teaching career, these works offer a more mature formulation of the thinker's position on key issues. Here the scholar was free to determine his own methodology and organization of the material. For Thomas Aquinas, the *Summa theologiae* or *Summa contra gentiles* offer the more developed positions and are far more central texts in our study today than his *Commentary on the Sentences*. Nonetheless, consulting his early commentary is useful when one wishes to trace the development of a position, or when we seek to identify alternate versions of an argument.

Because of his brief teaching career, Scotus's textual legacy is limited. Nevertheless, we can look to the three versions of his commentary on the *Book of Sentences* as signposts for positions that he fills out in slightly more detail in later works, such as the *De primo principio* or his *Quodlibetal Questions*. The three commentaries do shed light on one another in some particular cases. Fruitful studies examine his approach to the same questions at three distinct moments of his life. In addition, the central *Ordinatio* saw revision over a period of years, at Oxford and at Paris. Thus, while (despite important lacunae) it still has pride of place among Scotist texts, Allan Wolter insists that scholars should not consider it a single piece of work, or act as if its composition took place at one time.[17] It is not entirely clear, Wolter maintains, that the *Ordinatio* offers us Scotus's final word on certain questions. Indeed, there is currently some debate about the *Reportatio Parisiensis,* with Books I–IV begun by Scotus during the 1302–1303 academic year and Book IV completed when he returned to Paris sometime after April 1304. This text, the latest,

---

17. "What I would like to emphasize in what follows is that it is an even more serious and inexcusable mistake for scholars writing on Scotus today to regard his *Ordinatio* as a seamless garment rather than a work begun in Oxford and left unfinished when he left Paris for Cologne." Wolter, "Reflections about Scotus's Early Works," in *John Duns Scotus: Metaphysics and Ethics,* 39.

may hold the key to the final positions Scotus held. It has yet to appear in critical edition.

There exists a manuscript version of this third commentary, known as *Reportatio IA*, in which the term "examinata" appears. Scotus may have examined this text in view of a final revision. If true, this text, and not the *Ordinatio*, would represent the most reliable source for his final positions on a number of key issues. Charles Balic holds that it is based upon the best of Scotus's two series of lectures in Paris and was used by Scotus when he revised Book I of the *Ordinatio*. This text exists in a non-critical but safe version.[18]

Scotus leaves a few other authentic works as well. Among these the first and most significant is his major metaphysical work on the existence of God, *De primo principio (On the First Principle)*. This work dates from after 1305 and draws upon other proofs for God's existence found in *Ordinatio* I, distinction 2, qq. 1 and 3. His *Quodlibetal Questions*[19] records his scholarly disputation of 1306 or 1307. The *Questions on Aristotle's Metaphysics* is a commentary on the text of Aristotle that seems to have been composed over his years of teaching.[20] His commentary on the *De anima*[21] and the *Theoremata*[22]

---

18. Edited by A. B. Wolter and O. Bychkov, St. Bonaventure: Franciscan Institute, forthcoming 2004.

19. An English translation of these has been available for some time. See *God and Creatures: The Quodlibetal Questions,* trans. F. Alluntis and A. B. Wolter (Princeton: Princeton University Press, 1975).

20. The editors of the critical edition show clearly how the text was composed over several years. See *Quaestiones super libros metaphysicorum Aristotelis (Opera philosophica,* vol. 3–4, St. Bonaventure: Franciscan Institute, 1997), 3:xlii–xlvi. In addition, see T. Noone, "Scotus's Critique of the Thomistic Theory of Individuation and the Dating of the *Quaestiones super libros metaphysicorum* VII, q. 13," in *Via Scoti: methodologica ad mentem Joannis Duns Scoti,* ed. L. Sileo (Rome: Edizioni Antonianum, 1995), I: 391–406.

21. The critical edition of this is forthcoming in volume 5 of *Opera philosophica* (Washington, D.C.: Catholic University of America Press, 2004).

22. This work will appear with the remaining logical texts in volume 2 of *Opera philosophica* (forthcoming). On its significance, see Mechthild Dreyer, "Wissenschaft als Satzsystem: Die *Theoremata* des Johannes Duns Scotus und die En-

complete the non-logical writings on Aristotle's work. Among his logical works we have the *Quaestiones super librum Porphyrii, Quaestiones super librum praedicamentorum,*[23] *Quaestiones in I et II librum Perihermenias, Opus secundum sive octo quaestiones in duos libros Perihermenias,* and *Quaestiones in libros Elenchorum.*

Allan B. Wolter, OFM, longtime scholar of Scotus, has made various texts available in English, either taken from critical edition or, where not yet available, corrected on the basis of Codex A (the standard manuscript used in the critical edition). In *Duns Scotus on the Will and Morality*[24] he presents a collection of Scotist texts that deal with the nature of ethics as a practical science, the will's freedom, and moral goodness. The Franciscan Institute has published the translation of Scotus's teaching on the Immaculate Conception in *Four Questions on Mary* (2000), on his political and economic theory in *Duns Scotus Political and Economic Philosophy* (2001), and on *haecceitas* in *Duns Scotus' Early Oxford Teaching on Individuation.*[25] In *John Duns Scotus, Mary's Architect* (with Blaine O'Neill), Wolter offers a concise introduction to the overall thought of Scotus.[26] His complete translation (with Girard Etzkorn) of the *Questions on Aristotle's Metaphysics* appeared in 2000 as a companion to the critical edition. Finally, with William Frank, Wolter has collected and published the most important texts on metaphysics, cognition, and ethics in *Duns Scotus, Metaphysician.*[27] Wolter's text and translation of *Reportatio IA*

---

twicklung des Kategorisch-Deduktiven Wissenschaftsbegriffs," in *John Duns Scotus: Metaphysics and Ethics,* 87–105.

23. In *Opera philosophica,* vol. 1 (St. Bonaventure: Franciscan Institute, 1999).

24. Washington, D.C.: Catholic University of America Press, 1986 (Latin/English) and 1997 (English only).

25. This edition is forthcoming. Wolter published an earlier version in 1992 (Santa Barbara, CA: Old Mission). P.V. Spade presents the *Ordinatio* II, d. 3, qq. 1-6 text in *Five Texts on the Mediaeval Problem of Universals: Porphyry, Boethius, Abelard, Duns Scotus and Ockham* (Indianapolis: Hackett 1994), 57–113.

26. Quincy, IL.: Franciscan Press, 1992.

27. West Lafayette: Purdue University Press, 1995.

is scheduled for publication in 2004 (The Franciscan Institute). The interested reader could fruitfully consult any of these translations to get a better sense of how Scotus works his way through a question.

1.3 Scotus's Philosophical Context

As later chapters in this study develop Scotus's philosophical positions on epistemology, metaphysics, and ethics, it is helpful to consider here the state of these questions during the last quarter of the thirteenth century. In what follows, we sketch very briefly the major concerns of each of these philosophical domains at the time of Duns Scotus, both in the surrounding scholarly context and within the Franciscan tradition.

The vibrancy of university debate in Paris and Oxford was not diminished by the famous 1277 condemnation. Rather, it was revitalized with the encounter of dynamic circles of thought, and the return of earlier, more traditionally held positions. Political and ecclesiastical influences shaped the context of discourse, as did doctrinal and philosophical concerns.[28] Politically, the rector of the university (a member of the Faculty of Arts) became a more important figure than the chancellor (a member of the Faculty of Theology).[29] The theology faculty moved from the Cathedral chapter to the Quarter of St. Jacques and the Sorbonne.[30] Doctrinally, well-developed Aristotelian positions debated Augustinian and neo-Augustinian positions. The difference between the debates of the first quarter and those of the last quarter of the century, however, lay in the greater

28. See William Courtenay, "The Parisian Faculty of Theology in the Late Thirteenth and Early Fourteenth Centuries," in *After the Condemnation of 1277: Philosophy and Theology at the University of Paris in the Last Quarter of the Thirteenth Century,* eds. J. Aertsen, K. Emery, A. Speer (Berlin: Walter de Gruyter, 2001), 235–47.

29. William Courtenay, "The Parisian Faculty of Theology," 246, especially n. 29.

30. Ibid., 241.

theoretical precision and analytic sophistication that characterized the arguments, due primarily to the integration of Aristotelian thought by all sides. Scholars of these final years were more critical of Aristotelian conclusions than their predecessors. Indeed, it may very well be that the anomaly of the thirteenth century is not what occurred after 1277, but what had happened in mid-century, when Aristotle was so well received and when his thought flourished.[31]

By the closing years of the thirteenth century, the major figures were men like Henry of Ghent, Godfrey of Fontaines, and Giles of Rome. These men both represented and reacted to various aspects of the Condemnation. Henry, a strong neo-Augustinian voice and Regent Master from 1276 to 1292, had been one of the members of the commission that drew together the heterodox propositions. His student Godfrey, Master in Paris from 1285 to 1299 and in residence at the university c. 1303,[32] was a much stronger proponent of the Aristotelian and (to some degree) Thomist perspectives on philosophical matters. In his *Quodlibet* q. 12 (c. 1296), Godfrey questioned the validity of the continued condemnation for those articles that had been erroneously prohibited. Giles, Master from 1285 to 1291, had studied under Aquinas and had some of his own positions touched by the 1277 pronouncement. In the twenty years following the condemnation, Dominicans rallied around Thomas (at the Chapter of Paris in 1286) and Augustinians committed themselves to Giles (in 1287). In 1285, Giles enjoyed a formal rehabilitation. In 1323, Aquinas was canonized.

---

31. "Indeed, . . . the anomaly in thirteenth-century Scholasticism, the phenomenon begging explanation, may not be the later-decades spirit often manifested in opposition to presumed Aristotelian orthodoxy but rather the curious inclination towards a reputed Aristotelian purism from the 1240's to the 1270's." Steven Marrone, "Aristotle, Augustine and the Identity of Philosophy in Late Thirteenth-Century Paris: The Case of Some Theologians," in *After the Condemnation of 1277*, 280.

32. See John Wippel, *The Metaphysical Thought of Godfrey of Fontaines* (Washington, D.C.: Catholic University of America Press, 1981), xix.

By contrast, Franciscan masters, the more dominant group after the condemnation, had no strong school allegiance. They had been on the side of the critics rather than the criticized; they needed no defensive strategy.[33] This tradition was, nonetheless, more voluntarist in its basic intuitions and more inclined to pursue questions of moral rather than metaphysical import. William de la Mare's *Correctorium fratris Thomae*, a Franciscan correction of Aquinas's positions, was officially endorsed by the Order in 1282, and was required reading for anyone studying the *Summa*. Franciscan John Peckham renewed the condemnation as archbishop of Canterbury in 1284. Other influential voices included Richard of Middleton (a moderate and Regent master from 1284 to 1287) and Peter John Olivi (whose commentary on the *Sentences* dates from 1280 to 1282). These men did not represent a common school or position, with Olivi the most critical of Aristotelian positions and himself condemned by the Franciscan Minister General (c. 1280). Gonsalvus of Spain, regent of the Franciscan school in Paris (in 1302, when Scotus was a student there) worked toward a reconciliation between Aristotelian and Augustinian positions, in distinct contrast to his immediate predecessors. Scotus's years of study and teaching were influenced by this dynamic debate, both within the Franciscan scholarly community[34] and in the university at large.

The epistemological concerns of the time focused on two central questions: cognition of the particular and the constitution of the intellect. Both concerns involved the Aristotelian model of sense perception, the agent intellect, and imaginative phantasms. Both had to do with the way the mind (an immaterial substance) could have scientific knowledge of the concrete, extra-mental world (material sub-

33. See William Courtenay, *Schools and Scholars in Fourteenth-Century England* (Princeton: Princeton University Press, 1987), 175–78.

34. See Stephen Dumont, "William of Ware, Richard of Conington," in *John Duns Scotus: Metaphysics and Ethics*, 59–86.

stances). While Aquinas's generation had answered the question of the possibility of scientific knowledge of the particular through the essence of the being, or its *quidditas,* Scotus's generation faced the question of the mode of such knowledge. Franciscans, among them Mathew of Aquasparta and Peter John Olivi, advocated a direct intellection of the singular.[35]

The more foundational epistemological question had to do with the constitution of the intellect. Here the debate focused on the relative passivity or activity of the human intellect, and involved the merits of the Augustinian illumination model over against the newer Aristotelian agent intellect theory. Much philosophical debate over the course of the twelfth and thirteenth centuries (involving both the Arab and Latin traditions) had centered on the exact nature of cognitive processes, the role of mental representations and the emergence of the mental *species* (concept) as the concluding step in the process of understanding. Franciscan influences on Scotus such as Richard of Middleton, William of Ware, and Peter John Olivi all abandoned the illuminationist position in favor of an Aristotelian approach.[36]

Closely related to the epistemological questions were the metaphysical questions. The parameters for the possibility of natural knowledge of God, a point of convergence for the two domains, was framed for Scotus's generation by Henry of Ghent's brand of neo-Augustinian illuminationism. The pivotal discussion surrounding being as an analogical or univocal concept is a central piece of Scotus's epistemological-metaphysical insights that can only be properly understood in light of Henry's position on how the mind knows God naturally.[37]

35. See Camille Bérubé, *La Connaissance de l'individu au Moyen Age* (Paris: Presses Universitaires de France, 1964).

36. See Bonnie Kent, *Virtues of the Will: The Transformation of Ethics in the Late Thirteenth Century* (Washington, D.C.: Catholic University of America Press, 1995), 16.

37. An extremely helpful study on this point can be found in Steven Marrone's

The thirteenth century had witnessed years of debate regarding the science of metaphysics and its object. On this topic, Arab philosophers had a profound impact. Thinkers sought to determine whether metaphysics was, following Averroes, a divine science (dealing with God) or, following Avicenna, a science of being. After 1277, the metaphysical questions turned to being *(ens)* and to questions dealing with act and potency, essence and existence, form and matter and the principle of individuation.[38] For Franciscans, the significance of metaphysics in questions directly related to God (other than divine existence) was more narrow, due both to their preference to view theology as a practical (rather than speculative) science and to their interest in the contingent order. On other questions related to metaphysical categories, while university debates may have been inspired by theological questions (such as the principle of individuation as it relates to angels,[39] or the relationship between substance to accident in the Eucharist and in the Incarnation),[40] philosophical distinctions were central to their solutions.

Finally, after 1277 ethical questions related to the scientific nature of ethics, its connection to theology, the question of human free choice and, certainly, divine freedom as it relates to the created order. Whereas earlier discussions of the thirteenth century had fo-

"Henry of Ghent and Duns Scotus on the Knowledge of Being," *Speculum* 63, 1 (1988): 22–57.

38. Timothy Noone locates Scotus's position on individuation between Henry of Ghent's conceptualist tendencies and William of Ware's simplified ontology of individuals. See his study "Universals and Individuation," in *The Cambridge Companion to Duns Scotus,* ed. Thomas Williams (Cambridge: Cambridge University Press, 2003), 100–128. One may also fruitfully consult Stephen Dumont's "The Question on Individuation in Scotus's *Quaestiones super metaphysicam,*" in *Via Scoti,* 193–228.

39. Scotus disputed this question in 1305. His opponent was Dominican William Peter Godin. See A. B. Wolter, "Scotus' Individuation Theory," in *The Philosophical Theology of John Duns Scotus,* ed. Marilyn M. Adams (Ithaca: Cornell University Press, 1990), 68–97.

40. Dealt with in *Quodlibet* 19. See *God and Creatures,* 418–42.

cused on free choice as distinct from freedom, in Scotus we find these terms used interchangeably. On this point, his own Franciscan tradition, as well as the positions of Henry of Ghent[41] and Godfrey of Fontaines were a rich source of reflection for him. Among Franciscans, Peter John Olivi and William de la Mare affirmed the independence of the will in the strongest possible terms. In contrast to their positions, Richard of Middleton offered a more moderate discussion.

In short, philosophers and theologians in Scotus's generation faced questions about scientific knowledge, necessity and contingency, mediated and immediate cognition, autonomy, and freedom that were not precisely those encountered by Bonaventure and Aquinas before them. And, in a post-1277 world, these questions appeared as part of a single, coherent philosophical view of human nature and destiny that focused on the intellect and speculation. When Scotus takes up questions of epistemology, metaphysics, and ethics, they form a coherent whole whose center is the rational will and whose perfection is ordered loving. His approach offers an alternative that seeks to be just as coherent and just as philosophically attractive, without sacrificing the significance of revelation or the dignity of faith. Scotist thought focuses on this world and upon the epistemological, metaphysical, and ethical dimensions proper to the contingent order, founded ultimately on the act of divine rational freedom.

41. Henry's teaching as it appears in his Quodlibetal Questions can be found in *Henry of Ghent: Quodlibetal Questions on Free Will*, ed. R. Teske, S.J. (Milwaukee: Marquette University Press, 1993).

2. KNOWING REALITY

THIRTEENTH-CENTURY SCHOLARS had two cognitive models from which to choose: the first based upon Augustine's theory of illumination and the second based upon Aristotle's theory of the agent intellect in *De anima* III. While Augustine's spiritual, Platonic approach was, in principle, more compatible with the religious perspective, it grounded the objectivity of human cognition in a prior knowledge of the world of Ideas, which pre-supposed some direct access to the divine mind or innate ideas. Aristotle's theory seemed to do a better job of explaining the psychological experience of cognition via *phantasms* (mental representations of reality generated by the senses), yet could not reach the world beyond the senses. Indeed, when it came to language about God, this approach moved from created to uncreated being by means of inferential reasoning and the logic of analogy.

In this chapter, we consider how Scotus elaborates upon the Aristotelian approach in two significant ways. First, he expands the cog-

nitional act from abstraction to include intuition, a higher, more direct act of intellection within the power of the human mind in the
present state *(pro statu isto)*. Second, he shifts the focus from the
mental *species* or *quidditas* to the concept of being *(ens)* as the primary
object of intellection. This concept is indistinct and univocal: so basic to cognition that it mediates the realms of human and divine real-
ities, making possible natural knowledge of God. Taken together, the
univocity of being and the double cognitive activity (abstraction and
intuition) distinguish the science of theology as based upon but sur-
passing Aristotelian foundations. As science, theology is grounded
upon Aristotelian principles of logic and predication. It surpasses the
Aristotelian framework, however, insofar as, according to Scotus,
natural knowledge of God uses terms analogically but does not depend upon analogical reasoning. The two elements also offer the natural conditions for the possibility of the beatific vision: a direct vision of the divine that does not require a supernatural light of glory.

   Allan B. Wolter has identified Scotus's theories of the univocity
of being and of intuitive cognition as "two of the more original con-
tributions" the Subtle Doctor makes to the Scholastic reflection on
human knowing.[1] The two theories are more properly understood
as two aspects of a single theory, that is, of the Franciscan's position
on how the human mind is present to all that exists and, additionally, on the intricate way in which all that exists is present to the human mind.

   For Scotus, both object and knower contribute actively to the act
of intellection. The cognitive act involving mutual presence of the
knower with reality underpins Scotus's theory of knowledge and
makes it impossible for him to treat the activity of knowing in abstraction from what is known. Attention to the act of cognitive
awareness reveals the conditions required for such an act to take

---

1. In *Duns Scotus Metaphysician*, 174.

place. These conditions, both in the mind and in reality, reveal themselves not simply as the basis for everyday human understanding of the world, but, more importantly, as foundation for the possibility of any science of reality that lies beyond sense experience (metaphysics) as well as any science of God (theology).

A consideration of the epistemological question for Scotus cannot take place in the absence of the concomitant consideration of the metaphysical question, at least in its most foundational aspect. When he asks "What is the first object of the intellect?"[2] he raises the two questions simultaneously. In order to answer such a two-fold question, one must focus both on what presents itself to intellection at the most basic level *(ens)* and on how intellection moves out toward its primary object (via abstractive and intuitive acts).

For the purposes of an introduction to Scotus's philosophical vision such as this, the two-fold question is best answered in several carefully sequenced moments. The act of knowing, like an onion, is to be peeled, moving from what is most obvious and external to what is most hidden and obscure. Such an analysis reveals the foundation for any scientific knowledge of reality first, from the perspective of the knower and second, from the perspective of what is known. For Scotus's moderate realism, concepts exist in a relationship to reality that is best understood as *isomorphic*.[3] This means that the discussion of the object of cognition *(ens)* cannot be understood independently of the sorts of cognitive acts of which the human intellect is capable (both abstractive and intuitive). Reality and the mind exist in a dynamic relationship of mutual presence that gives birth to concepts and to the language within which such concepts are expressed.

2. In *Ordinatio* I, d. 3, nn. 137–39 (ed. Vat. 3:85–87).
3. Allan Wolter uses this term to explain how the realms of being and knowing are closely related in Scotist texts. See his "The Formal Distinction," in *The Philosophical Theology*, 27–41.

We have chosen to begin this study with the activity of intellectual awareness, because it is where common, ordinary human experience begins. It is also the point Scotus chooses to begin his treatise on divine existence, *De primo principio*.[4] The discussion in this chapter proceeds from a presentation of the two ways the intellect is present to reality (in 2.1), through a discussion of the way reality is present to intellection in the formal distinction (in 2.2), to conclude with an examination of the most basic requirement for ordinary as well as scientific knowledge: the univocity of being (in 2.3). The arrival at the foundational and univocal concept, being, brings us back to the activity of understanding and, most importantly, sets up the conditions within which any science of being (metaphysics) is possible.

2.1 Abstractive and Intuitive Cognition

Although as a Franciscan, Scotus stands within a tradition ordinarily identified with the Augustinian perspective, his theory of knowledge is profoundly Aristotelian. Despite the temporary resurgence of Augustinian and neo-Augustinian theories of illumination in thinkers such as Henry of Ghent after the condemnation of 1277, Scotus strongly rejects the need for any divine illumination or innate ideas in human knowing. He uses Aristotle's *De anima* III, 5 discussion of the agent and possible intellects to defend the possibility of abstract, scientific knowledge of the world and of the metaphysical characteristics that ground this knowledge. He follows the Aristotelian theory of the agent intellect and its role in producing the intelligible species derived from phantasms, those imaginative re-

4. Scotus begins the Treatise with a prayer that recalls the theophany of the burning bush, God's self-revelation to Moses as being ("I am who am"), the limitations of human knowing in the present state, and the primary object of human cognition. See *A Treatise on God as First Principle*, translated and edited with a commentary by A. B. Wolter (Chicago: Franciscan Herald Press, 1966), 1.2.

presentations of external reality as experienced by the bodily senses. Scotus agrees that abstraction is the most common way the mind knows reality. Through abstraction the human mind, an immaterial substance, knows material objects in the extra-mental world by means of the immaterial essence or *quidditas*. Abstraction begins with sense experience and involves various stages through which ideas are brought to birth in the soul. At a first stage, sense experience (vision, touch, smell, etc.) gives rise to the phantasm or mental image in the imaginative power of the soul. This phantasm is a sensible representation of the extra-mental object. In a second stage, this imaginative mental image is received by the potential intellect (the passive intellectual potency of the soul). By means of the light of the agent intellect (the active intellectual power of the soul) the intelligible likeness *(species intelligibilis)* is born. This intelligible *species* now replaces the sensible likeness of the object and leaves its impression on the possible intellect. At this final stage the possible intellect, actualized by the presence of the concept, gives birth to the act of understanding. At each level of the cognitive process, the activity of abstraction involves various moments of intellectual receptivity and activity, as the mind interacts with its object. The process itself begins with the external object, moves through the senses to the imagination, from the imagination to the intelligible *species,* and finally to the fullest light of intellectual activity birthing into the conceptual order. The entire process involves moments of mediated representation. While the activity of abstraction began with sense experience, the concluding act of abstractive understanding considers its object independently of any actual existence it might have in the extra-mental world. Indeed, for Scotus, abstraction does not require the real presence of the object itself, only "something in which the object is displayed."[5]

5. *Ordinatio* I, d. 3, n. 382 (ed. Vat. 3:232–233; see also Appendix A, 3:366–367).

Universals such as humanity, rationality, and animality, as well as the essence (or *quidditas,* the whatness) of common natures belong to this abstract, conceptual order. For example, my experiences of Peter and Paul as two distinct yet similar individuals translates into imaginative phantasms which, for their part, give rise to the concepts human or rational, Peterity or Paulity (these referring to the essence of the individual) as conceptual formulations of the reality of experience. The existence of such a scientific, conceptual order depends radically upon the extra-mental world, sense experience, and the intelligible *species.* However, once generated, the body of abstract knowledge is independent of sense data, insofar as it abstracts from the actual existence of the beings known. In this way, sciences like metaphysics and theology both pre-suppose and transcend common experience. They presuppose it because all abstractive reflection relies on sense experience. They transcend it because the objects of reflection lie in the conceptual order beyond the physical world.

In Scotist thought, abstractive cognition is not the only way in which the mind knows reality. As he develops his reflection upon this mode of cognitive presence at various levels of awareness, the Franciscan identifies a second act of cognition, belonging both to the senses and to the intellect. This act is immediate, with no representational species to mediate the mind's encounter with the object. Scotus calls it intuitive cognition and explains that it is like a vision *(visio),* an immediate awareness of an object in its entirety as present and existing. He offers two arguments in favor of such an act. The first is taken from the nature of sense experience. Our corporeal senses do experience such immediacy in relationship to the object of their activity as present and existing. Even the Aristotelian theory endows them with this immediacy. If the corporeal senses have direct access to a subject as present and existing, why, he wonders, deny this perfection to the intellect? His second argument is taken from the nature of the beatific vision and the human requirements for such a face-to-face encounter with God. Surely, if one seeks to explain the beatific vision in Aristotelian terms, then one must accord the intellect an object that is other than the *quiddities*.

When he presents the two acts of abstraction and intuition,[6] Scotus notes clearly that abstraction refers to the act by which one knows the object but abstracts from its presence or absence. Since knowledge obtained through abstraction uses the intelligible *species,* the continued presence of the extra-mental object is not part of the cognitive act, nor is it required. The object as known in the phantasm or *species* mediates between the mind and extra-mental reality. By contrast, intuition is not representational. Here one knows the object precisely as present and existing. As he presented intuition in its most developed form, it does not mean for Scotus, as it did for Henry, an act whose immediacy is opposed to discursive reasoning.[7] Rather, it is an act whose immediacy dispenses with the need for any mental *species*. It is a type of existential immediacy. It is the experience the human intellect will have in the beatific vision: an immediate encounter with God.

In sum, intuition has two main characteristics. First, it dispenses with the intelligible *species* and transcends the Aristotelian cognitional apparatus. Second, and because of this cognitive immediacy, it is an indubitable act. Unlike the act of abstraction, the act of intuition is accompanied by the certainty of the object's existence. In this way, the act of intuition includes all the perfection of abstraction along with the certainty of existence.

6. In *Lectura* II, d. 3, nn. 285-290 (ed. Vat. 18:321–323) and *Quodlibet* q. 6 (*God and Creatures,* 6.17–6.20, 135–137).

7. Although he seems to have used it in this way in the *Lectura* I, d. 3, discussion. See A. B. Wolter, "Duns Scotus on Intuition, Memory and Our Knowledge of Individuals," in *The Philosophical Theology,* 107, n. 29. As is true of most of Scotus's positions, Henry of Ghent's formulation of a question or a problem is the starting point for his critical reflection. In this way, Scotus uses much of Henry's conceptual framework and terminology.

Intuitive acts can be of two sorts: perfect or imperfect. In a perfect act of intuition, the mind knows an object as present at the very moment of cognition. In an imperfect act of intuition, the mind remembers an object that was known perfectly in the past, when it was actually present. In this way, the imperfect act calls to mind the perfect act of intuition. An imperfect act of intuition might also anticipate a future event, such as in a prophetic vision. Memory and foresight, then, belong to the category of imperfect intuitive acts.

Whereas his early texts attribute the possibility of such activity to the afterlife, Scotus's later teaching affirms that it does, indeed, belong to human experience *pro statu isto*. In his *Questions on Aristotle's Metaphysics,* Scotus suggests that intuition is not simply a cognitive experience we will have in the beatific vision, but that the intellect can and does have such acts of immediate awareness in this life. His argument is simple: our intellect is a power superior to vision in the eye. It would be unreasonable, he argues, to attribute immediate awareness to the power of vision and deny it to the power of intellection.[8] Intuitive cognition is a pure act of presence between the mind and the object.

Despite its immediacy and the certainty of the presence of the object, intuition has its limits. At no time does Scotus endow the act of intuition with an ability to grasp a singular object *qua* singular in its proper intelligibility. Intuition knows the singular *qua* existing and present. The act of abstraction seizes the nature of the object.[9]

8. "However, it seems that there is [i.e., intuitive cognition in the intellect in this life], because whatever is of perfection in an unqualified sense in an inferior power ought to be assumed of the more perfect." II, q. 3, n. 23. *Questions on the Metaphysics of Aristotle by John Duns Scotus,* trans. G. Etzkorn and A.B. Wolter (St. Bonaventure: Franciscan Institute, 1997), I:198.

9. "The intellect, in understanding the universal, abstracts each [of the attributes] [one at a time], so that it might eventually understand the singular, namely the nature which is [in fact] 'this' but not *qua* 'this.' But with the accidents proper to this, it [the intellect] composes a subject with accidents." *Questions on the Metaphysics* VII, q. 15, n. 8 (II:262–63).

Thus, neither act reaches the particular in all its essential particularity. What the intellect does understand, via both intuitive and abstractive activity, would be the universal or nature of the object, along with those accidents that are proper to it (via abstraction) and as it is presently existing (via intuition).

While the process of abstraction begins with the intuitive and immediate access of the senses to the world (sense intuition), intellectual intuition is not the first act of cognition, nor does it ground this theory. Unlike Ockham, Scotus does not hold that intuitive cognition is foundational to our understanding of the world. Rather, he holds that our first acts of cognitive awareness are based, as Aristotle explains, upon the process of sense intuition and the activity of abstraction that begins there. Only subsequently does intuition provide us with that immediate awareness of our own acts of sensing, intellection and willing. These have as their necessary foundation the actual presence of sense objects in the world. As the fulfillment rather than the source of human understanding, intuitive introspective acts include reflection upon acts of abstractive cognition as well as upon earlier acts of sensory intuition.

Finally, intuitive cognition plays an essential role in moral judgment. In *Ordinatio* III, d. 14 Scotus presents the intuitive act as a necessary condition for any affirmation of the truth of a contingent, existential statement. The act reveals the present state of affairs to the moral subject. Additionally, he affirms in *Ordinatio* IV, d. 45, that without the act of intuition, no certainty of the existence of the object of knowledge could be maintained. Indeed, the very possibility of deliberation about a contingent state of affairs depends upon an intuitive act. The activity of reflection upon past events of a person's life, so necessary for conversion or repentance, requires the sort of access to reality that intuition guarantees.

While not yet at the position Ockham would advance about the primacy of intuitive cognition, or even at the centrality of the question of certainty for any scientific endeavor, Scotus is clearly beyond the Aristotelian cognitional theory of abstraction that typifies someone like Thomas Aquinas. By the end of the thirteenth century, the cognitional question has shifted from "Can the singular be known?" to "Of what mode is knowledge of the singular?"[10] With his distinction between the acts of abstractive and intuitive cognition, Scotus contrasts the abstract order of metaphysical speculation with the contingent order of experience. He thereby concedes to the Augustinian tradition that there is indeed direct intelligibility of the singular as existing (intuitive cognition) and to the Aristotelian tradition that in the present state *(pro statu isto)* any scientific understanding of the singular would be indirect (abstractive cognition).

Taken together, intuitive and abstractive cognition explain how the mind is present to reality, both as to extra-mental and internal states of affairs. This two-fold act of presence is simultaneous and progressive, moving from the senses to the concept. Cognition begins with an initial, indistinct awareness of the presence of an existing reality on the part of the senses (sensible intuition). The mind progresses via phantasm and intelligible *species* toward a clearer and clearer grasp of the nature of what stands before it (in the act of abstraction). Because the mind is both present to the object as well as to itself, the process of awareness is accompanied by the consciousness of the knower as present. This reflective self-awareness is an act of intuition, which though immediate, is itself capable of leaving behind an impression in the memory. This impression is not a representational *species* of what is known, in the way that the intelligible *species* is present to the mind, but is rather the memory of the act of mutual presence between the mind and the object. In such an act of imperfect intuition one calls to mind both an event along with one's

10. For a seminal and in depth study on this, see Camille Bérubé, *La connaissance de l'individu au Moyen Age.*

presence to it (the earlier act of *perfect intuition*). At the level of judgment, the certainty of intuition provides the basis for the truth of any contingent proposition. This certainty grounds moral deliberation and makes possible certain knowledge of the self. It explains the possibility of regret and conversion as the result of self-awareness and reflection upon one's past actions.

Finally, this capacity for immediate presence, both to the object and to the self, offers the framework within which to understand the experience of the beatific vision as the fulfillment of natural perfection. Because the mind is equipped with all that it needs for such immediate knowing, the blessed in heaven require no light of glory or special revelation for the direct face-to-face vision of God. All that is required is from the side of God, that is, the immediate and voluntary divine self-revelation as object.

Scotus's discussion of abstraction and intuition is motivated by two main concerns. First, he seeks to explain how any science of reality can be a science of what lies beyond the powers of sense perception. Metaphysics can be the science of the transcendentals (being, true, good, one). Second, he wants to account for the beatific vision as the natural fruition of the conditions already present in human nature, that is, as an activity that does no violence to the natural constitution of the human person. While the act of abstraction can explain the conceptual framework required for scientific knowledge, it is the act of intuition that grounds such science in an objective, extra-mental order to which the mind has access, albeit indistinctly and confusedly prior to any deliberate reflection. The activity of human understanding is grounded on the certainty of the object as existing, as it appears to the mind via sensible and intellectual intuition.[11]

Finally, the distinction between abstractive and intuitive knowl-

11. Richard Dumont identifies the key difference between the Scotist and Kantian epistemology at this important point. ". . . [T]he crucial difference between the

edge reveals how the science of theology can exist *pro statu isto* as knowledge of God distinct from that of the beatific vision.[12] By identifying the face-to-face vision of God with the act of intellectual intuition, Scotus can point to abstractive cognition as that proper to theology as a science in the strongest Aristotelian sense.[13]

2.2 The Formal Distinction

The act of abstractive cognition has as its object the essence of an individual, not in its particularity, but according to its common nature or universal characteristic. This essence is expressed in the definition. In this way, the activity of abstraction gives rise to the idea of humanity as an aspect of the individual (a rational animal) or of rationality, animality, or any other concept by means of which an extra-mental individual can be considered. In a certain individual, Peter, humanity, rationality, and animality coincide and are inseparably bound to one particular person. These aspects can be considered distinctly or independently of one another. They can even be considered independently of Peter himself. They are inseparable in reality yet separable in thought. Considered in this way, such attributes are

---

Kantian and Scotistic noetic is the issue of intellectual intuition. Whereas Kant simply denies to the human intellect an intuitive access to reality, Scotus does not." "Intuition: Prescript or Postscript to Scotus' Demonstration of God's Existence," in *Deus et homo ad mentem I. Duns Scoti*, ed. C. Bérubé (Rome: Cura Commissionis Scotisticae, 1972), 86.

12. See Olivier Boulnois's discussion of the Scotist transition from analogy to univocity in "Duns Scot, théoricien de l'analogie de l'être," in *John Duns Scotus: Metaphysics and Ethics*, 293–315.

13. Stephen Dumont argues that the Scotist distinction between abstractive and intuitive cognition actually had as its primary goal the defense of the science of theology, rather than as an attempt to ground cognition on the certainty of intuition. It was, therefore, abstraction rather than intuition that was his main concern, and the reason why he continued to refine the distinction between the two over many years. See his "Theology as a Science and Duns Scotus's Distinction between Intuitive and Abstractive Cognition," *Speculum* 64 (1989): 579–99.

called the formalities within the individual. A formality is the objective, extra-mental basis for a concept, which represents a partial, intelligible aspect of the being under consideration. Abstractive cognition reveals that the mind is able to distinguish such formalities and consider them independently of one another. In this way, cognitive activity points to the formal distinction.

The formal distinction is best understood at a mid-point between the two distinctions known as conceptual and real. A conceptual distinction is purely mental and has no reality external to its mental existence. Two terms that are conceptually distinct have an identical referent in reality, but represent that referent according to different formulations. For example, the "morning star" is conceptually distinct from the "evening star," since both terms refer to an identical reality, Venus, known under two distinct conceptualizations. By contrast, two terms are really distinct when their meanings are different and their referents are capable of existing or actually exist independently of one another. For example, two individuals are really distinct, as are the body and soul, or a substance and its accidents. Between the conceptual and the real distinction we find the formal distinction. This distinction is more than conceptual, yet less than real. In other words, the formal distinction is based upon an existing aspect of the object (Scotus calls it a distinction *a parte rei*) and so is not merely mental, yet the aspect in question is not capable of existing independently from the object in which it is found. The object of the formal distinction is a potentially knowable aspect of the particular being in question.

The most common use of the formal distinction (and the only one Ockham admitted) is that between the persons of the Trinity and the divine nature. Each person of the Trinity is formally distinct from the divine essence, since the divine person cannot exist independently from the divine nature. The distinct conceptualization of each person is based upon something in the divine essence and can be considered distinctly from that nature. Similarly, Scotus holds that there is only a formal distinction between the soul and its faculties, intellect and will. The soul is identical to and inseparable from the faculties of knowing and loving. However, we can consider the soul both under the aspect of cognition alone, without volition, and independently of the aspects of volition and cognition. Such consideration terminates in a concept that is distinct and clear. An intermediate distinction such as this, between the conceptual and the real, explains how the intelligibility of what exists is based upon something about reality itself or, at least, about the relationship between an object and the mind's understanding of it.

Scotus refers to the formal distinction as more properly a "formal non-identity"[14] where an aspect is understood to be formally distinct, that is, distinct according to the order of thought. The distinction is *a parte rei*, however, which means that the ability of the mind to consider this formality depends upon the potential for such conceptualization, a potential that really belongs to the object under consideration. This type of distinction was not a Scotist innovation, for it corresponds to Bonaventure's *distinctio rationis* and Henry of Ghent's intentional distinction. However, Scotus points out that his formal distinction postulates what is required in things, in order to account for Henry's intentional distinction.[15] There must be something existing prior to conceptualization of it, in order to avoid a *fictio mentis.*

Allan Wolter gives the clearest explication of the distinction when he presents four central points of agreement among medieval thinkers about it:

1. There is an isomorphism between thought and reality in virtue of which the former may be said to be a likeness of the latter. This

14. In *Reportatio Parisiensis* I, d. 45, q. 2, n. 9 in *Opera Omnia* (Vivès 22: 503).
15. *Questions on the Metaphysics* VII, q. 19, n. 5 (II:316).

likeness is based upon what reveals itself in both the world of facts and the world of thought about that world.

2. Based upon this community of intelligibility, we can speak of a *ratio*, a *logos* or an Avicennian *intentio* as existing either in things or in the mind.

3. To the extent that this *ratio* is a property or characteristic of the object, we are justified in asserting that the individual in question is "this type of thing."

4. Despite the fact that these *rationes* can be conceived independently of one another, such that their definitions differ and that what is implied by one is not implied by another, in the extra-mental world they constitute one and only one thing. They are not really distinct parts, like bricks in a wall.[16]

Scotus holds that there is a formal distinction between generic perfection and specific difference (i.e., between animality and rationality in "rational animal"), between the *haecceitas* (thisness) or individuating difference of an individual and those features it has in common with others of a similar type (the common nature), between the transcendental attributes of being (good, true, one) as well as between being and those attributes.

Closely related to the formal distinction is the formal modal distinction. This distinction applies not to different attributes or aspects of a being, but to the distinction between a subject, such as intelligence in humans, and its mode, such as finite. In the human person, intelligence is a finite characteristic. Scotus also calls this modal distinction a distinction *a parte rei*, but yet less than the strict formal distinction. An intrinsic mode (such as finitude) is not a formality in its own right, insofar as it could not be conceived clearly as an independent concept, even though the line between the two sorts of distinction is very slim and easily crossed. A closer consideration

16. Wolter, "The Formal Distinction," in *The Philosophical Theology*, 30.

of two propositions reveals how the formal distinction and the formal modal distinction are not identical. When we consider the expression "a being is good," for instance, it appears to be identical to the expression "a being is infinite." Careful reflection upon the two reveals that they are not of the same sort, since infinity is a mode of being while goodness is a transcendental attribute. Unlike the attribute *good*, the mode *infinity* is incapable of terminating a definite, proper concept. And, while the concept *being* can be conceived without its intrinsic mode *infinite*, the concept without the mode is imperfect.

The significance of the formal modal distinction becomes clear when we understand its role as foundation for those concepts that are predicable univocally of God and creatures. Consider, for example, the concept *wisdom* as predicable of God and creatures. Scotus asks, "How can the concept common to God and creatures be considered real unless it can be abstracted from some reality of the same kind?"[17] In response, he explains the difference between the modal distinction and the strict formal distinction. A perfection and its intrinsic mode, such as infinite wisdom, are not so identical that we cannot conceive of the perfection (wisdom) without the mode (infinity). We can, indeed, conceive of wisdom independently of whether it is finite (human wisdom) or infinite (divine wisdom). The perfection and mode are not really distinct, however, because they cannot be separated in reality; nor are they formally distinct, because they are not two formalities each capable of terminating a distinct and proper concept. Nonetheless, they are still not identical, because the objective reality signified by the perfection with its modal intensity (infinite wisdom) is not precisely the same as that signified by the perfection alone (wisdom).

The formal modal distinction, then, actually safeguards the reali-

---

17. *Ordinatio* I, d. 8, q. 3, n. 137 (ed. Vat. 4:221–22).

ty of those concepts, such as being, that are predicable of God and creatures. Without the mode, these sorts of concepts are common and imperfect. They function semantically in a confused manner, designating only in a general way. With the mode, the concept is called proper, and has a more focused, specifying role. The referent (that is, the being designated as infinite) emerges more clearly within the field, like a figure against a background. The formal modal distinction, in a manner similar to the formal distinction, is linked to the activity of abstractive cognition. The modal distinction's specificity can be clearly seen when we reflect upon the experience of the beatific vision. The blessed in heaven, states Scotus, perceive the infinite perfection of divine infinite wisdom intuitively, not as two formal objects, but as one.[18] By contrast, no intuition in heaven erases the formal distinction between the divine persons and the divine essence, or between the divine intellect and the divine will. In short, the formal distinction is such that it remains even in the beatific vision, while the formal modal distinction does not.[19]

The formal modal distinction points to the intensity of perfection that differentiates the divine from created orders. It is this distinction of modes, rather than formalities that reveals most clearly what is foundational: the existence of common, imperfect concepts whose domain is exhausted by the disjunction of finite and infinite. Of these, the most perfect common concept, capable of univocal predication at the most common level, is being itself.

2.3 The Univocity of Being

Primo in intellectu cadit ens. Being is the first and most basic object of intellection. Avicenna's discussion of the primacy of being in

18. *Ordinatio* I, d. 8, q. 3, nn. 137–42 (ed. Vat. 4:221–24).
19. A. B. Wolter, *The Transcendentals and Their Function in the Metaphysics of Duns Scotus* (St. Bonaventure: Franciscan Institute, 1946), 25–27.

his *Metaphysics*[20] was the foundation for most thirteenth century speculation on Aristotelian insights as they relate to the question of knowledge and its relationship to reality.[21] Although it is the most basic and most general of all concepts, prior to all determination, being is not a genus. Indeed, being cannot be a genus because, if it were, then the modal intensity of finite or infinite would represent the specific difference. As we have seen, modal intensity represents not a species within being, but a perfection of being. Prior to logic, being is the foundational and necessary concept for any cognitional act, the horizon within which knowing inscribes itself. Non-being, while it can be represented linguistically, cannot be conceived in a manner other than the absence or negation of being. Thus, in order to be understood, even the concept of non-being requires the prior concept of being.

Our earlier reflection upon the modes of intellection (abstraction and intuition) revealed the formal and real distinctions that are based upon objective reality. Both the formal distinction and the formal modal distinction point to an objective order to which the mind is present. In addition, the mind's presence to itself and to its own activity reveals, at a most basic level, its primary object, being, whose presence to the mind is the necessary condition for any knowledge. For Scotus, the primacy of being as a univocal concept is revealed as the necessary condition for metaphysics, for any language about God and for any science of theology.[22]

A concept is univocal, states Scotus, that "has sufficient unity in

20. Avicenna, *Metaphysica* I, 6 (72rb) *Liber De Philosophia Prima sive scientia divina* I–IV, ed. S. Van Riet (Leiden: Brill 1977).

21. Scotus cites Avicenna's *Metaphysics* and names the author in *Questions on the Metaphysics* I, 1: "Is the proper subject of metaphysics being qua being as Avicenna claims or God and the Intelligences as the Commentator, Averroes, assumes?" (I:13).

22. He asserts this in both *Lectura* and *Ordinatio* versions of I, d. 3. The *Lectura* claim is found at n. 113 (ed. Vat. 16:266) and the *Ordinatio* n. 139 (ed. Vat. 3:87).

itself that to affirm and deny it of the same subject suffices as a contradiction. It also suffices as a syllogistic middle term, so that where
two terms are united in a middle term that is one in this fashion, they
are inferred without a fallacy of equivocation to be united among
themselves."[23] Despite the centrality of the univocity of being, Scotus discusses the nature of our concepts of God in terms of analogy
as well.[24] He admits that there are analogous concepts we do use to
think of God, yet maintains that analogy itself would be impossible
without some more basic, common concept that is univocal.[25] Without univocity of being, analogy would be merely equivocation, and
no language or understanding of God would be possible.

  Scotus sets forth his argument for the univocity of being in *Ordinatio* I, d. 3, q. 1.[26] The text deals specifically with the possibility of
knowledge about God and, by implication, of the existence of theology as a science. Here, the Franciscan develops his position on the
univocity of being in tandem with a discussion of scientific knowledge of God. Together, both constitute the *sine qua non* condition
for any possible theology: human cognition must have some natural
basis from which to reflect on the divine. This natural ground is, in
Scotist thought, the univocity of the concept of being. If, in his argument, Scotus can show that the human mind has foundational access to reality, and if that reality provides an adequate basis for natural knowledge of God, then theology can be understood as a
science, whose content does not exhaust the truth about God.

  23. *Ordinatio* I, d. 3 n. 25 (in *Duns Scotus, Metaphysician*, 109).
  24. In his *Questions on the Metaphysics* IV, q. 1, he notes that the metaphysician
(who deals with reality) attributes according to analogy, while the logician would
deem this equivocation. See n. 70 (I:271). Marginal notes in the manuscripts point
out that this was not his position in the *Sentences*. See also *Ordinatio* I, d. 8, q. 3, n.
83 (ed. Vat. 4:191). O. Boulnois offers a helpful discussion of analogy/univocity in
his "Duns Scot, théoricien de l'analogie de l'être," 293–315.
  25. This is his critique of Henry of Ghent's position.
  26. An English version of this text can be found in *Duns Scotus, Metaphysician*,
108–33.

Three points of this textual presentation are worthy of note.
First, Scotus reasons from the discussion of language about God to
the deeper consideration of the sort of foundation that would explain how such language is possible (namely, that being rather than
quidditas is the first object of the intellect). In this, he follows his
usual methodological procedure, moving from experience to what
grounds the possibility of that experience. Second, Scotus bases his
argument, as we would expect, upon the Aristotelian cognitive model, where sense knowledge, mental species and agent intellect form
the constitutive parts. Finally, the Subtle Doctor rejects Henry of
Ghent's proposed illumination theory, along with its argument from
analogy. For Scotus, Henry's position on analogy without an under-
lying conceptual univocity is simply equivocation. The Franciscan argues that when we conceive of God as wise, we consider a property
(wisdom) that perfects nature. In order that we might do this and in
light of the cognitive structure Aristotle provides, we must first have
in mind some essence in which the property exists. When we consider properties or attributes such as wisdom, we do not understand
them as pure abstraction, but as belonging to an essence. This more
basic, *quidditative* concept is the conceptual foundation for scientific
knowledge. Were such a concept not univocal, theology could not
be a science, nor would language about God be meaningful.

Scotus presents five reasons in favor of univocity, of which the
first is, in his mind, the most compelling. In his opening argument,
Scotus offers as the major premise a common experience immediately evident to any knower: that concepts of which we are certain
are distinct from those of which we are in doubt. Indeed, in the
mind of the knower, such concepts are distinguishable mentally. His
minor premise is taken from the evidence of philosophical disagreement. An individual in this life *(pro statu isto)* can be certain that God
exists, while in doubt as to whether this being is finite or infinite.
The concept of God as a being is therefore distinguishable from the

concept of God as this or that. And, although the prior concept (that God is a being) is included in the later one (that God is finite or infinite), it is in itself neither of them. Scotus then concludes that the more basic concept in this example is a univocal concept of being.

The argument for the first premise rests upon negative necessity. If there were no concept distinguishable, on the basis of its certainty, from other dubious concepts, then the human mind would have no certainty about any concept at all. Indeed, if all concepts were subject to doubt, then no scientific knowledge would be possible. Thus, the immediate subjective experience of concepts possessing differing degrees of certainty (an experience which Scotus asserts to be self-evident) is explained in terms of the deeper logical requirement for the possibility of any scientific knowledge.

Scotus proves the minor premise with historical evidence. Every philosopher of antiquity who proposed a first principle was certain that what he proposed as the first principle was a being: whether fire, water, etc. However, these philosophers were not certain about whether this being was created or uncreated, or whether it was first or not first. This point can also be confirmed by the obvious fact of philosophical disagreement. A third person (a student, for example), attempting to understand the nature of such a question, could conclude with certainty that what was proposed as first principle by these various philosophers was indeed a being, and yet, because of the many contrary philosophical opinions, still be in doubt as to whether the first principle was this or that sort of being. If, by means of a demonstration, this student could be shown that one or the other of the alternatives were false (that the first principle is not fire, for instance), this demonstration would not destroy the student's already certain notion that the first is a being. It would only eliminate the doubtful notion concerning fire. The certain notion would even be conserved in the resulting conception proved about fire (i.e., "that the first being is not fire"). Throughout the demonstration, therefore, the certain concept remains, both distinct from and related to the doubtful ones. This concept is the foundation upon which the reasoning depends. It is therefore, more basic than what is doubtful.

Scotus then introduces a possible objection that would arise from Henry's position. Against this argument that scientific knowledge requires some one univocal concept, the objection claims that such univocity is not necessary. Indeed, each thinker has in his mind two similar (certain and basic) concepts that only appear to be one concept because of their analogous relationship. This objection suggests, as would Henry, that no univocal concept is required for theology to be a science. One only needs concepts that are very similar, such as those relating natural knowledge to knowledge of God. In response, Scotus argues that if this objection were accepted, then the unity of any univocal concept would thereby be destroyed. Indeed, a concept such as human would not pertain univocally to Socrates and to Plato. The two would be related by two concepts that only seem to be univocal because of a great resemblance.

A second argument in favor of univocity, based upon the Aristotelian cognitive model of abstraction, rejects the possibility of analogy by means of an approach inspired by the *via negativa*. Because God is completely other, analogy attempts to explain concepts about God on the basis of their otherness. This approach, if true, would destroy the possibility of any natural knowledge or language about God, on the basis of the chasm that exists between human knowing and divine being.

Here, Scotus's first premise accepts that natural knowledge *pro statu isto* is the result of agents that move the intellect naturally. According to Aristotle, these agents are the object as revealed in the sense image (or phantasm) and the active intellect. The conclusion follows directly: given these two natural agents, there can be no way for the mind to give rise to a concept that is not related to them as effects to causes. In other words, there would be no possibility of a concept that is not univocal. The possibility of an analogous concept (one that would refer to God) could never be the result of natural cognitive powers and activity. Indeed, the analogous concept would be *other* to such an extent that it could have no foundation in nature. Thus, Aristotle's explanation of abstractive cognition offers no analogical basis for natural knowledge of God.

Scotus offers a first confirmation of this argument in the following manner. No object produces both a simple proper concept of itself and, in the same intellect, a simple proper concept of another object, unless the former contains the latter essentially or virtually. No created object essentially or virtually contains an uncreated object, because it is contrary to the idea of being posterior to contain virtually what is prior. Therefore, it is impossible that a created object could produce a simple concept that is proper to what is uncreated. Since all discursive reasoning requires a prior grasp of that toward which one reasons, there must be something to bridge the gap between created and uncreated. Since analogy plays upon the otherness of concepts that are proper to God, the only remaining solution would be univocity. Were the concept *being* not a univocal one, then no concept that is the result of natural cognition would be adequate to bridge the gap between our knowing objects in the world and our knowing objects that exist beyond sense experience. No analogous concept would arise, because there would be nothing on the basis of which the judgment of analogy could be made. There would be no natural concept of God and, *a fortiori*, no science of the divine, regardless of whether this be understood as metaphysics or theology.

A second confirmation follows. Every inquiry about God proceeds by means of formal notions (such as wisdom or intelligence) which, once freed from the imperfection and limitations of the created order, retain their formal meaning and are attributed to God.[27] In this way, wisdom and intelligence can be predicated of God in the most perfect way, according to a *via eminentiae*. Likewise, every inquiry about God proceeds, by means of a type of reduction, from ordinary human experience to a univocal concept common to the created and uncreated orders. In addition, every theological inquiry presupposes something common to God and the created order. And, were one to argue (as Henry of Ghent might) that such a formal notion is *other* as it relates to God, then one would have to conclude that there is no possible way to infer anything at all about God on the basis of creatures, thus destroying Henry's own argument in favor of analogy.

Following this, Scotus explains the precise sort of understanding we have of God in this life, its limitations, and how his position on univocity both takes this into account and explains the possibility of scientific knowledge of God. He agrees that in this life *(pro statu isto)*, no one has natural knowledge of God in a particular and proper way, that is, according to the divine essence as "just this" *(ut haec)*.[28] Such knowledge belongs only to the beatific vision, for it is God's self-revelation that makes this experience possible. In this way, the blessed enjoy knowledge of God, not as a natural object, but as an *obiectum voluntarium*. Accordingly, the position in favor of the univocity of being does not entail that this concept contains the proper and specific content within which God is understood. If the concept *being* had such positive content, then Scotus's position on univocity would be a type of illumination in disguise. Rather, notes Scotus, the univocation to which he refers obtains only in reference

27. Augustine argues in this way when he states "take this good and that good, remove this and that, if you can, and you will see God." *De trinitate* VIII, 3 (PL 42, 949) in *The Trinity*, intro., trans., notes by Edmund Hill, O.P. (Brooklyn: New City Press, 1991). Scotus cites this in *Ordinatio* II, d. 3, n. 399 (Vat. 7:564).

28. *Ordinatio* I, d. 3, n. 56 (*Duns Scotus, Metaphysician*, 115).

to general notions, on the basis of which some scientific reflection can take place.[29] The concept *being* is the most basic of these and the most minimal we have; it is the not-nothing, the formal category of something that is virtual in terms of what might fill it. The concept *being* is, then, most common, most basic and extends virtually to all that exists.

Scotus also argues that we can arrive at many concepts proper to God precisely because they do not apply to creatures: these are the pure perfections. This argument takes as its starting point a specific concept we can have of God, "infinite being" *(ens infinitum)* and proceeds, by means of reflection upon the concept, to the foundational concept *ens*. It is the mirror image of the reduction process noted earlier. We can, first, arrive at concepts proper to God by taking the concepts of all pure perfections to the highest degree. This *via eminentiae* would offer a descriptive and affirmative method for language about the divine. A less perfect, but simpler concept is also possible to us in the concept *infinite being (ens infinitum)*. *Infinite* does not function here as an attribute like goodness or truth, but as noted earlier, an intrinsic mode. The concept *infinite being* refers to "what is essentially one, namely, [it is a concept] of a subject with a certain grade of perfection—infinity."[30] Since, as noted in the first argument, one can be certain about the existence of a being and yet in doubt about its intrinsic mode, this most simple concept *ens infinitum* can be analyzed to reveal that about which one is certain, *ens*, as foundational to the discussion of the divine.

The fifth and final assertion based upon language about God is taken from the relationship between human acts of cognition and their connection to transcendental concepts as a bridge to knowl-

29. "For only in general notions is there univocation; imitation also is deficient, because it is imperfect, since creatures imperfectly imitate him . . ." *Ordinatio* I, d. 3, n. 57 (*Duns Scotus, Metaphysician,* 117).

30. *Ordinatio* I, d. 3, n. 58 (*Duns Scotus, Metaphysician,* 117).

edge of God. Since all scientific knowledge *pro statu isto* is abstractive, related to the impression of the species on the possible intellect, created objects can impress upon the intellect a likeness or species both proper to themselves and the species of the transcendentals. Examples here would be good, true, one. These can be applied commonly to themselves as transcendentals and to God. Scotus offers an example of how this might take place. The created intellect could use the species of good, of highest and of act to compose and conceive of "the highest good that is the most actual." This activity of composition and division is only possible on the basis of a concept that is common to both the created and uncreated orders.

In sum, Scotus offers a *sine qua non* argument for univocity in *Ordinatio* I, d. 3. Because of the nature of human cognition, and specifically the activity of abstraction as described by Aristotle's theory, were there no common or basic concept by means of which the finite intellect could consider all that exists, there would be no possibility of any science such as theology. The Franciscan also sees this argument as applicable to metaphysics. Since, for him, the transcendentals are the primary focus of metaphysical reflection and since, by definition, these lie beyond the categories of Aristotle and thus beyond sense perception,[31] were being not a univocal concept, no science of metaphysics would be possible. Therefore, the univocity of being is, first, the condition for the possibility of any metaphysics as well as of any theology.

A second implication follows from this argument. Being must also be the first object of the intellect, having a two-fold primacy: commonness and virtuality. In other words, everything that can be known either includes the notion of being (*in quid* or essentially) or is known via something that includes the notion of being (*in quale* or accidentally).

---

31. As the following chapter will make clear.

*And so it is evident that being has a primacy of community to the first
intelligibles—that is, to the quidditative concepts of genera, species, and
individuals, and to all the essential parts of these—and to the concept of
uncreated being; and it has a primacy of virtuality to all intelligibles
included in the first intelligibles—that is, to those qualitative concepts of
ultimate differences and proper attributes.*[32]

Our notions of God depend upon the univocity of being, as do
our notions of substance. Indeed, all that Scotus has argued about
the possibility of science and language about the divine he applies to
metaphysical knowledge. In his argument in favor of being as the
first object of the intellect, Scotus offers two reasons parallel to
those offered in favor of language about God. The first appeals to
our awareness of the difference between concepts about which we
are certain and those about which we are in doubt. Concepts that
are restrictive of other concepts and about which we are in doubt
presuppose the common concept of being that they restrict.

The second reason applies natural knowledge (based in the senses) to conclusions about what lies beyond physical appearances:
substance. If Aristotle's cognitional model is apt, then the intellect is
not moved immediately by substance any more than it is moved immediately by God. Rather, the intellect is moved by the accidental
attributes of a substance that are themselves known through the
senses. Our knowledge of substance and our ability to develop any
science of metaphysics depends upon the act of abstraction from
sense experience. This act of abstraction reveals the necessity of the
concept of being as foundational and most basic to all cognition, all
predication, and all use of language to describe reality. Scotus concludes, "and so nothing will be known of the essential parts of substance unless being is univocal to them and to accidents."[33]

32. *Ordinatio* I, d. 3, n. 137 (*Duns Scotus, Metaphysician*, 121).
33. *Ordinatio* I, d. 3, n. 145 (*Duns Scotus, Metaphysician*, 123).

Because of the way Scotus grounds the possibility of scientific knowledge on the relationship between the mind and reality, he affirms a three-fold certainty.[34] First, and foundationally, there is scientific certainty from analytic truths formally understood, where the predicate is seen to be contained in the subject. Such truths are primary and *per se nota,* such as "every whole is greater than a part." One need only understand the meaning of the terms whole and part to understand with certainty that every whole is greater than one of its parts. However, this certainty does not necessarily mean that in a given and particular set of circumstances, a particular whole will be judged to be greater than a particular part, since knowledge, dependent as it is on phantasms, can err. Thus, one can know with certainty that "a whole is greater than its part" and still judge wrongly, on the basis of faulty sense perception.

A second certainty arises from the perception of patterns in experience and, like analytic certainty, holds a formal truth. An example of this is the certainty that "every effect has a cause." This basic formal truth of scientific induction grounds the inferential reflection from effect to cause. Scotus offers the example of a lunar eclipse to explain how scientific reasoning, using the foundational cause/effect principle, inquires after the cause for a given effect, testing and removing explanations that prove unsatisfactory. In this way, the process of reasoning concludes to the affirmation that the moon cannot be the source of its own light and that the earth moves between the moon and the sun at certain intervals. Thus human experience and observation reveal patterns of events that are explained by means of the scientific certainty of the cause/effect relationship. Once again, this certainty of foundational truth does not remove the possibility of error, based upon faulty perception or reasoning.

A final level of certainty is found at internal or subjective states of

---

34. *Lectura* I, d. 3, nn. 172–81 (*Duns Scotus, Metaphysician,* 125–29).

awareness, such as "I am awake" or "I am thinking." These states are known with a certainty of immediacy, due to the intuitive powers of the intellect. Because no mental species or phantasm is needed, then no error of perception is possible. For this reason of immediacy, such propositions, when uttered, are not only true, but certain. Scotus holds that, were such immediate and certain knowledge not available to us, then no knowledge at all would be certain, no moral responsibility would be reasonable and, finally, no conversion possible.

Scotus successfully re-formulates and re-presents Augustinian cognitional conclusions within an Aristotelian framework and, by that fact, dismantles the theory of illumination as a viable alternative to the cognitional model based upon *De anima* III. He builds a natural bridge between philosophy and theology, showing that one can defend the formal, scientific dimension of theology on Aristotelian grounds and never sacrifice any central element of an Augustinian vision. Scotus extends the act of intuitive cognition from the senses to the intellect and offers an original integration of this theory into the Aristotelian noetic of his day. In doing so, he advances upon attempts by Vital du Four, Matthew of Aquasparta, and John Peckham before him. His cognitive theory provides the foundation for the certainty of subjective states and, more importantly (at least for him) explains how the beatific vision adds no perfection to the activity of the human intellect. No special illumination, no light of glory is needed to raise the human mind to enter the presence of God. Human nature is naturally constituted for the perfection that awaits it, even though that perfection surpasses its natural ability of attainment.[35] The experience of the beatific vision depends more on the divine will as *obiectum voluntarium* than on the human intellect.

---

35. On this aspect of Scotist thought, see Wolter's "Duns Scotus on the Natural Desire for the Supernatural," in *The Philosophical Theology*, 125–47.

In addition, Scotus re-frames the metaphysical question to focus on being and its transcendental attributes, true, good, and one. As the subsequent chapters make clear, this re-framing identifies metaphysics as a transcendental science that deals with cognition as it relates to reality. In this way, metaphysics prepares the way for theology, since both deal with the realm of being that lies beyond sense experience. The univocity of being grounds the unity of all human cognition and enables both the mind and language to say something about the realm beyond the physical.

3. METAPHYSICS AND NATURAL
KNOWLEDGE OF GOD

MEDIEVAL AUTHORS customarily began their study of a given discipline with a consideration of its scientific character. Therefore, before Scotus considers the specific content of Aristotle's *Metaphysics*, he first discusses the epistemological problems that are involved in metaphysical reflection. Not only does metaphysics claim to be a science, but since its earliest beginnings, it lays claim to the highest philosophical status. Metaphysics claims to be the first of all sciences. Its primacy results from the unique character of its object, as Scotus affirms in his *Prologue* to the *Questions on the Metaphysics*.[1] This connection of object to prima-

---

1. "In this way, therefore, it is clear how this science is concerned with what is most knowable. From this it follows that it is most truly a science and thus most to be sought, as was proved above." *Questions on the Metaphysics, Prologue* n. 21 (I:8). See also n. 26 (I:10).

cy is not accidental. Indeed, according to Aristotle's doctrine of the sciences,[2] every science is determined essentially through its object and all the sciences are related to one another through their respective objects. The most important science has the most important object. One understands the object of a science in advance, either in the form of a purely nominal definition or in terms of its existence. It belongs to a particular science to determine the qualities belonging to the object, or to demonstrate that certain qualities belong, in fact, to that object. If the object appears only in terms of its nominal definition, then the science must construct a proof for its existence along with its qualities. It is therefore no accident that Scotus opens his consideration of Aristotle's *Metaphysics* (in the *Prologue*) with the question of the dignity and nobility of the science. He answers this question within the context of a sustained reflection upon its object.

3.1 The Nobility of Metaphysics

The *Prologue* begins with a citation from Aristotle's work, according to which all men, by nature, desire to know (*Metaphysics* I, 1, 980a21). Scotus assumes that this passage contains the thesis regarding the nobility of the science. He first explicates this thesis and then offers a proof for the nobility of metaphysics, in order to bring Aristotle's text into dialogue with the position on the nobility of the science. The Franciscan begins as follows: "If all men by nature desire to know, then they desire most of all the greatest knowledge or science."[3] It is therefore necessary to identify that science which is the most noble. To answer this question, Scotus first formulates two

---

2. Aristotle's discussion in the *Posterior analytics* was definitive for epistemological questions in philosophy and theology during the thirteenth century. See *The Complete Works of Aristotle,* ed. J. Barnes (Princeton: Princeton University Press, 1984), 114–166.

3. *Prologue,* n. 16, *Questions on the Metaphysics* (I:6).

assumptions.[4] The first, or major premise, offers the Aristotelian definition in order to determine that precise object to which the greatest science corresponds ("those things that are most knowable"). His second, or minor premise has two parts. The first part focuses more closely on the definition of this object that belongs to the highest science. The second part maintains that metaphysics concerns itself with this object. From these premises, two conclusions follow. However, in order for these to be valid, the second assumption (the minor premise) must be demonstrated in both its parts. One does not need a proof for the first premise, since it is a definition taken from Aristotle. It is the second premise that is critical to this argument. In other words, if Scotus can show that the state of affairs posited by the minor premise is true for metaphysics, then the conclusion to the primacy of metaphysics will follow. Furthermore, it will also follow from this that metaphysical knowledge is the most noble.

The major premise defines the greatest science as one "which is about those things that are most knowable."[5] The minor premise states that, since the expression maximally knowable can be understood in two different ways, there are two different kinds of beings that are maximally knowable. On the one hand, the maximally knowable could be understood as that which is the first of all things known and without which nothing else can be known. On the other hand, the maximally knowable could be understood as that which is known most certainly. According to this minor premise, the science of metaphysics deals with the most knowable in both senses of this term.

Scotus now demonstrates the truth of both parts of the minor premise. He begins with the first part, that the object is prior in the sense that it is the first thing known.[6] He identifies this first thing with what is most common to all that is. This is being *qua* being and its properties, since one can predicate being of everything that is. If one considers any being solely from the perspective of the fact of its existence (however this might be construed), then one considers it as being *qua* being, or as an existing thing insofar as it exists. However, one can also say of everything that is, that it is an entity (a particular being), a subject-matter (for thought) or an object in reality. These three aspects follow upon the determination of being *qua* being and are only recognized after this first, more primary, determination. Insofar as they refer to the same conceptual range as does the first and most basic determination (being as such), they are no less common. In this way, *ens* (a being) and *res* (a thing) can also be understood as transcendentals, along with *bonum* (good), *unum* (one) and *verum* (true), because they do not fall within Aristotle's ten categories (the predicables), which are only valid in reference to independently existing beings.[7] On the contrary, these lie beyond the categories (from the Latin: *transcendere* and *transcendens*). That to which such transcendental properties refer appears first to the knowing subject, insofar as knowledge of them cannot be acquired through anything more common and therefore more knowable than themselves. On this point, Scotus cites Avicenna's interpretation of the *Metaphysics*.[8] Aristotle's authority as founder of the science of metaphysics is also brought to bear in this argument, when Scotus notes that all these properties, understood to be common to all beings, belong to the subject matter of metaphysics.[9] With Avicenna's

---

7. In contrast to Scotus, Avicenna considers the determination "entity" (*res*) among the transcendental determinations, as is shown by Scotus himself. Scotus uses the terms *ens* and *res* (thing) interchangeably. See *Duns Scotus, Metaphysician*, 179, note 33, as well as *Quodlibet* q. 3, n. 2. 3.8 in *God and Creatures*: 61.

8. "For Avicenna says in Book I, *Metaphysics* ch. 5: that 'being and thing are impressed in the soul with the first impressions, and they are not acquired from anything more knowable than themselves . . .'" n. 17 (I:7).

9. "These most common things are considered by metaphysics, according to the Philosopher in the beginning of Book IV of this work: There is a science which

help, Scotus has shown, first, what is maximally knowable. Second, with the help of Aristotle, he has demonstrated that this maximally knowable is the object of metaphysics.

The first part of the second assumption is not as yet sufficiently proven by means of such a consideration. Scotus has only shown by this argument that metaphysics is in fact concerned with what is maximally knowable. He has not shown that it necessarily concerns this object. He immediately turns to this task.[10] Again following Avicenna, Scotus states that the content of what is less common (or more particular) can only be known by means of the content of the more common. In other words, what is valid for the particular can only be known once one understands what is valid for all things. Those things which are less common, or only valid for certain beings, are treated by the various special sciences whose objects involve just these sorts of beings. If, therefore, the knowledge of the smaller group presupposes the knowledge of what is valid for all, then every specialized science would first be required to consider what is valid for all before it could consider what lies within its own domain. Following Aristotle, Scotus holds that the sciences relate to one another according to a division of labor. It would be unreasonable for each lower science to be required to deal with what is predicated of all beings at the level of the most common. Consequently, there must be one general science among all the sciences that deals with the transcendentals as such. This science is metaphysics. Scotus explains the name *metaphysics* on the basis that this science deals with the transcendentals, and is therefore the transcending science.[11] The first part of the term, *meta*, comes from the Greek root, beyond (or in Latin, *trans*). Scotus omits the second part of the term *(phy)* and

---

deals theoretically with being *qua* being and with what characterizes it as such" (*Metaphysics* IV, 1, 1003a21–22) n. 17 (I:7).

10. At n. 18 (I:7–8).

11. "It is, as it were, the transcending science, because it is concerned with the transcendentals" (n. 18, I:8).

focuses on the third part *(ycos)*, translating it (possibly relying on an older tradition) as science. Metaphysics is then that science that lies beyond all other sciences: the highest science.

The Franciscan next turns to the second part of the minor premise.[12] Here it is claimed that what is maximally knowable is what can be most securely known, or what can be known with the highest degree of certainty. This second part also claims that metaphysics itself deals with those matters that are maximally knowable and, therefore, knowable with the greatest certainty. Now, what is knowable most certainly involves the principles and causes for everything. The more constitutive priority they have in the order of being, the more certain they are.[13]

Several key ideas lie beneath this very simple statement. First, we see here the ontological and metaphysical conviction that (with the exception of God) all that is, both in its essence and in its existence, can be traced back to foundations that lie partially in principles or causes extrinsic to and independent of the being in question, and partially in dependent principles and causes intrinsic to the being, known by means of a separate reflection. For example, in the case of a marble statue, the block from which it has been hewn can be called the material cause and the form given by the sculptor can be called the formal cause. Both causes are dependent, because they only occur together with the marble statue. By contrast, the sculptor can be identified as the efficient cause and the person who commissioned the statue as the final cause. Both the sculptor and the person commissioning the piece are independent causes of the marble statue that are, nevertheless, essential for the formation of the work of art. All four causes exist prior to the statue, according to the constitutive order.

12. At n. 21 (I:8).
13. "What is knowable most certainly are principles and causes, and the more they are prior the more certainly are they known" (n. 21, I:8).

A second key idea is equally important. The principles themselves are more stable than that of which they are the cause or principle. The less something is subject to change, the more certain or secure is the knowledge obtained therefrom. Hence those principles and causes must be most certain that are already more stable and less subject to change than that of which they are the principles and causes. If one follows the chain of principles and causes back to the first cause or principle (assuming no infinite regress) then one reaches the first principle of all that is, and this would also be the most certain. At this point in the argument, a proof that this falls within the legitimate domain of metaphysics would be superfluous for Scotus, and he simply appeals to Aristotle who proves in his *Metaphysics* that this science is wisdom. Within the philosophical tradition, wisdom can only be that knowledge which deals with first causes and foundations.

Scotus has now completed the entire deductive proof. Metaphysics is seen to deal in a twofold manner with what is maximally knowable; there follows from this that it is a science in the highest degree. If all men, states Scotus following Aristotle, desire to know, then metaphysics cannot be surpassed as a science and is, in addition, that science most desired by all.[14]

3.2 The Subject of Metaphysics

For anyone familiar with metaphysics and its history, Scotus's argumentation in the *Prologue* of his *Questions on Aristotle's Metaphysics* remains ultimately dissatisfying. With his consideration of metaphysics as the science of the maximally knowable according to two aspects (that is, as first and most certain), Scotus refrains from mak-

14. "In this way, therefore, it is clear how this science is concerned with what is most knowable. From this it follows that it is most truly a science, and thus most to be sought, as was proved above" (n. 21, I:8).

ing a judgment about what, ultimately, constitutes the subject of the science. Is it a primary being, excelling all others in perfection? Is it what is most common to and valid for all that exists? The entire metaphysical tradition stemming from Aristotle finds itself confronted with these two alternatives, particularly insofar as Aristotelian metaphysics itself offers no *prima facie* unambiguous solution. If one follows Book I (983a5–8) or Book VI (1026a20–21) of Aristotle's *Metaphysics,* then First Philosophy is the science of the supersensible, unchanging sphere of being. Its subject is the separated and ontologically independent, i.e., those principles and causes of being. This is thus the first principle of everything, or theologically speaking, God. Under this aspect, the science of being is a *metaphysica specialis.* By contrast, if one follows Book IV (1003a21–22), then First Philosophy deals not with a special sphere of being, but with being insofar as it is being, making the claim to be a *metaphysica generalis.* How might these two apparently opposed interpretations be reconciled?

Because the problem of the determination of the subject of metaphysics arises from Aristotle's own conflicting assertions, Scotus rightly begins Question 1 of the *Metaphysics* with this topic. He offers, first, the arguments of the Commentator, Averroes, according to which God is the object of metaphysics, showing in what way *(modus)* this might be possible. The question of the *modus* emerges for Scotus because he distinguishes the different types of sciences.

Scotus, following Aristotle's understanding of science, holds that it refers to a disposition *(habitus)* of the rational soul developed to a habitual attitude.[15] In its ideal form, science consists in the

15. For this and what follows, see L. Honnefelder, *Ens inquantum ens. Der Begriff des Seienden als solchen als Gegenstand der Metaphysik nach der Lehre des Johannnes Duns Scotus,* in *Beiträge zur Geschichte der Philosophie und Theologie des Mittelalters* N.F. 16 (Münster: Aschendorff, 1979); ibid., "Scientia in se—scientia in nobis: Zur philosophischen Bedeutung einer wissenschaftstheoretischen Unterscheidung," in *Scientia und ars im Hoch- und Spätmittelalter* (Miscellanea Mediaevalia 22, Berlin: Walter de Gruyter, 1994, 204–14).

knowledge of a statement whose necessary truth is recognized in the conclusion of a syllogism. A syllogism is a unit of argumentation that consists of three statements: two premises and a conclusion drawn from them. In the strongest form, affirmations alone can function as premises and conclusions.

According to the traditional syllogism, premises and conclusions are formulated in such a way that they contain only a total of three concepts, whereby two premises have one common term (or middle term, *medium*) and two different terms (the outer terms). In the conclusion, these two different terms hold the subject and predicate positions; the middle term bridges the reasoning process between the two premises and disappears in the conclusion. Concepts that function as predicates can stand in the subject as well as the predicate position. The premise that contains the most universal of the three is called the major premise. The other premise is called the minor premise. A universal affirmative syllogism has the following form:

> All S are R.
> All R are P.
> Therefore, All S are P.

Premises relate to the conclusions as the foundation relates to what is founded. Any science that seeks as its goal the antecedent premises, or seeks to draw the conclusion from two given premises, is a science that seeks the reasoned fact *(propter quid)* and is called the *scientia propter quid*. Such scientific knowledge is not free of presuppositions—on the contrary, it rests on presuppositions. Scientific statements that belong to a *propter quid* science are therefore necessarily contained in their prior premises and deduced from them. Such premises are either conclusions that are derived from even more prior premises, or they are themselves first principles for which no further investigation is possible. For Scotus, such first principles have a claim to self-evidence in such a way that the predicate is contained necessarily in the subject. Ultimately, this means that all the propositions of a science are contained in a single subject of a proposition. This single subject is identical to the object of the science in question. In its ideal form, science is *propter quid,* and therefore the ultimate reasoned explanation for the object or topic, elaborated into an axiomatic system. The object in its unity constitutes, on the one hand, the unity of the science. On the other hand, the object is also the criterion for distinguishing one science from another. According to Scotus, this sort of *scientia propter quid* is only possible for an intellect whose cognitive power is unlimited.

When Scotus refers to the object of a science, we should not confuse this term with our contemporary notion of the object of a science. Indeed, what we understand as the object of a science corresponds to what Scotus understands as the subject of the science. Insofar as science refers to a disposition *(habitus)* of the rational soul formed into an attitude, it can be understood as a power *(potentia)* that is moved by an object *(obiectum).* The first object of any power is that which is perfectly commensurate to it, i.e., that which can cause all cognitions of which the power is capable, and thereby bring about the habitual knowledge. The ideal form of science *(scientia in se)* is one where the first *subiectum* and the first *obiectum* correspond. To attain this ideal form, two conditions must be fulfilled simultaneously: the first *subiectum* must be fully known (that is, regarding all qualities that can be contained in it through the mode of possibility) and the first *obiectum* must be grasped by an understanding that is perfectly commensurate to it. Both conditions are fulfilled only in the case of an intellect whose cognitive powers are unlimited.

It is important, however, to distinguish factual from ideal science. The former *(scientia quia)* is that science that is possible for the human mind, based upon its earthly composition *(pro statu isto).* Scotus refers to this as *scientia in nobis.* In this case, the limits within which the first *obiectum* is reached by the power in question are identical to the limits of the first *subiectum*. Accordingly, the human mind under its current conditions can only cognize on the basis of sense perception.[16] That which cannot be experienced by means of sense perception is only accessible in the form of reductive conclusions from the conditioned to the unconditioned, from the caused to the cause. Such a science of reductive inference knows only the simple fact *(quia)* of a thing; for this reason it is described as *scientia quia* as distinct from *scientia propter quid*. And, since it infers from effect to cause, it is also *a posteriori* science. *Scientia propter quid,* since it infers from cause to effect, is by contrast an *a priori* science.

Although *scientia quia* proceeds not deductively but reductively or by means of resolution, it still has a claim to necessary knowledge. According to both Aristotle and Scotus, necessity is one of the essential qualities belonging to all scientific knowledge, and *scientia quia* is no exception. However, the necessity of such a science is only given within the mode of possibility. In addition, its knowledge is fragmentary with reference to its subject and is measured by *scientia in se*. This is because knowledge of this type *(quia)* can never infer all predicates in the way that *scientia propter quid* can. What is more, it can only produce the connection of propositions with their *subiectum* in a reductive manner. Both sciences, however, must be treated as a single science, since for Scotus the first *subiectum* of the propositions of that science that is possible for the human mind in the present life *(scientia in nobis)* is identical to the first *subiectum* of the propositions of the ideal science *(scientia in se)*.

3.2.1 Is God the Object of Metaphysics?

In the first question from his work on Aristotle's *Metaphysics,* Scotus argues that God can be the object of a science, if science be understood precisely as habitual knowledge of conclusions.[17] Such a

---

16. See the discussion of cognition *pro statu isto* in chapter 2.1 above.
17. *Met.* I, q. 1, n. 131 (I:49–50).

definition applies both to the deductive conclusions that become habitual (the cause/effect inference of *scientia propter quid*) and to the reductive conclusions that develop into habitual knowledge (the effect/cause inference of *scientia quia*). Scotus reprises some arguments when he asserts that God can be the object of a science *propter quid*. Earlier,[18] he had noted the many qualities of God, for example desirability, immovability, immutability, and the role of prime mover. This title of prime mover can be understood and considered in itself as an absolute quality of the divine essence insofar as it relates to all that is not God. Scotus had earlier[19] pointed out that the qualities of God that are also his perfections are (because they are unlimited) identical with the divine essence, since God is absolutely simple. These qualities can be distinguished from God either conceptually as they are in themselves or according to the divine essence that is formally distinct from them.[20] By contrast, this identity between essence and quality is not the case for creatures, because of the imperfection of their qualities. These two insights (divine simplicity and the conceptual distinctions of qualities) are critical for the assumption that God is the object of metaphysics. Only that which has qualities can be the object of a *scientia propter quid*, since it belongs to such a science to demonstrate that certain qualities must be ascribed to its object according to its essence (and therefore, necessarily). If God had no qualities or if the divine qualities were not at least conceptually distinct from the divine essence, then God could not be the object of such a science.

Scotus is quick to remind his readers that he has already considered an unsound objection to Averroes' position that God is the object of metaphysics. This objection[21] stated that a science *propter quid*

---

18. *Met.* I, q. 1, n. 25 (I:21).
19. *Met.* I, q. 1, n. 26 (I:21).
20. See the discussion of the formal distinction in chapter 2.2 above.
21. Presented in *Met.* I, q. 1, nn. 30–31 (I:23–4).

is more certain with regard to its conclusions than is a science *quia*. There can be no science of God as first object and there can be no science that considers him as first cause, because God causes nothing of necessity. Therefore, no science can treat God, either as cause or as first principle. Scotus confirms this argumentation in the following way: one does not know anything about God on the basis of any cause prior to God (since God is the first cause). But if one assumes that a cause is the middle term of a syllogism, then this is precisely what occurs, so that one might infer from the concept of God to an absolute quality such as wisdom, power, or eternity, which one attributes to God in terms of his internal activity *(ad intra)* or his external activity *(ad extra,* as first cause, first mover, etc.). What is essentially identical with God has nothing in it that is essentially prior to God. A cause, however, is always other than the caused and essentially prior to it. Consequently, nothing in God can be demonstrated by means of a cause, since there is no cause different from or prior to God.

Scotus holds that this objection is not convincing.[22] Indeed, if an essentially prior and distinct middle term is used in a syllogism in such a way that it leads one to understand something essentially posterior and distinct from what is prior, then it does not, in fact, function as a middle term insofar as it is different from the posterior (for this aspect is incidental), but insofar as it is understood as a *distinct* aspect, essentially prior to and in itself known prior to what follows from that knowledge. This is in fact the case with those unique features and attributes of God.

God can function not only as the *subiectum* of that science that is habitual knowledge of deductive conclusions *(scientia propter quid)*, but also as the *subiectum* of a science that involves habitual knowledge of reductive conclusions *(scientia quia)*.[23] In this case, a nomi-

22. *Met.* I, q. 1, n. 131 (I:49–50).
23. *Met.* I, q. 1, n. 132 (I:50).

nal definition of God must be presupposed. If God is considered as cause and there is an effect belonging to this cause, then one can infer from the effect to that which is described through the nominal definition. This reductive inference is possible both with regard to the essence or the essential qualities as well as with regard to the unique features. In this way, what is inferred from the effect is understood as its necessary condition, or as its cause.

God can also be the object of a type of science that consists of a collection of such habitual dispositions, whether by means of deductive *(propter quid)* or reductive *(quia)* inference.[24] On the one hand, such inferences can only have to do with God. The unity of the science is given by the unity of its single object. Such a science, the conclusions of which refer only to God, is the absolutely first type of science for this object, since it considers God under the first possible perspective, according to the divine essence.

On the other hand, such a collection of habitual dispositions (to deductive and reductive inferences) has to do with God and, in addition, with everything that is to be attributed to God.[25] Those things attributed to God only emerge in the science from this perspective, and the unity of the science is guaranteed from this attribution. By the term *what is attributed to God,* we mean everything created or caused which is understood as that which is ordered toward God. More precisely, these are ordered toward God not insofar as God is substance, but insofar as God is First Being. A science of everything created, that considers all that is insofar as it is ordered toward the first being, is logically the first science of this being. And, if (as Aristotle states) metaphysics is the first of all sciences, then it is identical with this science.

When one considers a metaphysics of all created beings, understood insofar as they are ordered to the first being, two possibilities

24. *Met.* I, q. 1, n. 133 (I:50).
25. *Met.* I, q. 1, n. 134 (I:50–51).

must be distinguished. The first takes cognition of God as the starting point for knowledge of reality, the second takes cognition of created reality as the starting point for knowledge of God.

If we begin with knowledge of God as the starting point for scientific knowledge, then we are dealing with a science that proceeds deductively *(scientia propter quid)*. Such a metaphysics assumes, however, that the created being must initially be suited to be completely understood deductively by the one who possesses the science.[26] In addition, implied by what has been said, the cognition of the essence of this created being is attained insofar as the being is ordered to God. Those who possess such a science *propter quid* would be minds that would know all that differs from God by means of a natural knowledge of God. Such scientific knowledge of what differs from God is discursive, i.e., it would come through logical inference from one thing to another. God indeed has such knowledge that corresponds to this *propter quid* metaphysics, i.e., God knows the essence of all created being and understands this also as it is ordered to Himself as the first being. But God does not have such knowledge discursively, by means of logical inference. God knows immediately and intuitively, not by means of an inference from divine self-cognition.

One might attribute such *propter quid* and deductive metaphysics to angelic beings, if they had been pilgrims on earth. In contrast to humans, angelic beings are not limited in their cognitive determinations, since they are immaterial beings. For an angel, a purely rational cognitive act would be possible relative to every being: each can know everything that is free of matter (e.g., God) without limitation. If we think of them as pilgrims on earth (that is, with no access to an immediate, intuitive perception of God) then angels could, by means of their intellect, come to a first and natural cognition of

26. *Met.* I, q. 1, n. 135 (I:50).

God, i.e., one attained through their own natural capacities. This natural cognition of God would serve as a prerequisite for *propter quid* metaphysics, which then infers to a cognition of the essence of created beings, albeit discursively, considering created beings only in terms of their ordering to God.

If, however, we consider the knowledge of created being as the point of departure for the reductive knowledge of God, then the science in question is a *scientia quia*.[27] In this text of Scotus, such metaphysical knowledge belongs only to humans, since only the human mind knows reality by means of sense perception. When an act of knowledge comes about because of the senses, then the appropriate object of such an act would be corporeal reality. Anything that is incorporeal, however, can only be known by means of the process of abstractive cognition.[28] In contrast to angelic knowledge, human cognition is in no position to know God immediately by means of the natural intellect. The human mind requires, initially, cognition of a corporeal being in order to infer the existence of a first, immaterial being. Such a metaphysics-*quia* does not begin with a cognition of the existence of God. Rather, it is far more likely that it presupposes only a nominal definition of God, inferring from the cognition of created, material reality to the existence of God and to divine qualities.

Scotus tries to come to terms with a series of doubts directed against the thesis of Averroes that God is the object of metaphysics. The sixth of these[29] argues as follows: whatever the human mind (given the earthly conditions of existence) can know of the divine essence is really nothing more particular than being itself. Any process of cognition that proceeds to parts of anything, states Scotus, proceeds by means of descriptive concepts. Here he provides the example "the living being capable of laughter" as a descriptive concept

27. *Met.* I, q. 1, n. 136 (I:51–52).   28. See above, chapter 2.1.
29. *Met.* I, q. 1, n. 154 (I:56).

for the human person. Likewise, the concept First Being, by means of which we would know God's essentiality, would also be such a descriptive concept. Such concepts, however do not touch the essence of the being, but only its accidental qualities. Consequently, a metaphysics that has God for its object and is possible for the human mind cannot be understood as that which provides knowledge of the divine essence. This is, however, what a science *quia* claims to do.

Scotus takes the argumentation against Averroes' position even further: If it is to be proven of a being that it is the first being, then the concept First Being must be presupposed as a non-self-contradictory concept. If not, a self-contradictory concept could be the subject of this science.[30] This non-contradictory concept First Being presupposes that the term refers to both existence and essence. If one says that metaphysics demonstrates the being of God and understands by this the actual existence of God, then it cannot mean that God's existence is demonstrated deductively, since the science is *quia*, not *propter quid*. This science must proceed by means of reductive inference. Nor can such a claim necessarily presuppose God's existence. Nonetheless, Scotus holds that metaphysics does indeed demonstrate that God has essential being. How does he sketch this out?

3.2.2 *Being qua Being as the Object of Metaphysics*

According to Scotus, we do not acquire the concept of a first being that serves as the presupposition for metaphysics by abstraction from the existence of creation. Rather we begin with the concept of a quality that must necessarily be attributed to creation from which we then deduce that the concepts first, highest and best belong to the concept of being. This means that the determination of a first being (to which one gives the name God) is not self-contradictory.

---

30. *Met.* I, q. 1, n. 155 (I:56–7).

It therefore has essential being. Such an argumentation is problematic: the demonstration of the inference from the concept of being to that of First Being is *sui generis,* since it concerns a particular being. It cannot, therefore, follow immediately on the basis of the nature of being, understood universally. Therefore, before one can demonstrate that the concept of a first being is contained in the concept of being, it must be shown that transcendental determinations belong to the concept of being. Consequently, a science of being and its transcendental determinations must precede a metaphysics that has God as its object. In this way, the historically later distinction of *metaphysica generalis* from *metaphysica specialis* is already anticipated by Scotus. If a double metaphysics is in fact required, then one can no longer speak, with Aristotle, of three speculative sciences (namely, physics, mathematics, and metaphysics). Instead, one must hold that there are four: three speculative sciences (physics, mathematics, and theology) and one universal speculative science, the science of transcendentals (metaphysics).

Scotus can now answer the doubts directed against the position of Averroes that God is the object of metaphysics. He states that it belongs to one and the same science to demonstrate a universal and special argumentation.[31] If one seeks to prove that there is a first being—the task that belongs to metaphysics understood as theology—then one implicitly holds that there are secondary beings, or that there is at least one second being. Qualities such as first being or second being are disjunctive attributes. They are mutually exclusive but, taken together, they can be predicated of several or all beings. In addition, one can identify other contradictorily disjunctive attributes, such as finite and infinite, limited, and unlimited. These disjunctions are distinct from others, such as prior and posterior or cause and caused.

31. *Met.* I, q. 1, n. 156 (I:57).

Because Scotus seeks to demonstrate the scientific dimension of such a metaphysical reflection, he turns to a consideration of the syllogistic reasoning required. He considers the question, specifically, of the appropriate middle term that such a syllogistic form would require. If one wishes to prove that there is such a first being, one must assume (as noted above) that there are second beings. This presupposes, however, that being is ordered. Now, how should the middle term appear, if one wishes to prove that all being is either first or second? If one can identify no suitable term, then one must deny that being is ordered. Does the affirmation of such an order itself not require, in addition, a further assumption about multiple essences? In other words, the affirmation of the order of being presupposes a plurality of beings. How does one demonstrate this?

These reflections show clearly that the predicates first and second being are not an appropriate disjunctive pair for such a demonstration, since there are too many assumptions connected with them. Each of these assumptions would require a separate demonstration. By contrast, as Scotus shows, it is far better to distinguish between first and not-first.[32] With this, one has an analytically true statement that requires no further proof: every being is either first or not-first. Furthermore, it is also immediately evident that every not-first being presupposes a first being. The origin of this first being must now be demonstrated on the basis of firstness.

From these considerations, it follows that whichever of the two disjunctive predicate-pairs one favors, and however the search of a middle term proceeds, if one wishes to prove a special quality of one being (e.g., that it is first) then this quality cannot be grasped categorially.[33] A categorial quality is one that falls under one of the ten Aristotelian categories and is therefore not predicable of all being. Such a quality presupposes (as noted above) the knowledge of spe-

---

32. *Met.* I, q. 1, n. 157 (I:58).
33. *Met.* I, q. 1, nn. 158–59 (I:58).

cial essences. These do not, however, belong to the domain of metaphysics since this is a science of the universal. Only those qualities that are convertible with its subject can be demonstrated by metaphysics. Thus, the object of metaphysics would be being and the attributes that can be demonstrated. These include the transcategorial or transcendentals, those that are valid of all being and are simple in themselves, such as good, one, and true. The disjunctive attributes (finite/infinite, for example) would also be included. Such a metaphysics can demonstrate nothing about God as God, or about the other separated substances (that is, those separated from matter) as they are in themselves.

Scotus raises two arguments against these considerations of metaphysics as the science of being *qua* being.[34] First, the goal of metaphysics is the knowledge of the wholeness of being. God belongs to this, however, as the First Being. Since the First Being possesses all the qualities of being to an eminent and perfect degree, all other beings must be understood in reference to this first. Second, according to the *Nicomachean Ethics,* the happiness of human persons consists in a cognitive act that is metaphysical in nature: namely, the understanding of the First Being.

Scotus responds to these objections in the following manner. If one denies the assumption of the four speculative sciences (that is, physics, mathematics, and metaphysics, understood both as a science of transcendentals and as theology) and if one considers all the points listed above insofar as they deal with God (rather than being), then it follows that all that is naturally knowable about God in this science are the divine transcendental qualities. The goal of this discipline is a perfect knowledge of being which, since being is first in perfection, must involve knowledge of this first being. One must then distinguish between God as first being (and goal of meta-

34. *Met.* I, q. 1, n. 160 (I:58).

physics) and being in general *(ens in communi)*. This latter is what is most familiar to human cognition and what is known first. In the course of all knowing, the human mind first knows something as being before it knows the thing as this thing or that thing. It is then shown that, on the basis of this being in general, there is a first being, etc. In the cognition of this first being one discovers simultaneously the fullness, the perfection, and the summit of metaphysics.

Scotus ends his considerations of this question with two remarks on this way of understanding metaphysics. The second remark relates to the relationship of beings in reality, i.e., that in addition to metaphysics, physics also deals with God.[35] Physics demonstrates that something is a first mover and that such a first mover is unmoved, immutable, etc. In contrast to metaphysics, however, physics deals with God in a secondary or accidental way. What physics demonstrates about God has less to do with the divine essence than what metaphysics can know about God. Although the two disciplines approach God differently in their propositions, the same conclusion, namely that God is the first being, can be proven with the help of a middle term, proper to physics or to metaphysics. The argumentation must, however, be described as physical or metaphysical depending upon how close the middle term comes to the divine essence. In other words, the middle term used by metaphysics will be closer to the essence of God than will the middle term used in a physical demonstration. Finally, in closing, Scotus asks which science demonstrates that the first mover is the first being? In other words, must there be a third science, beyond physics and metaphysics, that proves that each science deals with the same object, albeit in a partial manner? Wouldn't this problem continue *ad infinitum*, as we seek to identify that on the basis of which the sciences are partial approaches to a single reality?

35. *Met.* I, q. 1, n. 163 (I:59).

From Scotus's consideration of the first question in his *Questions on Aristotle's Metaphysics*, we can conclude the following. The metaphysics possible for the human mind *pro statu isto* proceeds according to a method of resolution, that is, a *quia* method. God is the object of this metaphysics, or its subject insofar as the science is ordered toward an understanding of God, and finds its fulfillment in such an understanding. All metaphysical knowledge, however, begins with being in general. Thus being is the proper (or actual) object of that metaphysics of which the human mind is capable, *pro statu isto*.

3.3 The Proof of God's Existence

The problem of the natural knowability of God is not only a theological problem but also, as the first of the Scotist *Questions on the Metaphysics* shows, a central question of philosophy.[36] Since the human person, under the present conditions of earthly existence *(pro statu isto)* knows only on the basis of sense perception, that object proper to the human mind is what can be perceived by the senses or, in other words, what is corporeal. Therefore God as an incorporeal, purely spiritual being can be neither the first object of human understanding nor, as a consequence, the proper object of that metaphysics that is possible for the human being in this life. Notwithstanding, according to Scotus, God is the fulfillment of the entire human cognitive effort. How is a natural cognition of God

36. On Scotus's proof of God's existence cf. A. B. Wolter, "Duns Scotus and the Existence and Nature of God," in *The Philosophical Theology*, 254–77; T. O'Connor, "From First Efficient Cause to God: Scotus on the Identification Stage of the Cosmological Argument," in *John Duns Scotus: Metaphysics and Ethics*, 435–54. A. Ghisalberti, "Ens infinitum e dimostrazione dell'esistenza di Dio in Duns Scoto," in op. cit., 415–34; L. Honnefelder, "Metaphysik und Transzendenz. Ueberlegungen zu Johannes Duns Scotus im Blick auf Thomas von Aquin und Anselm von Canterbury," in *Transzendenz: Zu einem Grundwort der klassischen Metaphysik*, ed. L. Honnefelder, W. Schüßler (Paderborn: 1992), 137–61.

possible, then, for the human person under the conditions of our earthly existence?

In the first of his *Questions on Aristotle's Metaphysics,* Scotus suggests his solution to the problem: he begins, as we saw earlier, with cognition of the corporeally existent. From this starting point, one infers (through a process of abstraction) the existence of an incorporeal being and then the existence of the characteristics of a first immaterial being. The proof of God's existence is thus *a posteriori,* using human experience as its point of departure. Apart from this experience, the proof presupposes only a nominal definition of God. Scotus wants to make cogent that, apart from the many finite beings that one can know, there is a single infinite being that exists of itself and is the absolute ground of all reality that causes everything that exists finitely, and is both intelligent and capable of free choice.

Within the framework of the now extant writings from Scotus's commentaries on the *Sentences,* we find three versions of the proof for God's existence: one in the *Lectura* (the early Oxford commentary),[37] a second in the *Ordinatio* (revised on the basis of both the Oxford commentary and Paris commentary), and a third found in the *Reportatio* IA, the transcript of the Paris lectures on the *Sentences,* corrected by Scotus.[38] Finally, Scotus treated the theme monographically in *De primo principio.* These four versions are essentially the same in content. For our purposes here, we will focus on the *Ordinatio* I, d. 2 version.[39]

In his investigation of the question of God's existence, Scotus presupposes a series of theoretical elements that he has developed

37. *Lect.* I, d. 2, p. 1, q. 1–3 (ed. Vat. 16:111–57).

38. *Rep.* IA, d. 2, p. 1, q. 1–3, in A. B. Wolter and M. M. Adams, "Duns Scotus's Parisian Proof for the Existence of God", in *Franciscan Studies* 42 (1982): 248–321.

39. In ed. Vat. 2:125–243. An English translation of the first question can be found in A. B. Wolter, *Duns Scotus: Philosophical Writings* (Indianapolis: Hackett, 1987), 31–81.

elsewhere.[40] To these belong the univocity of being (that is, the doctrine of the common application of the concept being) and the doctrine of the transcendentals.[41] In addition, he presupposes that human understanding can know its first proper object (being as such) on the basis of sensible perception coupled with the process of abstraction.[42] Several concepts gained through abstraction, such as the transcendentals being, one, true (among others), can be predicated univocally of everything, both sensibly perceivable and nonsensible, as long as this does not involve a contradiction. In this way, God can be known by means of the concept of being. To know God as being, however, is unsatisfying insofar as this does not offer distinct knowledge. It is therefore necessary to find a concept through which God can be known in terms of his difference from other beings. Infinite being *(ens infinitum)* is such a concept. What is noteworthy here is that the concept infinite does not add anything new (in the sense of its own reality) to the concept of being; it only determines the degree of intensity of the being.[43]

With the formation of the concept of an infinite being nothing yet has been said as to whether something that corresponds to this concept actually exists. From this perspective, Scotus rightly raises the question at the beginning of his investigation into the proof of God's existence (in the *Ordinatio*) as to whether among beings something exists that is actually infinite.[44] Scotus begins this question by introducing the most varied arguments for and against the

---

40. Cf. L. Honnefelder, *Scientia transcendens. Die formale Bestimmung der Seiendheit und Realität in der Metaphysik des Mittelalters und der Neuzeit (Duns Scotus—Suárez—Wolff—Kant—Peirce)* (Hamburg: Felix Meiner, 1990), 158–99.

41. See chapter 2.3 above.

42. See chapter 2.1 above.

43. Finite and infinite are the modes within which being can be understood. This mode of intensity is discussed in chapter 2.2 as one aspect of the formal distinction.

44. *Ord.* I, d. 2, p. 1, q. 1 in *Duns Scotus: Philosophical Writings,* 35.

assumption of the existence of such a being.[45] Unable to resolve the question at this time, he turns to Question 2, where he considers whether the proposition "An infinite being exists" is a self-evident (and therefore true) proposition.[46] A proposition is known to be self-evident when the truth of what is said follows solely on the basis of the understanding of the terms involved, i.e., when one needs no additional information and thereby no proof in order to know the proposition is true. An affirmative answer to this question would solve the earlier question, since if the proposition is self-evident, then an infinite being exists. After he has adduced the arguments pro and con, Scotus answers this question in the negative, providing three arguments for this.

Following this, he returns to the first question, left open, whether among beings something exists that is actually infinite.[47] Despite the fact that the proposition "there is an infinite being" is not self-evident, one may still demonstrate its truth by means of concepts related to it and without recourse to experience, thus a priori. However, it is not possible for the human mind in its present state to proceed in this way. We can only demonstrate this proposition from the created order, i.e., on the basis of an experience of what exists, whereby one understands the created (or a characteristic of the created) as an effect, inferring from this to its cause. However, in order for such an a posteriori proof to be compelling, one must assume a self-evident and necessary truth about it, i.e., that the given effect stands in a necessary connection to the cause. Only on this condition is it guaranteed that the truth about the cause can also be demonstrated as self-evident and necessary. Finally, the entire proof must proceed by means of univocal concepts.

45. Cf. *Ord.* I, d. 2, p. 1, q. 1, nn. 1–9 (*Philosophical Writings*, 35–36).

46. "Utrum aliquod infinitum esse sit per se notum, ut Deum esse" (*Ord.* I, d. 2, p. 1, q. 2, ed. Vat. 2:128).

47. *Ord.* I, d. 2, p. 1, q. 2, n. 39 (*Philosophical Writings*, 37).

Scotus's first proof presupposes a necessary connection between an effect and its cause and proceeds from the effect to its effective cause. In this way he demonstrates the existence of an infinite being on the basis of relative properties belonging to it: these relate to created being *(proprietas relativae entis infiniti ad creaturas)*.[48] Since these properties only belong to infinite being, he is able to show that such a being actually exists. In his second proof, Scotus considers the absolute property of actual infinity.

According to Scotus's first proof, the relative properties of an infinite being can be divided into those of causality *(proprietates causalitatis)* and of eminence *(proprietates eminentiae)*.[49] The features of causality can be subdivided into features of efficiency *(proprietates efficientis)* and of finality *(proprietates finis)*.[50] This initial division provides the basis for the procedure in this first proof.[51] The proof itself is made up of three steps. The first step involves three separate proofs to be undertaken.

STEP 1: Among beings there is one that is absolutely first
    (a) from the viewpoint of efficient causality,
    (b) from the viewpoint of final causality, and
    (c) from the viewpoint of eminence.

Once this is demonstrated for each order, each proof opens to

STEP 2: The first in the manner of one conceptual order of firstness is also first in the manner of the other two.

---

48. *Ord.* I, d. 2, p. 1, q. 2, n. 39 *(Philosophical Writings,* 37–38).

49. Scotus's methodology here takes its inspiration from Henry of Ghent, who declared that all valid demonstrations of God's existence developed in the thirteenth century could be reduced to two basic ways, one using the principle of causality and the other using the way of eminence. See A. B. Wolter, "Duns Scotus on the Existence and Nature of God," in *The Philosophical Theology,* 258.

50. *Ord.* I, d. 2, p. 1, q. 2, n. 40 *(Philosophical Writings,* 38).

51. *Ord.* I, d. 2, p. 1, q. 2, nn. 41–42 *(Philosophical Writings,* 39–45).

At this second stage, the first in the order of efficiency is shown to be identical to the first in the orders of final causality and eminence. There follows

STEP 3: This threefold primacy can only belong to one essence.

The demonstration concludes with this point.

The first step of each of the three proofs of step 1 (that there is a being that is absolutely first in that particular order) depends in its turn on three sub-proofs:

SUB-PROOF STEP 1: There is a first in the order under consideration (efficiency, finality, or eminence).
SUB-PROOF STEP 2: This first is uncaused.
SUB-PROOF STEP 3: This first actually exists.

Looking at the argument as a whole, then, the first step of the proof requires a total of nine individual sub-proofs. In what follows, we shall consider only the first of the three sub-proofs: that from the order of efficient causality. The arguments from finality and eminence are similar in structure.

The proof from efficient causality appears at I, d. 2, nn. 45, 57 and 58. SUB-PROOF STEP 1 begins at n. 45 with the fact of experience that there are beings capable of being effected, beings that are produced or that can be the result of a causal process. If one inquires after the cause of such a causal process, there are three possibilities:

1. either something is brought about from nothing, or
2. through itself, or
3. by another.

The first two possibilities are rejected by Scotus with the help of arguments taken from authority. If one follows Aristotle,[52] then noth-

---

52. Cf. Aristotle, *Physics* I, 4 (187a29), in *The Complete Works of Aristotle*, I:320.

ing can come from nothing: if one follows Augustine,[53] then nothing can produce itself. Therefore, one must take the third possibility, according to which an efficient cause must be assumed for something that is capable of being brought about by another. Here the single cause/effect relationship presupposed by Scotus must be understood as a necessary one. Cause and effect do not stand to one another in an accidental (or contingent) connection but in a necessary one. Only in this case is the compelling inference from caused to cause possible.

If this efficient cause is a first being, such that it is neither caused nor is its causal power exercised with the help of another efficient cause, then the goal of the proof has been reached. If this efficient cause is not the first, then it is a subordinate cause, which in turn points to a preceding cause to which it stands as an effect. If this preceding cause is a first being in the sense described, then the proof is complete; if not, the indicated argumentation is applied again. In this way, one ascends, as it were, the causal chain. Since Scotus, along with Aristotle, rejects an infinite progression from effect to cause, there must be a first in the chain, and in this beginning the first being is given: itself neither caused nor is its causal power exercised with the help of another cause.

SUB-PROOF STEP 2 (at n. 57) shows that this first causal power cannot be caused. According to the Aristotelian doctrine of causality, which Scotus also follows, one can name at most four different causes for everything that can be caused. The two intrinsic causes are the material cause *(causa materialis)* and the formal cause *(causa formalis)*. The two extrinsic causes are the efficient cause *(causa efficiens)* and the final cause *(causa finalis)*. For example, in the case of a house, the material out of which it is built is the material cause; the

---

53. Cf. Augustine, *De trinitate* I, 1, in *The Trinity,* 66 and Aristotle, *De anima* II, 4, in *The Complete Works,* I:660–63.

plan according to which it is constructed is the formal cause; the person who builds it is the efficient cause, and the ability-to-live-in-it is the final cause. This present proof must show that the first cause able to produce an effect cannot itself be traced back to any of the four causes.

It can be assumed from the preceding proof that the first cause capable of producing an effect has no efficient cause. Scotus now has to show that the First Being, if it is unable to be caused, at the same time can be neither finally, formally, nor materially determined. That an uncausable being cannot be determined in terms of its end can be concluded from the following: A final cause is only active in such a way that it moves, as it were, an efficient cause to its effect. It follows, though, from this that a final cause is only given in the case where something caused by it depends upon it essentially as upon a prior cause. Since, however, the being unable to be caused—as the preceding proof has shown—does not depend on anything prior, there can be no final cause for it. Next it must be proven that the being that cannot be caused, if it has no extrinsic cause (efficient or final), has no inner cause either. The intrinsic causes (form and matter) belong, as the term intrinsic makes clear, to the caused thing itself. Consequently, these are not independent causes; they are imperfect, while the extrinsic causes, insofar as they are independent, are perfect. What is imperfect, however, presupposes by virtue of its concept that there is something perfect, since it is determined by what is perfect. If, however, in the case of the being unable to be caused there are no perfect extrinsic causes, then there can also be no imperfect, intrinsic causes. Additionally, intrinsic causes do not constitute themselves but are caused by the extrinsic causes. With this conclusion, Scotus has demonstrated that the first being capable of causing an effect has no causes and thus is itself uncaused.[54]

54. At this point, we leave open whether Scotus here transposes relations from the level of concepts to the level of things.

SUB-PROOF STEP 3 (at n. 58) shows that the first being capable of producing an effect (the first efficient cause) exists in actuality. If it contradicts the concept of a being to be caused, and if its existence is possible, then it is also possible that this being exist of itself. Now this is precisely the case for a first being capable of causing an effect. In addition—and Scotus appends this to his consideration—it would not be fitting for a universe that exists as a perfect whole in which all levels of being exist to lack the highest form of being.

The second proof for God's existence in this text (nn. 131–39) takes up the absolute property of actual infinity. The first demonstration, outlined above, has shown the existence of an infinite being from the perspective of its relative properties. The second demonstration shows that there exists an actually infinite being.[55] For this, Scotus must show that the infinite being, the being capable of the triple primacy demonstrated above, must be both rational and free. Knowledge and love or volition are attributed to it, however, in such a way as to reveal that this first being able to produce an effect is infinite. Scotus shows that an infinite being exists in actuality from four different perspectives:[56] two arguments from efficient causality, one from final causality, and one from eminence.

The texts under our consideration here are taken from the fourth type of argumentation: that of eminence or excellence.[57] The goal of this demonstration functions as the conclusion of a syllogism that has the following two premises:[58]

MAJOR PREMISE: *It is inconsistent with the most excellent being that something should be more perfect than it.*

MINOR PREMISE: *It is consistent with the finite that there exists something more perfect than itself.*

55. *Ord.* I, d. 2, p. 1, q. 2, n. 74 (*Philosophical Writings*, 52).
56. *Ord.* I, d. 2, n. 111 (*Philosophical Writings*, 62).
57. *Ord.* I, d. 2, nn. 131–39 (*Philosophical Writings*, 71–74).
58. *Ord.* I, d. 2, n. 131 (*Philosophical Writings*, 71).

If it can be shown that both premises state a necessary truth, then the conclusion is thereby proven as a necessarily true proposition, and the proof is complete. A proof of both premises, however, is required. Neither is a self-evident statement.

Scotus has already demonstrated the major premise in an earlier context.[59] The minor premise of the syllogism can be demonstrated as follows: The concept of the infinite does not stand in contradiction to the concept of being, since infinite and finite are qualities of being that determine it more closely, whereby what is infinite is more than what is merely finite and is more excellent than it.[60] If, therefore, there is no contradiction in the concepts being and infinite,[61] then it is possible for the most perfect being to be an infinite being. Another line of argument runs as follows: If the concept of an intensively infinite being entails no contradiction, then a being is only fully complete (or perfect) that is infinite not only in possibility but also in actuality.

These considerations, however, do not convince Scotus. What is to be proven can only be shown to be true through an analysis of the concepts in question. An argumentation would be compelling if one could trace what is to be proven back to something that is undoubtedly true. Being is, however, the most common and at the same time the most well known concept—the first thing we recognize about something is that it exists. Consequently, it cannot be discovered by analysis that it is derived from a more common or more well known concept. In addition, the concept infinite can only be understood from its opposite finite. One cannot refer the concept back to something obviously known.

Scotus therefore develops several other arguments.[62] In the first, he shows that being and infinity are not inconsistent concepts. He

59. Ord. I, d. 2, nn. 59, 63, and 67 (Philosophical Writings, 48, 49, 51).
60. Ord. I, d. 2, n. 132 (Philosophical Writings, 71–72).
61. In other words, if the term infinite being is meaningful.
62. See Ord. I, d. 2, nn. 133–36 (Philosophical Writings, 72–73).

begins as follows: just as one can assume that something not obviously impossible is possible, one can also take to be consistent what is not obviously inconsistent. In the case of the concept being (as has already been shown) the concepts that cannot be employed together with it (i.e., those which are inconsistent with it), are those that describe the first and convertible characteristics of being and therefore belong to the same conceptual range. One *(unum)*, true *(verum)* and good *(bonum)* belong to this class. Finite and infinite, on the other hand, designate characteristics of being, nevertheless their conceptual range is specified and not identical with the conceptual range of being. Consequently they can be employed together with the concept being.

In the second argument, Scotus points out that the infinite does not stand in contradiction with extension. To the contrary, it is imaginable that the infinite absorbs extension into itself incrementally. No contradiction whatsoever arises if one thinks of being and infinite together, since everything that has extension is always already a being. If *infinity* and *being* are considered together, then (as Scotus suggests in his closing remarks) this will be thought of as a perfection, namely the perfection of being.

The third argument involves the consideration of quantity once again. Here we must distinguish quantity as extension from quantity as intensity or power. If one assumes along with Scotus that intensity (or power) is more perfect than extension, and if the preceding argument has shown that an infinite mass is possible, then an infinity of intensity (or power) must also be possible, since it belongs to the infinite to be the most perfect. However, if an infinity of intensity (or power) is possible, then it is also actual. The validity of the conclusion from possibility to actuality that was proven in the textual passage at n. 58 (seen earlier) appears again at n. 138.

Scotus offers a fourth and final argument for the proof of the minor premise, i.e., that it is consistent with the finite that something is more perfect than it. Here, too, one must show that infinity and being do not stand in contradiction, this time from the perspective of cognition and perception. What is most perfectly knowable appears immediately to be infinite being. The fact that the intellect encounters no contradiction in this as an object is all the more compelling, given the sensitivity of the cognitive power. Indeed, the mind reacts to dissonances, as our aural experience demonstrates. If hearing, as a subordinate perceptual process, shows such a clear sensitivity to inconsistency, then all the more must the intellect possess the capacity to react in this way. In every case the activities of the intellect are decidedly superior to those of auditory perception.

These considerations show, first, that being and infinite are bound to one another in a non-contradictory conceptual unity. Second, they make it clear that if an infinite being is possible (that is, if it is a conceptual non-contradiction), then it must also exist, since if it did not, it would not be an infinite being. Scotus's attempt here to retouch *(colorare)*, i.e. to modify, the famous ontological proof for God's existence of Anselm of Canterbury, must be understood against this background.[63] In his *Proslogion*, Anselm had attempted to develop a proof for God's existence that begins with the proposition that God is "that than which nothing greater can be thought."[64] Anselm tried to prove that this being also must exist in actuality by means of the following consideration in the form of a *reductio ad absurdum:* If "that than which nothing greater can be thought" exists only in the intellect, then it can also be thought to exist in reality; therefore something greater than it can be thought that is both in the intellect and in reality—a self-contradiction. Therefore there undoubtedly exists something greater than which nothing can be thought, both in intellect and in reality.[65]

63. *Ord.* I, d. 2, n. 137 *(Philosophical Writings,* 73–74).

64. Anselm, *Proslogion,* II. See Anselm, *Monologion and Proslogion,* trans. with an intro. by Thomas Williams (Indianapolis: Hackett, 1995), 99–100.

65. Ibid., 100–101.

A modification of this proof appeared necessary to Scotus because Anselm had left himself open to the objection made later by
Kant, among others, that existence as a real predicate adds nothing
to the characteristics of something: ten thalers in thought (to for-
mulate it as Kant did) are not different in their formal content from
ten real thalers. Scotus modifies the Anselmian definition of God in
such a way that he inserts *sine contradictione* twice into the formulation. God is "that than which, if it can be thought without contradiction, a greater cannot be thought without contradiction." "Without contradiction" here means that two objects of thought unite to
form a single object of thought, the one more closely determining
the other. With this double insertion of *sine contradictione,* the Anselmian argument becomes a proof that argues by means of modal
levels.

That the highest conceivable also exists in actuality without contradiction is proven by Scotus in two ways. The first argument refers
to the content of what is stated in the concept of the highest being
that can be thought as infinite being, i.e., the essence of the being so
described. Scotus points out, against the background of the philosophical tradition as well as the tradition of Christian faith, that the
intellect finds its peak of achievement in thinking the highest being
that can be thought, insofar as one does not desire to know anything beyond this. If this is the case, then, on the one hand, the essential determination of the specific object of the intellect must be
contained in the content of the concept of the highest being conceivable. That is, however, precisely what is provided by the concept, being. Additionally, this essential determination, infinite being, must be contained to the greatest degree in the concept of the
highest being that can be thought; otherwise the intellect would
never come to rest in it. The highest being that can be thought—so
runs the second proof—cannot exist in the intellect alone, since in
this case, it would be caused by it and dependent on it. This would

contradict the already proven determinations of infinite being. In addition—as the first proof (in its triple primacy) demonstrated—for everything conditioned there must be a first unconditioned: the cause of the conditioned, itself uncaused. If the infinite being is conceivable without contradiction, then it must exist in actuality, independently of the mind.

Scotus concludes his consideration of the Anselmian proof for God's existence by pointing out that a being that exists outside the mind is more accessible to thought than one that does not.[66] Concepts can only be known through abstraction, beginning with what is outside the intellect. Actually existing beings can be known either through sense perception or by the act of intuitive cognition. In this way, that which is most perfectly knowable must actually exist.

66. *Ord.* I, d. 2, n. 139 (*Philosophical Writings,* 74).

4. MODES OF BEING

WILL AND NATURE

FOLLOWING ARISTOTLE, medieval philosophers understand by a contingent being one which is not necessary, in
other words a being that possesses the (symmetrical) possibility of existence or non-existence.[1] The domain of the contingent
represents both a logical and an epistemological problem. If all that
exists is subject to change, what can the human mind know with certainty? Ancient as well as medieval philosophers point out that it is
possible to have certain knowledge of a being in itself as well as of
its essential qualities. Such knowledge is possible only where one
has knowledge of the causes of the being and where the causes are
so constituted that they cause necessarily. With this knowledge of
the relevant causes, one can attain scientific knowledge about the being in question (as already caused) and any changes that will occur

---

1. Cf. *Prior analytics*, I, 13 (32a15–32b35), in *The Complete Works of Aristotle*,
I:51–53.

(the future states of the being). In the case of contingent beings, however, this is not helpful. Contingent beings are not the result of necessary causes. In the absence of such causes, the human mind can know contingent things as necessary only at the moment when they are known; not, however, what they will be in the future.

This epistemological problem has logical consequences: one can only say that propositions about contingent states of affairs are true or false at the moment they obtain. In the case of propositions that refer to a future contingent state of affairs, one does not know in the present whether what is said will come to pass or not. One does not know whether these statements are necessarily valid or not. In principle, such propositions can be only true or false. However, in the present one cannot know whether a given statement about the future will be determinately true or false. Aristotle treats the problem of the relation of contingency and necessity in his treatise *On Interpretation* in terms of what would become the famous example of an impending sea-battle: "I mean, for example: it is necessary for there to be or not to be a sea-battle tomorrow; but it is not necessary for a sea battle to take place tomorrow, nor for one not to take place— though it is necessary for one to take place or not to take place."[2]

4.1 The Problem of Contingency

While one might grant that the puzzle of future contingents reveals the boundaries of finite human understanding, this logical knot is particularly difficult where divine knowledge is concerned. Christian doctrine affirms that God is both omnipotent and omniscient. If, however, God is omnipotent and omniscient, then God must know the future situation of all contingent states of affairs. This means that God knows the truth and falsehood of all proposi-

2. *On Interpretation* 9 (19a29–32) in *The Complete Works of Aristotle,* I:30.

tions about the future. But how is this possible? A second problem follows from this. As suggested above, ancient philosophers held (and on this point the thirteenth-century schoolmen agreed) that one can only have certain, i.e., necessary knowledge of what is necessary. In other words, only what in itself is necessary can be known necessarily. One must therefore ask whether God has a necessary knowledge of contingent states of affairs.

Scotus develops his position on contingency as a preliminary investigation, so as to be able to solve these two more theological problems.[3] In what follows, we look more closely at the treatment this receives in his *Reportatio* IA, d. 39–40.[4]

In his initial investigation, Scotus seeks to clarify whether or not there is contingency in things.[5] For this purpose, he must first determine what is meant by the term *contingency*. The Franciscan begins with necessity as the contradictory opposite of contingency, showing that it can be considered under two different forms. He then applies this difference to the conceptual contents of contingency. Ne-

3. On the Scotistic doctrine of contingency, cf. the following from the Scotus scholarship of recent years: L. Honnefelder, *Scientia transcendens*, 56–108, as well as "Die Kritik des Johannes Duns Scotus am kosmologischen Nezessitarismus der Araber: Ansätze zu einem neuen Freiheitsbegriff," in *Die abendländische Freiheit vom 10. zum 14. Jahrhundert*, ed. J. Fried, 249–63 (Sigmaringen, 1991). A. Vos Jaczn et al., *John Duns Scotus: Contingency and Freedom. Lectura I, 39. Introduction, Translation and Commentary* (Dordrecht, 1994); M. Sylwanowicz, *Contingent Causality and the Foundations of Duns Scotus's Metaphysics,* Studien und Texte zur Geistesgeschichte des Mittelalters 51. (Leiden: Brill, 1996). C. G. Normore, "Scotus, Modality, Instants of Nature and the Contingency of the Present," in *John Duns Scotus: Metaphysics and Ethics*, 161–74. J. R. Söder, *Kontingenz und Wissen. Die Lehre von den futura contingentia bei Johannes Duns Scotus,* Beiträge zur Geschichte der Philosophie und Theologie des Mittelalters NF 49 (Münster: Aschendorff, 1998).
4. This text does not as yet exist in English translation. An edited version with commentary can be found in J. R. Söder, *Kontingenz und Wissen,* 224–65. References in the text will be to that version of the question. A. B. Wolter discusses Scotus's position on this as well as the *Lectura* and Apograph versions of the question in "Scotus's Paris Lectures on God's Knowledge of Future Events," in *The Philosophical Theology*, 285–333.
5. *Rep.* IA, d. 39–40, nn. 26–30 (Söder, *Kontingenz und Wissen:* 246–47).

cessity can be understood first as immutability: a thing is necessary when it cannot act otherwise than it is acting. Necessity as immutability belongs to a being according to its essence or nature. One says, for example, that God is a necessary being because God is immutable according to the divine essence. Secondly, necessity can be understood as inevitability. Here, something may be contingent by nature, but necessarily connected to another event. Its occurrence is therefore inevitable. All natural events are necessary in this sense, according to Scotus.

In the same way, the two forms of contingency are to be distinguished: one related to the essence of a being, and the other to the circumstances or events connected with it. If a being is by nature subject to change, then the contingency of mutability belongs to it. This type of contingency belongs to all corporeal beings, since they are subject to generation and decay. This form of contingency is distinct from that which refers to what is not inevitable. Examples of this second form of contingency are events that can be avoided, or actions resulting from free choice that might not occur.

From these distinctions, we can infer the following. If a being is contingent according to its nature (such that the contingency of mutability belongs to it), then events or circumstances that are connected with it are either necessary in the sense of inevitable or contingent in the sense of avoidable. If, however, a circumstance or event is contingent in the sense of avoidable, then its foundation is also contingent, yet now in the sense of mutable.

At this point, though, how can one prove that anything is contingent? Scotus would like scientific, that is, certain knowledge of the answer to this question. Such knowledge, however, can only be independent of any experience *(a priori)*. After several attempts, he concludes that such an *a priori* proof is impossible. In one of his attempts, Scotus seeks to introduce contingency into the definition of the contingent being, as a qualitative attribute. One can identify being as the most common bearer of the qualitative attribute. Accordingly, one would thus have to define the concept *being* in terms of this qualitative concept.

According to Aristotelian logic, definitions presuppose the doctrine of the division of concepts. This assumes that in relation to a concept A, another concept B can be produced by abstraction. As a concept, B is both more general and one in which the first concept A is contained. In addition, there is an even more general concept C in which both A and B are contained. In relation to A, B is a species-concept and C is a genus-concept. In relation to B, C is a species-concept. In this way a conceptual tree can be formed. On the assumption of such a conceptual order, a definition is built in such a way that for the concept to be defined, the next higher genus-concept is sought within the conceptual hierarchy. The specific difference that distinguishes the concept to be defined (according to its content) from the genus-concept is added to this.

A problem clearly arises when one attempts to determine being according to this definitional schema from the viewpoint of the contingent. There is no common concept (i.e., no middle term) to connect being with contingency. Being is, as noted earlier,[6] precisely not a categorical concept that belongs to the conceptual order presupposed by the definitional schema. Instead, it is a transcendental concept that lies beyond this order.

Another possible approach for an *a priori* proof that there are contingent beings consists, according to Scotus, in the inference of contingency from other attributes of being. Thus, the concept contingency might be included in an attribute of being that is ontologically prior, i.e., more universal than it, and that therefore implies it. However, such an attribute is not given in the case of contingency, because every being is either necessary or contingent. There is no be-

6. See chapter 3.

ing left over that is not comprehended in one of the two concepts. Consequently, no concept can be identified that would be more general than both, or would include them along with other attributes.

A third possible proof would consist in the case of a disjunctive attribute that has a correlate, inferring one correlative attribute from its alternate. If the attribute *causal* is assumed, then there must also be something of which the characteristic *causal* can be predicated, so that from the assumption that the quality *caused* belongs to something, it can be inferred that there exists a being to whom the quality *causal* belongs. In other words, if we assume that there is a being to which a correlative disjunctive quality belongs, it follows that there also exists at least one being to whom the correlatively more noble attribute belongs. Such a procedure is not possible, however, in the case of the attribute *contingent,* for numerous reasons. First, *necessary,* the fitting disjunctive attribute for *contingent,* is not correlative but rather a contradictorily disjunctive attribute. Second, even if *necessary* were the correlative disjunctive attribute for *contingent,* it would not follow from the assumption that there exists a necessary being that a contingent being also exists. This is the case, since in the case of correlative disjunctive qualities, one can conceive of a being to which the more noble of the two attributes would belong. Yet this does not entail that the existence of the correlative less noble being follows from the existence of a more noble being. We can make this clear with the example of caused and causal. A being can be thought of as causal without at the same time being forced to think of another being as caused, since a causal being must not necessarily be active as a cause. Additionally, even in the case mentioned above where one can infer from the assumption of a being to whom the less noble quality can be attributed to another being to whom the correlating more noble disjunctive quality belongs, there still remains a problem. How is one to demonstrate the assumption of the first being? According to Scotus, this is not possible independent from experience, i.e., *a priori.*

As a result of the foregoing we conclude that without recourse to experience, one cannot demonstrate that contingent beings exist. Experience by contrast shows quite clearly that contingency exists, as Scotus then explicates.[7] Indeed, the human experience of reflective planning, of intentional discussion with others about one's actions, reveals that there are contingent events. Otherwise, one could act blindly and random actions would always produce successful outcomes. But, despite this or other *a posteriori* evidence, should someone still doubt the existence of contingent beings, Scotus recommends a radical but swift remedy: the doubter should be struck until he admits that it is not necessary that he be struck; that, in other words, it is quite possible not to strike him.[8]

4.2 Contingency and the Divine Will

After this first investigation is complete, the second seeks to identify the first cause of contingency.[9] Scotus answers this question in advance, proving it in what follows. The foundation of contingency lies in the act of the divine will directed toward all that is not God *(ad extra)*.

Scotus offers an indirect proof for this thesis. He proceeds from the contradictory assumption according to which God necessarily causes everything *ad extra*. The first inference that arises from this assumption would be that nothing in the universe is contingent. Scotus accounts for this inference on the basis of three assumptions:

1. In the universe, there exists a series of causes that are ordered and related to one another in such a way that a first cause causes a second cause or moves it to act, which causes a third cause or moves it to act, etc.

7. *Rep* IA, d. 39–40, n. 30 (Söder, *Kontingenz und Wissen*: 247).
8. This was Avicenna's remedy for the skeptic, in order to convince him of the truth of the principle of non-contradiction. Cf. *Metaphysics* I, 8 (Van Riet: 62).
9. *Rep.* IA, d. 39–40, nn. 31–38 (Söder: 248–49).

2. What is caused or moved to act in this causal chain in turn causes or moves in the same way as that by which it was moved or caused.

3. The first cause moves or causes by necessity.

If these assumptions are all true, then the second cause, since it is necessarily caused or moved to activity by the first cause, must move or cause the third cause necessarily. The same holds for the third cause and all further causes in the chain. Thus, everything in the universe is necessarily caused or moved. What Scotus said earlier on the question of an *a posteriori* proof of contingency already suffices to show that this statement cannot be correct. Indeed, our everyday behavior shows us that neither do we always cause things by necessity nor is everything in our surroundings caused by necessity. According to the rules of logic, whatever entails a falsehood must itself be false. Therefore, God does not cause everything by necessity.

The second inference that arises from the assumption that all that God causes *ad extra* is caused by necessity affirms that there is no second cause in the universe. Here, too, the account takes previously formulated presuppositions as the point of departure:

1. The first cause must, as its name indicates, cause or move prior to the second, subsequent cause.

2. The first cause is first because it is more perfect in its activity than any of the causes subordinate to it, and thus it produces more perfect effects than do these.

3. The first cause causes or moves necessarily.

If these three assumptions hold, then there is no effect that is not the result of the first cause. Therewith, however, every second cause is superfluous. Once again, our experience helps to prove that this proposition cannot be true. In our world we see numerous causes.

The third and final inference that follows from the assumption that God causes everything *ad extra* necessarily affirms that there is no deficiency and no evil in created being. The proof for this builds off of the following presuppositions:

1. Deficiency or evil in a (created) being comes about by the absence of a perfection that it actually could have.

2. God is, as the source of creation, the first cause and acts perfectly, because of divine perfection.

If one assumes the correctness of the two presuppositions, all effects that God produces are perfect such that everything God produces is as perfect as God, thus lacking nothing. This third inference, too, is quite obviously false, since in our world everything is afflicted with some flaw.

From the falsehood of these three inferences it follows logically that God, or more precisely, the divine will *ad extra*, acts not necessarily but contingently. There follows the question: Is the divine will the cause of this contingent behavior, or is it the divine intellect? Indeed, if there were a cause prior to the divine will, it could only be the divine intellect. According to Scotus, the intellect is a power for cognition that, like sense perception, routinely knows what is present to it, provided sufficient conditions obtain. The intellect cannot therefore refrain from knowing; it is by nature, i.e. necessarily, directed toward cognition. The will, by contrast, is different: the will can not only will something *(velle)* or not will it *(nolle)*, it can beyond this also not will *(non velle)*; i.e., it can withhold its own execution. If the act of a power and thereby the power itself is subject to necessity, then such a power cannot be the cause of contingency; since what acts necessarily by nature can bring forth nothing contingent. Consequently, the divine will must be the first cause of all contingency in the universe.

Since everything that belongs to the universe can not only be traced back to a single cause, but also to the activity of second caus-es, the question arises how the divine will as first cause works to-gether with a second cause. On this, according to Scotus, there are four conceivable combinations, using the framework of necessary/contingent, from which only two are actually possible.

1. The first and the second cause both operate contingently. This is, for example, the case when the divine and human wills work to-gether.

2. The first cause operates contingently and the second cause by nature (or necessarily). An example of this occurs when the divine, contingently operating will prevents a flood as the consequence of massive precipitation that otherwise would have occurred, since the causal powers of nature operate by necessity.

3. The first cause operates necessarily, the second cause contin-gently. This case is not possible, on the basis of the presupposition proven above that the divine will always operates contingently *ad ex-tra*.

4. The same holds for the fourth combination: both causes oper-ate by necessity.

The result of Scotus's second investigation can be stated as follows: God's will acts *ad extra* constantly in a contingent manner. It is the first cause of all contingency in the universe. Second causes, by con-trast, can operate contingently or necessarily. No created thing is necessary in itself—this is only the case for God—since everything created is the object of divine will, which, *ad extra,* only operates contingently. Necessity in the domain of the created exists in a rela-tive manner in such a way that one thing necessarily causes another.

The third investigation deals with the question of how the di-vine will can be the first cause of all contingency when it is true that God Himself and thereby also the divine will is immutable.[10] To un-

10. *Rep.* IA, d. 39–40, nn. 39–44 (Söder: 250–52).

derstand what follows, one must keep in mind that the will, according to the ancient/medieval conception, is a power *(potentia)*. A power is the predisposition to an activity, to an act *(actus)*. This activity or act is the actualization of the power; i.e., in this activity, what has possibility, or natural disposition, becomes actualized. Thus John, for example, has a predisposition for playing the piano. When he actually plays the piano, a merely present possibility becomes actualized. The act of the will is that activity to which the will as power is ordered. This act accompanies all intentional behavior.

In his solution, Scotus proposes first to proceed from the basis of human willing and its act. Then one could abstract from all imperfections and only concentrate on the perfections that can belong to the act. These perfections should then be transferred to God. This process takes the implicit assumption that the human person as creature is similar to the Creator *(imago Dei)*, at least in the perfections that he possesses, so that one can infer from the perfections belonging to the human being to the divine qualities.

The human will can will or attend to all possible actions. It is in itself not a power having pre-determined acts, as is the intellect which always stands in relation to the cognitive act and cannot restrain itself from cognizing in the case of sufficient conditions. The human will is indifferent to contrary acts and not determined with respect to them. It is also indifferent and undetermined with regard to possible objects and the effects of actions. Scotus regards the indifference of the human will in the face of contrary acts as a sign of imperfection. Here he refers to the circumstance that the human will can produce different acts, but not simultaneously two contrary ones. In other words, at any one time, the will can produce one of two contrary acts. Thus it cannot simultaneously love and hate (i.e., not love) someone in the same way. By contrast, Scotus considers the indifference with regard to objects as a perfection, since the human being can in his willing refer to numerous objects. For example, he can, like Buridan's ass, want to eat one thing and another.

If it is the case that all of the perfections (and none of the imperfections) of the human will belong to the divine will, then the divine will can be characterized as one that is not indifferent to contrary acts but that is, however, indifferent with regard to differing objects. Unlike the human will, the divine will has the simultaneous capacity for contrary acts. Like the human will, the divine will has the simultaneous capacity for different objects. God behaves necessarily toward willing as such; i.e., God wills necessarily. With regard to what He wills, however, God behaves contingently. Since in the case of God the act of willing in itself is unlimited (insofar as the will actualizes itself as will), God can will contrary things with regard to the same object. This is not possible for the human will, for whom "to will something" is a different act from "not to will something."

At the end of his third investigation, Scotus thematizes the peculiarity of the will in its ability to be ordered toward the contrary simultaneously.[11] One can be ordered toward the contrary in two ways: either serially or simultaneously. The human will can be ordered toward the contrary serially, in that it first wills one thing and then another. In this way changes occur: one state is replaced by another. Thus one can, for example, first want to work and, after a while, want to take a rest. This contingency is then called *diachronic* contingency. The human will can, however, also be ordered toward the contrary simultaneously. Scotus accounts for this as follows: A cause causes either contingently or necessarily. The human will wills contingently in the moment in which it produces an act of willing; since it could also (at that moment) produce an act of willing that is ordered toward the contrary. Thus a human being can want to sit down and want to remain standing at the same time. He can, to be sure, not sit down and remain standing at the same time, but he can, before he executes the one or the other willed action, want both.

11. *Rep.* IA, d. 39–40, nn. 41–4 (Söder: 251–52).

The ability to want two contrary actions before one actually wills them is evidence that the will wills contingently and not necessarily. This contingency is called *synchronic* contingency.

What Scotus develops here with a view to the ability of the human will to will contraries simultaneously, holds also for God. In one moment of eternity, God wills something and is thus cause of a certain effect. In that moment in which this certain effect is there, the contrary effect could also be there, if God had willed to cause it. The effects that God produces are thus not necessary; He could also produce other effects.

Clearly, in the presence of these considerations, one must see the will, whether human or divine, as a power that, before it produces a concrete act of willing (before the activity A or not-A is willed), can be ordered simultaneously toward doing A and not doing A. This *before* must however not be understood temporally, since that would mean that the will is contingent in this respect. Rather, one must understand it in such a way that the will by its nature is in this position: that it is an essential characteristic of the will to be able to order itself toward doing A and not doing A. In terms of this double ordering it behaves necessarily and thereby immutably. The will is necessarily free in this respect. If one applies this to the divine will, this means that even when God behaves contingently *ad extra,* the divine will is nevertheless by its nature immutable. In addition, it orders itself as a power toward contraries simultaneously.

The result of Scotus's considerations of the problem of contingency can be summarized as follows. The contingency to which beings are subject is not a consequence of their materiality; rather, it belongs to them by reason of their being; it is one of their essential ontological characteristics. Such an ontologically understood contingency has its ultimate source in the free will of the first cause, i.e., of God, over against all that is not divine, the contingently constituted *ad extra.*

4.3 Modality

Scotus follows the tradition when he understands God as a rational being with voluntary self-determination. Prior to any act of creation, a divine volition must be presupposed, the execution of which is the actual act of creation. Prior to this volition, one must also presuppose a divine cognitive act where God knows what he is capable of producing. Only what has been cognized can be willed. The creatable must be known according to its essence as something that is possible in itself, regardless of whether it is actual at that time. "To be possible" here means to be a metaphysical possibility. The divine intellect thus produces the possible essence of what the divine will chooses to create or not. What God can create depends upon what God can cognize. The power of cognition is the naturally active capacity, in contrast to the will, which Scotus defines as the capacity for free self-determination. Consequently, the metaphysical possibility of the particular is a consequence of an act of the intellect that is necessary by nature. The metaphysically possible is thus not necessary in itself. At the same time, it is something whose existence is not impossible *(non repugnantia ad esse);* it is therefore also the logically possible. There is a current scholarly debate on the extent to which Scotus did or did not hold that either the logically possible or the logically necessary depends on divine free choice. There is also a debate on whether the discussion of necessity or possibility can only make sense with reference to a divine essence or a divine intellect; hence, independently of a given actuality.

The metaphysically possible is the creatable, the not yet actual, that which can be or exist. When created, it is a contingent being, one that at one time did not exist but that does indeed exist now. It is a non-necessary being. Nonetheless, there is still a level of necessity within such a contingent being: this level refers to the aspect of its logical possibility, its non-repugnance to being. Such a dimension is a necessary aspect of every being; it cannot be given in one case and not another. The non-repugnance to being, characteristic of all contingent beings, belongs above all and to the highest degree to God as the necessary being, whose actual existence is intrinsic to the divine essence.[12] Beyond all the differences that are revealed by the disjunctive transcendental determinations necessary/contingent, being reveals that which is common to both God and creation, namely, that for each the act of existence implies no contradiction.

4.4 Common Nature

The concept of the common nature *(natura communis)* reaches its specifically philosophical meaning in the Latin Middle Ages through the reception of the Arabic philosopher Avicenna (Ibn Sina, ca. 980–1037). The nature or the essence *(natura, essentia, quidditas)* of a thing is, for the philosophical tradition, what makes it what it is, what remains the same in all its transformations (with the exception, of course, of the transformations of this being). Thus the essence or the nature of an individual person, Peter, consists in being a human being; the essence of this individual cat, Mimi, is in being a cat.[13] According to Avicenna, the essence or nature of a thing can be considered in various ways: first, one can consider the nature of the thing as it is in itself *(natura secundum se, natura communis)*; next, one can consider the nature of the thing as it occurs in an individual *(natura in singularibus)*; and finally, one can consider it inso-

---

12. *Ordinatio* I, d. 36, q. un, n. 50 (ed. Vat. 6:291).
13. On this aspect of Scotist thought, see T. M. Rudavsky, "The doctrine of individuation in Duns Scotus," in *Franziskanische Studien* 59 (1977): 320–77, 62 (1980): 62–83; A. B. Wolter, "John Duns Scotus," in *Individuation in Scholasticism: The Later Middle Ages and Counter-Reformation, 1150–1650,* ed. J. Gracia (Albany: State University of New York Press, 1994), 271–98; "Scotus's Individuation Theory," in *The Philosophical Theology,* 68–97; T. Noone, "Universals and Individuation," in *The Cambridge Companion to Duns Scotus,* 100–128.

far as it is an object of intellection *(natura in intellectu)*. Among
these three ways, Avicenna is most interested in the first, the common nature *(natura communis),* because it helps to explain how universal concepts can be predicated of individuals. The common nature, as described by the concepts *human being* or *cat,* is distinctive
insofar as, in itself, it is neither universal/general nor singular/indi-
vidual. If these concepts were of themselves universal, they could
not, as concepts, be predicated of individuals. If they were in themselves singular, they could not, as concepts, be predicated commonly of several individuals. This indeterminacy of the common nature
with regard to both universality and singularity is what is meant
when one speaks of the common *(communis)* nature. The common
nature is found in the definition of a thing.

Scotus deals with the problem of the common nature in his
Commentary on the Sentences at the beginning of the question of individuation, because, as we shall see, both questions are closely connected. In what follows, we will look more carefully at *Ordinatio* II,
d. 3, q. 1: "Is a material substance individual or singular from itself—
that is, from its nature?"[14]

The problem of individuation can be formulated as follows: how
can we explain the merely numerical difference between two instances of the same species? This problem traditionally appears in a
Sentences commentary within the context of the doctrine of angels,
the first beings created by God. The Judeo-Christian texts refer to
Gabriel and Raphael, individual angels who appeared as messengers
from God to human beings. If all angels belong to the same angelic
species, how are we to understand their different personalities as distinct from one another? Before this problem can be answered, we
must first clarify the schema of the numerical difference among be-

---

14. An English translation of this text appears in P. V. Spade, *Five Texts on the
Mediaeval Problem of Universals: Porphyry, Boethius, Abelard, Duns Scotus, Ockham,*
57–113.

ings belonging to the same species according to Scotus, with a view to those creatures who, unlike angels, possess material bodies. Accordingly, the problem is this: Is a material substance of its very nature numerically one, incapable of division into several individuals? Following Aristotle, Scotus understands substance, i.e., what stands beneath (as one would literally translate *sub-stare*) as the bearer of qualities. Substance is that through which a thing is what it is. The term signifies the essence or nature of a thing.

Scotus develops his doctrine on common nature in connection with the solution to this problem of individuation. The initial arguments presented offer both pro and con approaches to the question. On the one hand, nature is individual because it is proper to the thing of which it is. From its nature the thing is unable to be anything else.[15] To the contrary, if, for instance, it were the nature of stone to be just this individual, then it would be the selfsame individual (this stone) in anything that was stone, and hence there could not be several stones.[16] Consequently, it would be nonsensical to continue to use the concept of determinate singularity, since singularity presupposes the concept of universality, and there is no universal concept here. Another argument can be given against the individuality of nature: If a nature were of itself numerically one, then it could not simultaneously belong both to this individual and to the multitude.[17] In addition, one would not need to look for the cause of singularity in anything other than the cause of the nature. Scotus clarifies this consideration by means of a simile: Of itself, a nature has true being outside the soul. Only when it is known by the intellect, does the nature take on the characteristic of a universal.[18] Only as a universal can the nature be predicated of different individuals of

---

15. II, d. 3, q. 1, n. 2 (Spade: 57).   16. II, d. 3, q. 1, n. 3 (Spade: 58).
17. II, d. 3, q. 1, n. 4 (Spade: 58).
18. The Vatican editors attribute this position to Franciscan Masters Peter of Falco and Roger Marston.

the same species. Thus, universality belongs to it only in a qualified manner, that is, in the soul. In other words, the nature is not universal in an unqualified sense. The cause of its being universal in the soul is the intellect itself. If a nature in the soul were of itself a singular, then it would follow from this that one need not look for the cause of its individuation, since this singularity would belong to the nature in itself.[19]

Scotus argues against this position in two ways. Considered in itself (that is, independently of its being known), the object of the intellect is prior by nature to the act by which it is understood, for the object is the cause of the act. If this object were of itself a singular and if the intellect knew its nature as a universal, then the intellect would understand the object under an aspect opposite to the object's very notion (i.e., a singular).[20] In other words, the understanding of the thing *qua* universal would be an intellection opposed to the proper notion of the object. Thus the nature of the thing itself cannot be a singular. In addition, the nature existing in things (in the external world) possesses a unity of being, so that one can say that several individuals within the same species possess a unity of nature. This unity is, however, less than numerical. The unity of the stone-nature, which the stone has of itself, is not a numerical unity.[21] Consequently, the nature existing in things (in the external world) is not, of itself, singular.

When Scotus turns to offer his own position, he reaffirms that the unity characteristic of stone as stone is not a unity of singularity. If it were, the stone could not be thought of without conceiving it under an aspect opposed to its essence. The object of the act of understanding (a universal) would be opposed to the nature of the being (a singular).[22] The unity that is not numerical exists independ-

---

19. "Rather, the same causes that are the causes of the unity of a thing are also the causes of its singularity." II, 3, q. 1, n. 6 (Spade: 58).

20. II, d. 3, q. 1, n. 7 (Spade: 59).   21. II, d. 3, q. 1, n. 8 (Spade: 59).

22. II, d. 3, q. 1, n. 7 (Spade: 59).

ently of any intellect; it belongs to the nature insofar as it is a nature. Because this unity of nature is different from numerical unity, one can distinguish between two instances of the same nature. The unity of nature points to the fact that a nature is not something composed in such a way that it could be decomposed into determinate principles. This special less-than-numerical unity of nature is undetermined both with regard to the numerical unity of the individual being and with regard to the universality that inheres in the nature as known. In other words, because the nature is *per se* one, it can be both singular in the individual and universal (i.e., predicable of many instances) in the intellect.

In order to illustrate his position, Scotus points to a passage of Avicenna in which the latter develops his doctrine of common nature.[23] "Equinity is only equinity; of itself it is neither one nor several, neither universal nor particular." The common nature of horses, equinity, is in itself neither one nor many. It is neither universal nor particular. These determinations belong to the nature as it exists in a particular individual or as it is in the intellect, but not as it is in itself.[24] Nature essentially precedes such determinations. Because of this, the nature or essence *(quidditas)* that is the object of the intellect belongs to the study of metaphysics. The definition of a being expresses its nature or essence.

When philosophers speak about the essence or nature of a thing, they distinguish between those statements that have to do with the essence or nature in an unqualified sense, that is, independently of any logical determination, and those statements in which nature is understood as genus or species, i.e., logically. True statements that refer to the essence or nature of something in an unqualified sense belong to the first mode *(propositiones verae primo modo)*. These are true insofar as they refer to the nature or essence *(quidditas)* *per se*.

23. II, d. 3, q. 1, n. 31 (Spade: 63).
24. II, d. 3, q. 1, n. 32 (Spade: 63).

Affirming only what belongs to it essentially, these propositions abstract *(abstrahere)* from everything that does not belong to the nature itself.

But just as the nature is not a singular, it is also not a *per se* universal.[25] Indeed, just as stone is first presented to the intellect as something in its own right and not as universal or singular, neither is universality part of its primary concept. As a universal, i.e., understood as the species or genus of something, nature would be a second order concept or second intention *(secunda intentio)* and an object of logic. First intentions refer to things; second intentions refer to concepts. Metaphysicians understand *nature* according to a first intention, while logicians understand nature (as the species or genus of something) as a second intention. Of itself, nature is not universal in the knower, nor is it singular in the individual. In its extramental existence, stone has its own proper unity that is less than the unity pertaining to a singular. "Therefore, the first intellection is an intellection of the nature without there being any co-understood mode, either the mode it has in the intellect or the one it has outside the intellect."[26] Universality belongs to it accidentally, insofar as only a universal can be an object of reason. Since universality as well as singularity are determinations that do not belong essentially to nature, it is not contradictory for nature to be independent of them. Thus just as nature, when it is an object of the intellect, has true intelligible being, it also has true real being outside of the activity of the intellect. Outside the intellect, nature has *per se* unity insofar as it subsists in itself. As we have seen, this unity is less than numerical and indifferent with regard to singularity or universality.

Scotus raises the objection that this position seems to claim that the universal is something real in the thing according to which it would pertain to several individuals. To this he responds: The uni-

25. II, d. 3, q. 1, n. 33 (Spade: 64).
26. II, d. 3, q. 1, n. 33 (Spade: 64).

versal in act has some *indifferent* unity in its intelligible content. Because of this, it can be predicated (or said) of each suppositum. The universal is, according to Aristotle, "one in many and said of many."[27] Nothing in reality is such that it can be said of an individual according to a *precise* unity by a predication that says "this is this." For example, being human can be predicated of Socrates and Plato, but not in a way that both individuals are themselves the universal. Nor do they both participate in the universal as if in a real third individual. Because the universal has an indifferent unity, it can be predicated of individuals. It is no contradiction that something universal in a determinate individual (Socrates) could also be in another individual (Plato). As an object of the act of understanding, the universal has numerical unity, according to which it itself, the very same, is predicable of every singular by saying: "This [determinate universal] is this [individual]."

Scotus then turns to considerations based on the epistemological distinction between agent and potential intellect, as well as the role of the imaginative image (phantasm). As we saw earlier,[28] Scotus accepts the Aristotelian model in which the cognitive process begins with an object affecting the senses and thereby setting the process of perception in motion. In perception, a sensible perceptual image (*phantasma*) arises from the perceived object. This forms the basis for the activity of intellection. The intellect, like the power of sensible perception, is not constituted through the act of knowing an object. Instead, it is always (i.e., before any actual completed cognition of an object) a power for cognition and thereby stands in possibility toward every knowable object; it is *intellectus possibilis*. However, unlike the way in which sense perception is initiated by its object, the intellect constitutes its own object, the universal, into something to be known, just as light makes what is perceivable by the eye visible

27. *Posterior analytics*, I, 4 (73b26–33), in *The Complete Works*, I:119.
28. See above, chapter 2.1.

so that the eyes can perceive it. This is the task of the *intellectus agens*, which makes the universal (contained in the sensible representations) into something presently knowable so that the *intellectus possibilis* can receive it and know it.

The active intellect thus constitutes the universality in things. Indeed, the nature or essence of every being, itself the goal of the process of cognition, exists in a sensible perceptual image and in another individual, as that in view of which the image is known. The active intellect causes the universality in things insofar as this aspect of the cognitive power reveals the nature within the phantasm. In other words, the universality of nature is extracted or abstracted from the particular material conditions of the phantasm through which the individual is grasped. The nature, free from the particular material conditions, has an objective being *(esse obiective)* in the possible intellect, i.e., it is the object as known by the intellect. Before this moment, however, regardless of whether it exists in a thing or in a phantasm, the nature cannot be predicated of many. In individuals of the same species or genus there is therefore something common *(commune)*, a common nature that of itself is not numerically one. Such a common feature *(commune)* in the individual must, however, not be conflated with the universal *(universale)* that belongs to the nature as known by the intellect. In the individual, nature does not possess the indifference that is necessary to be predicated of many, for this individual does not embody the nature as a whole.

4.5 The Principle of Individuation

Against the background of these remarks about *natura communis*, Scotus then engages with the position of Aristotle, which he introduced at the beginning of the Question. According to Aristotle, the substance of a thing, that through which it is what it is (its essence or nature), is only proper to the thing to which it belongs. For this reason it cannot simultaneously belong to another. With this interpretation, Aristotle—according to Scotus—rejects the Platonic thesis that a determinate nature understood as existing in itself and as an Idea, is the universal for all individuals of the same species or genus. According to Scotus, the Aristotelian doctrine is true if Aristotle understands substance in the sense of nature. That means, however, that the Platonic Idea is not the same as nature or the Aristotelian substance. This is especially true, according to Scotus, if one understands substance as first substance. According to Aristotle, one understands by first substance the individual, e.g., a certain horse or a certain cat. This substance belongs of itself to the thing to which it belongs and cannot at the same time belong to another thing.[29]

The closing section of Question 1 reprises the original question of the cause of the individuality or singularity of material substances. Community (communitas), like singularity (singularitas), belongs to nature outside the intellect. The quality of community belongs to the nature, thus answering the question of the thing's cause. The quality of singularity, by contrast, belongs to the nature only through something in the thing that contracts the nature. At this point in the text, however, the actual cause of the singularity of material substances has yet to be determined.

The second question is taken up immediately in an effort to discover the intrinsic principle of the singular, and cause of its singularity. Scotus engages first with the position of Henry of Ghent. In his *Quodlibet* V, Henry had argued that the cause of individuation is no inner positive principle but rather consists in a double negation, a privation of division.[30] If someone says of something that it is individual or one, this means only that it is in itself neither divisible (*pri-*

29. II, d. 3, q. 1, n. 41 (Spade: 67).
30. II, d. 3, q. 2, n. 44 (Spade: 68).

vatio divisionis in se) nor identical with others *(privatio identitatis ad aliud)*. According to Scotus, the fact that the assumption of an inner positive principle of individuation stands in contradiction with our concept of being speaks in favor of this view. If, namely, *one* expresses a positive determination, it must, on the one hand, be different from the determination *being;* otherwise speaking of one being would be unnecessarily repetitive. On the other hand, no determination other than *being* can be expressed with *one;* otherwise in every being there would be entity added to entity, which is nonsensical.

Before Scotus rejects Henry's thesis of the individuation of material substances,[31] he makes his own direction of inquiry more precise, whereby he clarifies what he means to find. His question, what makes a nature an individual, does not refer to nature in the sense of a second intention.[32] He is not looking for a conceptual entity. Nor is he looking for the numerical unity by which a nature is formally one. Rather, he wants to discover the intrinsic positive principle on the basis of which the nature of something cannot be further divided. Scotus states his question thus: What is it in this stone, by which as by a proximate foundation it is absolutely incompatible with the stone for it to be divided into several parts each of which is this stone, the kind of division that is proper to a universal whole as divided into its subjective parts?[33]

Scotus wants to prove, contrary to Henry of Ghent, that the cause of individuality understood in this way cannot be a double negation but must be understood as a positive intrinsic principle. In

31. II, d. 3, q. 2, nn. 49–56 (Spade: 69–71).

32. As noted above, the Latin tradition—following Avicenna here—distinguishes between concepts of first and second intention *(prima et secunda intentio)*. A concept of first intention is the result of the direct cognition of a thing and refers to the nature or essentiality as cognized by the intellect (the object outside the mind); a concept of second intention follows from the reflection on this nature or essentiality, insofar as it represents a universal and is predicable of several things (a mental object).

33. II, d. 3, q. 2, n. 48 (Spade: 69).

this context, individuality means that it would be a contradiction for the essence of a thing to be divided into parts that could themselves underlie another thing. Scotus presents five arguments against Henry. First, a negation can, to be sure, take away the proximate potency to acting and being acted upon. However, this does not establish the formal incompatibility of that being with anything. Since negations are not beings, they remain external to the essence or the nature of the thing to which they are ordered, so that the opposite of this negation can also be connected with this essence or nature. Scotus clarifies this with the example of vision: negation (privation) of vision means "to be unable to see." If it is said of a certain person that he cannot see, then this means only that this particular human being is unable to see. The nature of the human being remains untouched by this privation, and for this reason there can and must be other human beings who can see. In other words, both the quality "to be unable to see" and the quality "to be able to see" are consistent with the nature of a human being. It follows from this consideration that a mere negation in a nature cannot suffice to oppose its being divided into parts that themselves can underlie another being. Additionally, an imperfection, and this is the case of a privation or negation, can only contradict the form or essence or nature of a thing, i.e., it can only militate against something formally, if there is something positive in the essence of a thing against which it militates.

The second argument against Henry is based on the Aristotelian distinction between first and second substance.[34] Already in a first rejection of the thesis of double negation as principle of individuation, Scotus had made reference to this distinction. By *first substance* Aristotle understands the individual substance, for example a certain horse or cat; by *second substance* the species or genus to which an individual belongs. First substance is substance to a higher degree

---

34. II, d. 3, q. 2, n. 53 (Spade: 70).

than second, because it occurs in the reality that surrounds us as independent and acts of itself, while second substance cannot subsist
of itself but is always bound to particular instances that represent it.
So first substance is more perfect than second. However, whatever is
more perfect than something else cannot (according to Scotus) have
reached this higher degree of perfection through negation, because
a negation neither is nor brings about anything positive. Consequently, individuality cannot be the result of a negation.

The third argument follows.[35] Of a singular there is predicated
per se in the first mode *(per se primo modo praedicari)* that of which it
is a singular. But nothing can be said of a being with regard to its
wholeness that is grasped through a double negation. For the mere
negation does not yet guarantee the wholeness of what is grasped.
This unity is, however, necessary in order to be able to speak of a
single essence.

The fourth argument decisively exceeds the precision of the earlier considerations.[36] Independent of the falseness of Henry's theory,
there is a further problem connected with it. The theory does not
answer the question. If one asks, "through what does the double
negation belong to the individual?" and obtains the answer that the
double negation in itself is the basis for it, then this is no answer to
the question at all. The question of the principle of individuation is
namely the question of the positive cause for the fact that it contradicts the nature of an individual to be divided into many particular
natures and to be identical with another individual. So the question
of the double negation is: Through what positive principle are the
opposites of these negations incompatible with this individual? On
what basis does this negation belong to the individual? Henry's position fails to answer this question. A fifth argument against Henry's
thesis completes the attack. If the same double negation always

35. II, d. 3, q. 2, n. 54 (Spade: 71).
36. II, d. 3, q. 2, n. 55 (Spade: 71).

makes Socrates into the individual Socrates and Plato into the individual Plato (rather than making Socrates into Plato and Plato into Socrates), then there must be something about the double negation that lets this individual come into being. This is, however, only possible through something positive.[37]

These considerations sufficiently convince Scotus that the cause of individuation must be an intrinsic positive principle. Even if Henry's theory is correct, a positive principle must also be connected with the double negation. This positive principle provides the basis for the double negation's belonging to the individual. More generally, it can be affirmed that every form of unity has its final basis in something positive, thus the numerical unity of the individual must also have such a basis.

After Scotus has demonstrated (in the subsequent three questions) that neither the existence nor the quantity nor the material can be the principle of individuation, he proves in the final (sixth) question that the material substance becomes individual through a principle that contracts the common nature *(natura communis)* to singularity. Scotus calls this principle the individuating entity *(entitas individualis)*. In the literature on Scotus, this is as a rule described as thisness or *haeceitas*, a term that Scotus uses in his *Questions on Aristotle's Metaphysics*.[38]

Scotus offers two reasons in favor of his thesis. The first emphasizes that everything to which the determination *being* belongs also carries necessarily the determination *one*.[39] Elsewhere, Scotus makes clear that the connection of the determinations *being* and *one* is so close that they are interchangeable or convertible. One can infer from this that the unity of the individual in itself necessarily follows

---

37. II, d. 3, q. 2, n. 56 (Spade: 71).
38. Cf. *Met.* VII q. 13 n. 61 (*Questions on the Metaphysics,* II:208–209) and 176 (II:240–41). In the new critical edition, the term is found in these passages with the orthography *haecitas*.
39. II, d. 3, q. 6, n. 169 (Spade: 101).

from its being. How is this being constituted in the case of an individual? According to Scotus, it cannot be the common nature *(natura communis),* because this already possesses a unity—as he has shown—which is, nevertheless, less than the numerical unity of the individual. We seek that principle which contracts the common nature into a unity. The individual to which the nature and principle belong is perfect as an independent being.

In his second justification, Scotus argues that if a distinction is given regarding different beings, then there must be a cause of this distinction.[40] Otherwise, one could progress infinitely. This holds, as well, for distinctions that are given through individuality. This first cause of the difference between individuals cannot, however, be the common nature, because this only explains why two species-distinct individuals are different from one another. It does not explain why two species-identical individuals differ. Two species-distinct individuals (a man and a dog) differ from one another in reality by reason of their different natures, while two species-identical individuals (two men) agree in reality in the same common nature. The question regarding individuation is precisely this: "What grounds the numerical difference between two individuals within the same species?" Since by reason of Scotus's foregoing considerations neither a double negation nor accidents are candidates for the principle of individuation, it can only be something positive distinct from the common nature.

In order to make clear how this principle of individuation is constituted, Scotus first distinguishes it from specific difference.[41] The specific difference is the difference between a species and its higher genus. Thus the disposition toward reason is, according to the traditional philosophical interpretation, the specific difference that exists

40. II, d. 3, q. 6, n. 170 (Spade: 101–102).
41. II, d. 3, q. 6, n. 176 (Spade: 103).

between the species *human* and its higher genus, *animal*. Scotus compares the specific difference with what is subordinated to it in the species-genus hierarchy, namely, the individual. It stands in contradiction to specific difference and numerical unity to be divided into parts *(partes subjectivae)* that can in turn be bearers of qualities. Since the unity of a common nature is less than that of the individual, a division of the nature is ruled out only in terms of essential parts. By contrast, the unity of an individual excludes all division. Because the less than numerical unity of nature has its own being, it follows for Scotus that the more perfect unity of the individual must also possess its own being.[42]

In a second step, Scotus compares the specific difference with the genus.[43] What designates the genus is formally (not materially) other than what designates the specific difference. This is seen in the definition *rational animal,* where reference is made to the next higher genus (animal) and the specific difference (rational). If genus and specific difference were not formally different, then one of the two of them would be superfluous in the definition. The specific difference is related to the genus as actuality *(actus)* is related to possibility *(potentia)*, i.e., the specific difference determines the genus and limits it to a species. As the specific difference is to the genus, so is the individual to the specific difference. The individual also determines the species in act and limits it. The specific difference and the principle of individuation differ in that the former is always added to the genus, while the latter is always the ultimate reality of a form *(ultima realitas forma)*.[44] The two are also distinct in that the specific difference (such as *rational*), in contrast to the principle of individuation, can be common to many and predicated of many.

Finally Scotus compares the specific difference with what is coor-

42. II, d. 3, q. 6, n. 177 (Spade: 103–104).
43. II, d. 3, q. 6, n. 179 (Spade: 104).
44. II, d. 3, q. 6, n. 180 (Spade: 104).

dinated with it in the species-genus hierarchy. This other type of specific difference is the ultimate difference in the hierarchy immediately prior to the individual.[45] Just as species are distinct from one another, so are individuals distinct from one another, so that ultimate specific differences and individual differences are comparable.

Scotus must now answer the question whether the principle of individuation or the individual entity *(entitas individualis)* is identical with matter, form, or their composite.[46] All three are ascribable to diverse specific differences and thereby to nature *(natura)*. The individual entity cannot be equated with any of them, however, insofar as the nature is not in itself individual but rather precedes all individual determinations. Since the individual entity is the last rung of the reality of a being, it can only be equated with those three that stand as the last rung of their order, namely where matter is *this,* the form is *this* and the composite is *this.*

In relation to the many individual beings, the common nature *(natura communis)* is to be distinguished from the individual entity *(entitas individualis)*. While the common nature is the reason that individuals of the same species have something in common, the principle of individuation is the cause of their difference, uniqueness, and numerical unity. This distinction of the common nature from principle of individuation is a formal one; the two are merely formally distinct *(formaliter distinctae)* in the individual. While two individuals are in themselves really distinct, two formally distinct entities are not in themselves distinct in reality; instead, they only become distinct through the intellect, i.e., they can be conceived independently of one another. Nevertheless, they are not mere concepts because the intellect does not produce them.[47]

45. II, d. 3, q. 6, n. 183 (Spade: 105).
46. II, d. 3, q. 6, nn. 187–8 (Spade: 106–107).
47. See above, chapter 2.2.

5. THE FOUNDATIONS OF
A SCIENCE OF 'PRAXIS'

$\int$ cotus's ethical insights, with their emphasis on freedom in the will, belong to the generation of thinkers writing after the Condemnation of 1277. In response to an overly intellectualized depiction of human perfection on the part of those he simply calls "the philosophers," Scotus examines traditional moral elements from the perspective of freedom, for both the human and divine wills. The will is central for Scotus because it is love, not knowledge, that perfects the human person as rational animal. Following Augustine, he locates the fulfillment of human nature in the act of right and ordered loving. With other mainline Franciscan thinkers he places sin not in the intellect as an error of judgment but in the will as disordered desire. Although he attempts this reformulation of ethical matters in the wake of 1277, Scotus's particular form of voluntarism is not simply reducible to his teaching on the freedom of the will. It is part of a much larger effort to ground the moral order on love.

Thirteenth-century reflection upon ethics centered upon the nature of a science of *praxis*, in light of the strong Aristotelian canons for a scientific argument found in the *Posterior analytics*.[1] Scientific reasoning requires premises that are necessarily true and, in addition, the syllogistic method of deduction to insure that the conclusions are also necessary. As we have seen in chapter 4, contingent states of affairs that result from choice do not admit of the necessity required for such conclusive scientific certainty. A science of ethics must be both scientific and practical. In his own elaboration of the contours of such a practical science, Scotus attempts to balance both scientific and practical spheres to offer a solid foundation for moral deliberation and to allow for the indetermination of the contingent realm of human choice.

Scotus understands moral science to be a unified body of knowledge, derived both from a first practical principle and acquired through experience. Moral truth can be rationally known and objectively verified. While particular moral judgments deal with contingent matters, the science of morals, *qua* science, requires an objective and necessary foundation that grounds the certainty of moral judgment in the intellect. As a scientific body of knowledge, then, ethics can claim to be more than a composition of truths that "hold for the most part," as Aristotle notes in *Nicomachean Ethics* I (1094b22). The truth of moral judgment is grounded objectively on the metaphysical relationship that exists among created goods, as established by the divine will. These goods possess a given value based upon their nature. This value can be known by the human intellect without any need for special illumination or revelation. As we saw earlier in chapter 2, the human intellect reaches out to reality by

---

1. Aristotle, *Posterior analytics* I, 6 (74b5–10), in *The Complete Works of Aristotle,* I:120.

means of a two-fold act: abstraction and intuition. This twofold cognitive capacity strengthens the objectivity of intellectual, rational reflection and judgment about moral matters.

Moral science is grounded logically in the form of its first practical principle, *Deus diligendus est* (God is to be loved). This first truth of practical reasoning is, according to Scotus, a necessary proposition, self-evident *(per se nota)* to all rational agents.[2] All moral propositions, all precepts of natural law, contained as well in the Decalogue, stand in harmonious relationship to this first, necessary, practical truth. As foundational to rationality, the first principle and all those derived from it are, as it were, "written on the human heart." They reveal themselves in human reflection and judgment. They are never lost, not even in the damned.

This first practical principle grounds, additionally, the objective order of moral goodness. Since God's will is good and ordered, whatever has been established in the act of creation is both good and ordered. Rational goods such as truth, life, or integrity are appropriate objects for human desire and reveal the objective ground for moral judgments. Because the natural order is rational, the goodness of its various elements is apparent to human reason. The Augustinian tradition understood this order according to the Stoic framework of the two categories of good. There are first, those goods whose value depends entirely on the use one makes of them. These are the useful goods, the *bonum utile,* such as money or power. Beyond these, there are goods whose value is intrinsic and inde-

---

2. Although he never presents the argument in a straightforward manner, Scotus appears to rely upon an Anselmian-like argument when he argues that the negative formulation of this principle, "If God is God, then God ought not to be hated" expresses the self-evidence of the proposition in a manner clearer than its affirmative formulation. He clearly intends the sort of formulation that reveals the logical impossibility of conceiving of God as the highest good and, under that *ratio,* hating God. Anselm's second version of the ontological argument comes to mind with this move.

pendent of use. These goods are valuable for themselves alone. They are worthy of respect because they are the goods of value, *bonum honestum*. Examples of such intrinsic goods would be truth, integrity, the person, God. These goods stand at the top of the ontological hierarchy and are the standard for human judgments and choice.

Scotus's moral theory links the scientific level of foundational principle and objective moral goods with the level of particular moral judgments. The validity of moral conclusions depends upon objective goodness, rationally known and understood. Because the moral foundations are so stable, practical moral judgments appear as scientific conclusions that can admit of a high level of certainty. Because of this certainty, the moral act as executed resembles a work of artistic performance. The morally perfected agent is compared to the artisan or musician who knows the principles and rules for the art, and who attempts to realize these principles to the best of her ability within the best performance possible. In this way, concrete moral judgments involve both a scientific dimension (their foundation in objective goodness and in necessary rational principles) and an artistic quality (their realization in a concrete, practical situation). It is the intellect, with its powerful cognitive acts of abstraction and intuition, which mediates this movement from the highest level of principle to the judgment immediate to choice.

Scotus's ethical insights are best understood when framed by three large perspectives: the nature of rational perfection, the object of a practical science and, finally, the role of the divine will as moral foundation. The first two perspectives can be found in the *Prologues* to his *Commentary on the Sentences* in the *Lectura*[3] as well as the *Ordinatio* versions. The third perspective appears in *Ordinatio* I, d. 44 and III, d. 37.[4] The three perspectives are related hierarchically to

3. A portion of this text is translated into English in A. B. Wolter, *Duns Scotus on the Will and Morality* (Washington, D.C.: Catholic University of America Press, 1986), 127–43.
4. These texts appear in *Will and Morality*, 255–61 (I, 44) and 269–87 (III, 37).

one another, moving from the human person as subject for moral science, to the activity of willing as object for moral science,[5] finally to the divine exemplar as ground for the perfection of right willing. The present chapter develops this three-fold perspective.

5.1 The Perfection of a Rational Nature

In his consideration of the elements that are involved in practical reasoning, Scotus affirms clearly that the subject of moral reflection is not an abstract notion such as happiness, but the human person.[6] The person, he argues, is the subject for moral science in the same way that he is the subject for the science of medicine. It is not health, but the healthy person who is the focus for medical reflection. Similarly, it is not an abstract definition of happiness or perfection, but the perfected and completed person who is the focus for an ethical science.

In the *Prologue*'s opening question, Scotus presents what he calls the "controversy between philosophers and theologians" that raged in the last quarter of the thirteenth century.[7] This controversy centered on the idea of human perfection or happiness and upon the need for revelation. Scotus summarizes the arguments of the two sides with his characteristic verbal economy. The philosophers held that no revelation was needed for human perfection, because the

5. According to Scotus, the subject of a science finalizes that science and transcends human knowing, while the object of a science is the subject as understood. See *Ordinatio Prologue* Pars III, q. 1–3, n. 142 (ed. Vat. 1:96). The subject of metaphysics is being in general *(ens commune); its object is ens in quantum ens,* or any being considered insofar as it exists. The subject of theology is the divine essence *(deitas);* its object is *ens infinitum,* or infinite being, the most perfect concept of which the human mind is capable. Accordingly, the subject of a practical science would be the human person as rational; its object would be *praxis,* the domain of activity by which the moral agent reveals her rationality.

6. *Ordinatio Prologue* Pars V, qq. 1–2, n. 262 (ed. Vat. 1:177).

7. An English version of this can be found in Wolter, "Duns Scotus on the Necessity of Revealed Knowledge," *Franciscan Studies* 11, 3–4 (1951): 231–73.

Philosopher (Aristotle) had adequately accounted both for the nature of human fulfillment in his *Nicomachean Ethics* X, 6–9, and for the powers of human cognition in the *De anima* III. As Arab commentators such as Averroes developed Aristotle's thought, Latin scholars found an independent, natural framework for a way of life that was seen as a viable alternative to that of the theologian.[8] Aristotle offered both a moral goal *(eudaimonia)* and a natural means to that goal in the life of virtue *(arete)*. Book X, 6–9, of the *Nicomachean Ethics* identifies the life of speculation and contemplation as that life which most completely fulfills the human natural desire to know. Aristotle presents the virtues as constitutive of this goal and therefore the natural and necessary means whereby such fulfillment is reached. The philosophical alternative to theology appears in its most complete form with the complete reception of Aristotle's text in the second half of the thirteenth century.[9] It was this alternative defended by members of the Faculty of Arts that prompted the condemnations of both 1270 and 1277. Propositions listed as heterodox embodied both Aristotelian and Arab models of human moral perfection.[10]

Against this naturalistic vision of human perfection based upon the intellect, the theologians of Scotus's *Prologue* emphasize the true nature of *beatitudo* in the beatific vision *(visio Dei)*. They claim that philosophers err in their understanding of the ultimate goal and, because of this, err in their assertion about the way such a goal is the result of the natural life of virtue. To err about the end is to err

8. Alain de Libera, *Penser au Moyen Age*, 214–227.

9. Georg Wieland, "Happiness, the Perfection of Man," in *The Cambridge History*, 673–86.

10. L. Honnefelder, "Die Kritik des Johannes Duns Scotus am kosmologischen Nezessitarismus der Araber: Ansätze zu einem neuen Freiheitsbegriff," in *Die abendländische Freiheit vom 10. zum 14. Jahrhundert. Der Wirkungszusammenhang von Idee und Wirklichkeit in europäischen Vergleich*, ed. J. Fried (Sigmaringen 1991), 249–63.

about the means needed to reach that end. Philosophers cannot know what God will reward with blessedness, since the divine will lies beyond the human capacity to understand. Indeed, the experience of the beatific vision is wholly supernatural and exceeds any capacity of the natural order.

Scotus attempts to mediate both positions in his determination of this question. With the philosophers, he affirms the dignity of human nature and the ability of the human intellect to know reality. With the theologians, he defends divine freedom and liberality, the primacy of love for God over knowledge of God and, additionally, the need for revelation in order that human reason might truly understand the God it seeks to love. Scotus concludes that the human person has a natural destiny that can only be reached with supernatural help. It is this, he affirms, that most clearly reveals the dignity of human nature.[11]

Although he does not entirely side with the theologians, Scotus does offer a sustained critique of the philosophical perspective in which he identifies the weaknesses of Aristotle's intellectualist, teleological theory. The heart of this critique is the inadequacy of the cognitive model they use. This is the representational model presented earlier (in chapter 2), where phantasms derived from sense perception give rise to intelligible *species* in the agent intellect. If abstractive cognition were the only possible mode of human knowing, then the fullest realization of human perfection would have to be supernatural to the point of transformation. Indeed, the conditions required for the beatific vision would not belong to human or angelic natures as presently constituted. God would have to create these

11. "But I go further when I say that there is another, higher form of speculation that can be received naturally. Consequently, nature in this regard is honored even more than if one were to claim that the highest possible perfection it could receive is that which is naturally attainable." Wolter, "Duns Scotus on the Necessity of Revealed Knowledge," 265.

conditions in eternity. This new nature would not be the perfection of the present nature, but rather a supernatural transformation into another nature altogether.

Scotus's act of intellectual intuition, however, saves both human dignity and the natural requirements for the beatific vision. This act lies beyond representational cognition and can only be affirmed as belonging to the highest human perfection on the basis of revelation.[12] Because the human intellect is in potentiality to all being, it already possesses the natural capacity to see God face to face. However, the divine essence is not the natural object of the human intellect. The vision of God that constitutes the fullest realization of human potential involves the free choice on the part of the divine will to reveal itself to the human mind. In heaven, God is the *obiectum voluntarium,* or voluntary object of human cognition. With his addition of intuitive cognition, Scotus can argue that human nature has a natural desire for a perfection that it can only achieve supernaturally, as a gift.

Accordingly, the conclusions of the philosophers skew the understanding of rationality and its perfection in a two-fold manner. First, they draw faulty conclusions about the nature of the highest being, based upon sense perception. They hold, for example, that the first cause causes necessarily. They also affirm the superiority of intellection to volition, of the life of knowledge to the life of love, and so set themselves a goal that will not bring them truly to the sphere of the divine or eternal. In truth, God is not merely infinite knowledge, but, more precisely, infinite love. Second, in their assumption that the present human condition (*pro statu isto*) is itself human nature, the philosophers fail to identify the higher perfection of a rational nature and settle for the lower. Because they are igno-

12. See Wolter's "Duns Scotus on the Natural Desire for the Supernatural," in *The Philosophical Theology,* 125–47.

rant of revelation, philosophers have no knowledge of the fall, of original sin and its consequences for human powers of knowing and willing. Because Aristotle thought that his cognitive experience was definitive of human nature, he concluded that reflection upon the experience of sense perception was sufficient to reveal the nature of all that exists. The human condition may reveal something of human nature, but not enough to conclude to the state of perfection to which the human person is destined. Human perfection, known best by means of revelation, is actually superior to anything Aristotle had imagined.

Because God is not the Unmoved Mover as Aristotle held, but rather unconditional love as Scripture teaches, a far more effective philosophical effort would begin with love rather than knowledge, and consequently with the will rather than the intellect. In this sort of effort, natural reasoning could provide useful information that would, in fact, lead one to a better understanding of human perfection than provided by Aristotle. Accordingly, human fulfillment would be understood as the perfection of ordered loving, founded upon the natural human desire to love the highest good above all and for itself alone. This is the Augustinian vision of human fulfillment, into which Scotus integrates Aristotelian insights.

Aquinas had argued that the fulfillment of human perfection (happiness) involves the highest activity of the highest faculty toward the highest object.[13] Scotus's ethical discussion takes this for-

---

13. Thomas Aquinas, *Summa theologiae* Ia–IIae, q. 3, art. 5 (I: 599). An interesting aspect of this article is the third objection and response. The third objection holds that happiness consists in the activity of the practical rather than speculative intellect. In his response, Aquinas maintains that, were man his own ultimate end, this argument would be valid. Since the ultimate end is extrinsic (i.e., God) human happiness consists in speculation. Scotus's approach takes seriously that God can only be the true end of human happiness when the true nature of God is known, that is, by revelation. In this way, Scotus would argue that the teleology used by Aquinas in his rejection of this objection is that of the theologian, not the philosopher.

mal definition and uses it to explain how human rational perfection is primarily the perfection of right loving, rather than the contemplative goal of speculation and understanding. The highest activity is love, the highest faculty is the will and the highest object is God. Consequently, loving God above all things and for God alone is the act that most completely perfects human nature and fulfills the human desire for happiness.

In assessing Scotus's position on freedom in the will, it is important to note that he responds to a specific vision of human nature and human rationality that masters of the Faculty of Arts in Paris presented and defended as validly Aristotelian.[14] He grounds his discussion upon the nature of the divine will as exemplar of rational, ordered, and self-determined generous freedom. He sees the human will as a finite image of that infinite will. It too, aided by grace, is capable of rational, ordered, and self-determined acts of generous freedom. In his presentation of the will, Scotus seeks to bring together the domains of objectivity and subjectivity as they relate to the moral order. Moral objectivity (the rightness of an action) is based upon the order created by God and upon the ability of human reason to understand something of that order. Moral subjectivity (the goodness of a person) is taken from the perspective of the human will, with its rational constitution and natural tendency to cooperate with the judgments of right reason.

The divine will plays a central and foundational role in Scotus's ethical insights. Divine creative free choice has established the objective order of goods and their natural relationship to human rationality. In addition, the divine will serves as model for the human will. Notwithstanding the central place held by God's will, however, Scotus does not present a divine command moral theory. Moral conclu-

14. I develop this in much more detail in "Duns Scotus, Morality and Happiness: A Reply to Thomas Williams," *American Catholic Philosophical Quarterly* 74 n. 2 (2000): 173–95.

sions do not require an understanding of their foundational basis in God in order to be moral. First practical principles are analytic in nature and require no foundation other than their logical necessity. The principles and conclusions of moral science can be known naturally, on the basis of rational reflection upon the created order.

5.2 The Science of *Praxis*

If a correct understanding of the human person defines the subject of a practical science, its object is the act of *praxis* in the will. The act of volition is the essential starting point for Scotus's discussion of the domain of a practical science, from its ultimate first principle to the concrete act of judgment. In the moment of judgment and choice, the moral agent brings forth the act as a type of giving birth. This moment of birthing requires the immediacy of moral knowledge and free choice. Without such immediacy, moral knowledge is not practical. With it, all levels of moral awareness and judgment, from the highest levels of principle to the concrete matter at hand, are brought into dynamic relationship within the will. In this way, the act of *praxis* lies completely within the power of the will and the moral domain is entirely framed by freedom.

As noted in chapter 2, Scotus identifies three levels of certain knowledge: first principles, scientific understanding based upon observation and experience, and immediate internal self-awareness. Likewise, knowledge of practical matters falls into three categories: first practical principles, the domain of moral science, and the deliberative judgment about a concrete matter for choice. The first principle of *praxis,* "Do good, avoid evil," appears in Scotist thought as *Deus diligendus est* ("God is to be loved"). This principle is an analytic truth, known with certainty on the basis of its terms. The domain of moral science is comprised of moral propositions whose truth is known on the basis of experience and reflection upon one's own behavior as well as upon the requirements of rational perfection. This science is both learned and can be understood to form a coherent and consistent body of knowledge that expresses the first practical principles. It stands between the two domains of ultimate moral principle and concrete moral decision.

The truths of moral science are necessary truths about contingent states of affairs. These truths can be ascertained by noticing the patterns that obtain in the created order, in the same way that scientists identify patterns of cause and effect in nature. In this way, the truth of the proposition "lying is wrong" can be known on the basis of personal experience and the requirements of rational perfection. The proposition is true and necessarily so, even though the act of telling a lie is contingent. Scotus compares the truths of moral science to the truths of physics, for example, when he notes that the truth about gravity is necessary, even though the fall of a stone is a contingent act.[15] The scientific habit that deals with necessary truths is distinct from the deliberative habit that deals with a concrete particular. This latter habit of moral judgment is immediate to action and is expressed as the dictate *(dictamen)* of right reasoning, the judgment of prudence. This judgment is related to choice in an immediate manner, unlike moral science that has a mediated and remote relationship to choice.

In some ways, Scotus's discussion of the science of *praxis* reverses that of Aristotle. The Stagirite understood the natural order as existing of necessity. There can only be one world and this is it. Against this background of metaphysical necessity, he presented ethics as a science of the contingent whose truth was defined by its

---

15. "Therefore, I say there are necessary truths about contingent things, because while it is contingent that a stone fall, nevertheless there are necessary truths about its descent, such as that it seeks the center and that it descends in a straight line." *Lectura Prologue,* in *Will and Morality,* 139. In this context, Scotus distinguishes between a scientific habit (moral science) and a deliberative habit (prudence).

object, a contingent state of affairs framed within a larger order of natural necessity. By contrast, Scotus understands the larger frame to be contingency, not necessity. This world does exist, but its existence is contingent. It is the result of a free act of choice on the part of the Creator and might have been different. Indeed, what currently exists might be other than it is. This larger frame of contingency influences the way Scotus seeks to ground moral science on logical necessity of first principles, and upon the divine will in contingently creating this sort of world with natures of these sorts and relationships of the kind that we find. On the basis of these already existing relationships, natural reason draws inferences and conclusions about moral behavior in its general dimensions. These conclusions have the coherency of science and admit of a necessity that particular moral judgments may not.

While Scotus develops his discussion of the requirements for a practical science against the foundation of contingency, he argues that moral science possesses an objective certainty which is to guide choice. Because he provides the will with a broad exercise of freedom, Scotus does not hesitate to give the intellect the power to come to moral conclusions with a high degree of certainty. With its twofold acts of abstraction and intuition, the intellect is able to understand a present situation reflectively, to identify the moral demands that are present, and to conclude to the best course of action. Reasoning back and forth among principles, the scientific body of moral knowledge and the present situation, the moral agent can conclude with certainty to what should be done.

In both *Lectura* and *Ordinatio Prologues,* Scotus presents the contours of a practical science, based upon the rational will and the relationship of cognition to action. He sets forth three conditions required for *praxis,* all on the basis of Aristotle's discussion in Book VI of the *Nicomachean Ethics.* These are:

1. It must be the act of a power other than the intellect,

2. That naturally follows intellection, and

3. Whose act must be elicited in such a way that it be in accord with right reasoning so that [the act itself] be right.[16]

Praxis is the act of a power other than the intellect because the intellect cannot extend beyond itself unless directed to do so by another power.[17] *Praxis* must, therefore, be an act of willing, either elicited or commanded, following intellection. It is an act that lies in the power of the agent such as one finds in artisans discussed by Aristotle in *Ethics* VI.[18] Indeed, remarks Scotus, if this relationship of cognition to action be true of the artisan, how much more apt of the morally mature *(prudens),* since prudence is the form of all the virtues. The third condition for *praxis* joins moral desire and choice to the judgment of right reasoning. *Praxis* is an act of willing in tandem with right reasoning. This means that when an act is not accompanied by right reasoning, it is not *praxis.* It also means that when an act of reasoning is not followed by an act of willing, the cognition involved is not practical.

Aristotle's discussion in *Nicomachean Ethics* VI[19] helps Scotus conclude from these three conditions that the primary object of a practical science such as ethics must be volition insofar as it conforms to rationality, or right and ordered willing. According to this perspective, the will's activity always involves cognition (conditions 1 and 2); its goal is right choice (condition 3). The will for Scotus is the locus for the discussion of moral science, both as the source and the perfection of ethics. The scientific domain of *praxis,* understood in this way, has an extension that can be defined from its source in rational volition to its completion in right choice and right action.

16. The *Lectura* version of this is found in *Will and Morality,* 127.
17. *Lectura* in *Will and Morality,* 127.
18. *Ordinatio* Prologue n. 231 (ed. Vat. 1:156–7).
19. *Ordinatio* Prologue n. 233 (ed. Vat. 1:158).

The will plays the triple role here as the principle, the object, and the perfection of the order of *praxis*.

Once he has focused his discussion of *praxis* on the will and rational choice, Scotus handles the scientific dimension of such a practical science. He does this by means of a discussion of practical cognition and its important relationship to *praxis*. Here again, a key reference to *Ethics* VI opens the discussion with its affirmation that cognition extends to *praxis* by a double relationship of natural priority and conformity.[20] Cognition is prior both temporally (because no volition takes place in the absence of intellection) and naturally (because rational moral principles are logically prior to the act of the will). Such moral principles carry the force of rational certainty. They are revealed in the judgments of reasoning about choice. There is conformity between choice and cognition insofar as the practical truth reveals the rectitude of desire (right loving) in the concrete moment of choice. Thus, right reasoning offers both the certainty of moral judgment and the norm for moral rectitude.

In order to understand practical reasoning precisely as practical (and not merely as reasoning), Scotus turns from the focus on the end *(finis)* to a consideration of the object *(obiectum)* of *praxis*. This focus on the object entails a consideration of the activity of moral reasoning from the perspective of efficient, rather than final, causality. When we shift our perspective from final to efficient causality, we see that the object of *praxis* contains all that is needed for the moral judgment. These elements are listed by Aristotle in *Ethics* III as those matters of which the voluntary agent should be aware: who the agent is, what the action is, who is affected, what means are used, the result intended and the manner of action.[21] This object offers all that is required for moral deliberation.

20. *Ordinatio* Prologue n. 236 (ed. Vat. 1:161).
21. *Nicomachean Ethics* III, 1 (1111a3–7) in *The Complete Works of Aristotle*, II:1757.

How might we understand this Scotist framing of the moral domain? Instead of viewing moral choices from a large perspective as means leading up to an end that transcends human knowledge, Scotus views moral choices insofar as they exemplify elements that can be rationally identified by the moral agent in the present situation. Among these elements we find the two most important: what one is doing and how this relates to one's moral purpose or intent. In the moral determination, reason identifies a course of action that is seen to fulfill the moral purpose. Right reasoning, considering first principles, the body of moral knowledge or science, and the particular situation at hand, issues a moral dictate or command. When the judgment is right, that is, when the course of action (the object) actually does promote the moral purpose (the end) and, additionally, when the will chooses freely in accordance with right judgment, then both choice and reasoning unite in a single object. Reasoning makes the choice right and the choice makes reasoning practical. The truth of the choice is truly a practical truth because choice follows from it. The choice is truly good because it conforms to the practical truth. Morally good choices unify the moral agent's desire and reasoning in a concrete, particular course of action, whose objective goodness is not determined on the basis of a transcendent end (ultimate human fulfillment or perfection), but from the conditions already present and identifiable in the matter for choice.

5.3 Moral Foundations: Natural Law and the Divine Will

We come to the final dimension required for Scotus's discussion of practical science: its ultimate foundation in the natural order as created by the divine will. In several texts, Scotus presents the concrete act of moral choice as a type of artistic judgment on the part of

the human rational will.[22] Such a judgment, in order to be morally
good, cannot depend merely on a subjective and personal foundation, even that of personal experience. It must have an objective and
indubitable moral foundation. This first moral principle, Scotus asserts, is *Deus diligendus est,* God is to be loved. Here is the analytic
principle that grounds every rational choice and defines the moral
order in a foundational manner: it points to an act whose intrinsic
goodness is self-evident. In this proposition, the good and the true
are identical. Since good is the object of love, then infinite goodness
is worthy of infinite love. God's essence is infinite goodness, therefore God is worthy of all love. "Si Deus est Deus, amandus est ut
Deus."[23] *Deus diligendus est* is the first practical principle that directs
all choice and admits of no exception. Its truth is necessary by virtue
of the essence of God as object of love.[24] This principle governs the
choice of the divine and human wills.[25]

Scotus's position on the relationship of the concrete moral judgment to its objective foundation in self-evident truth might be understood better if we consider the relationship of music to mathematics. Musical proportions are mathematical in nature; harmony is
defined independently of any musical performance and in terms of
precise numerical relationships, such as the octave, the quarter, etc.
The harmonic third is a natural sound that anyone can reproduce,
even someone who has not studied music. In this way, just as the accurate and (therefore) beautiful performance of a musical piece on a
stringed instrument depends ultimately and foundationally upon
the mathematical relationship of the notes to one another, so too
the accurate execution of a moral judgment depends ultimately

22. See M.B. Ingham, "Duns Scotus: Moral Reasoning and the Artistic Paradigm," in *Via Scoti:* II:825–37.
    23. Ordinatio III, d. 37, q. un., n. 5, in *Will and Morality,* 277.
    24. See Ordinatio III, d. 37, q. un., n. 2, in *Will and Morality,* 273.
    25. Ordinatio IV, d. 46, q. 1, n. 3, in *Will and Morality,* 241.

upon the self-evident truths foundational to the rational order, even when these truths have not been the object of formal training.

Medieval thinkers held that human reason exists in a two-fold relationship to the moral order. First, natural reason has access to knowledge of moral truth by observation and reflection upon the world around us. In addition to this, knowledge of moral truth can be found in revelation. Creation and the Bible are two books written (as it were) by a single, divine author. In both, human reason can read the order of what exists (the *cosmos*) and conclude something about divine goodness and about appropriate moral action. In the words of Peter Lombard, "That the truth [about the *invisibilia Dei*] might be made clear to him, man was given two things to help him, a nature that is rational and works fashioned by God."[26] Natural law refers to those moral truths to which human rationality has access by its very constitution. Moral behavior is rational behavior; reflection upon the goods proper to rationality reveals moral truths.[27]

Because the foundational first principle is rational, it can be known naturally by every rational agent. Moral perfection, therefore, is not the domain of believers only, but is open to every person. The precepts of natural law, traditionally held by medieval scholars to be synonymous with the commands of the Decalogue, can be known naturally on the basis of a reflection upon the nature of rationality, the nature of goodness and the perfectibility of rational beings. This is what it means to say they are "written on the hu-

26. *Sentences* I, d. 3, c. 1, 69, cited in *Will and Morality*, 25.

27. My interpretation on this point differs from that of Thomas Williams. He argues that Scotus's discussion of moral goodness in its natural foundations makes no reference to the agent, only to the act as measured by the divine will. See his "From Metaethics to Action Theory," in *The Cambridge Companion to Duns Scotus*, 332–51. To be sure, Scotus clearly distinguishes his discussion of moral goodness from that of the Aristotelian-inspired philosophers of the *Ordinatio Prologue*. However, the reference to the agent in his thought has strong Stoic antecedents. Understood in this way, Scotus does make reference to the agent and to the perfection of rational judgment. It is not the model of Aristotelian teleology, however.

man heart." Moral action has its natural grounding in rationality and human reasoning.

Nevertheless, moral action has an ultimate and supernatural foundation in the divine creative will. The precepts of natural law can also be known insofar as they are revealed in the Ten Commandments. In this way, the believer has an additional support for moral decision and behavior. The Decalogue can be understood as two separate commands: the first relating to God (commands 1–3) and the second relating to the neighbor (commands 4–10). According to Scotus, the commands of the Decalogue that relate to God directly belong to natural law *stricte loquendo* and thereby admit of no exception.[28] These commands are directly related to the analytic first principle that requires love for God above all. The last seven commands that relate to the neighbor belong to natural law *large loquendo* and can admit of dispensation.[29] These are not derived from the first analytic principle in such an immediate manner, but rather express the will or desire of the divine lawgiver. Their moral significance is derivative and not absolute. Their truth is not immediately evident as analytic truth. Nonetheless, the truth of the commands about the neighbor is in harmony *(consona)* with the first principles.

Because their truth does not depend necessarily on the meaning of their terms, there can be dispensations from and exceptions to the commands of the second table. There can never be a dispensation from the commands of the first, however. For example, Scotus notes, if there were a devastating epidemic and the survival of the human race were threatened, one might be allowed to practice bigamy. This dispensation from the sixth commandment (Thou shalt not commit adultery) would be rational in light of the particular circumstances. By the same token, private property under certain dire circumstances might not be reasonable. A dispensation from

---

28. *Ordinatio* III, d. 37, q. un., n. 5, in *Will and Morality*, 277.
29. Ibid., n. 8, in *Will and Morality*, 279–80.

the seventh commandment (Thou shalt not steal) might be war-
ranted.

Why does Scotus defend such a distinction within natural law?
The distinction of natural law into *stricte* and *large loquendo* appears
as part of a much larger (and more troubling) theological question
raised by the thorny issue of divine dispensations recorded in Scripture. In certain instances recorded in the Bible, God apparently
commanded someone to go against natural law. So the question is
an important one for the believer: Did God act irrationally in asking
Abram to sacrifice his son Isaac or in telling the Hebrews in Egypt
to despoil their captors as they prepare to leave for the Promised
land? If such commands were counter to necessary commands of
natural law, then the divine will cannot be counted on to act in a rational manner. Indeed, God might at any time command something
of the believer that would go against the best of natural, moral reasoning.

In his solution to the question, Scotus defends God against the
charge of irrational or arbitrary behavior.[30] When the divine will dispenses, the Franciscan argues, he does not set the law aside. Rather,
he actually makes the formerly illicit act licit in the present instance
as a command of the divine will. In other words, obedience to the
command to steal (in the case of the Hebrews leaving Egypt) actually fulfilled the first command to love God in a manner more immediate than obedience to the commandment not to steal would have.
The divine will can and does dispense because it alone is the lawgiver.[31]

This divine activity of legislation and dispensation is explained

30. Aquinas had also attempted to defend divine action. However, in *ST*
Ia–IIae, q. 100, a. 8 (I:1045), he argued that what God commanded actually fulfilled the command more appropriately than a literal following of the letter of the
law. In other words, on this point Aquinas distinguishes between the letter and the
spirit of the law. Scotus affirms divine power in a much stronger manner.

31. *Ordinatio* III, d. 37, n. 3, in *Will and Morality,* 275.

by Scotus in *Ordinatio* I, d. 44, by the two powers of the divine will: *potentia absoluta* and *potentia ordinata*. Both are rational and belong to God as creator. God's absolute power extends to all that does not imply a contradiction; God's ordained power extends to a particular state of affairs as created and ordered.[32] So, for example, God could *de potentia absoluta* create any type of world in which any sort of creature could exist (as long as the creature was not logically impossible). However, *de potentia ordinata*, God has created our world. And, *de potentia ordinata*, God abides by the creative decision made relative to us. The logical implications of divine creative choice are expressed in natural law and in those goods proper to the sort of rational beings we are. So, even though the commands of the second table do not admit of the logical necessity of those belonging to the first table, they do have a necessary relationship within the present natural order, and to human nature as created.

When considered against his discussion of natural law and the commands of the Decalogue (in III, d. 37), Scotus's analysis of the law and its relationship to the will of the lawgiver (in I, d. 44) provides a discussion in which we recognize a structure more familiar to modern moral philosophy: the existence of foundational moral propositions and their hold upon a rational will that freely follows the dictates of moral reasoning as a type of law to which it freely submits itself. In creating and sustaining this world, God models a type of autonomous moral self-legislator. Even the divine will acts according to the fundamental moral principle: *Deus diligendus est*. Here is clearly a structural similarity that anticipates the moral framework offered by Kant.

32. *Ordinatio* I, d. 44, n. 3 (ed. Vat. 6:535). *Potentia ordinata* is defined as the ability to act in conformity with some right and just law. *Potentia absoluta* is defined as the ability to act "beyond or against such a law." The latter exceeds the former. This double power belongs to every free agent who is not constrained to act in accordance with such a law. This would refer to any lawmaker who stands above the law, such as a monarch.

Scotus is a moral foundationalist in a manner that Aquinas is not. He affirms the existence of an act whose intrinsic moral goodness can be known prior to any concrete circumstance of choice. This act of love for the ultimate good can be expressed propositionally as a moral imperative. This proposition can be known as an analytic truth by any rational agent. Propositions consonant with this truth can be determined by means of mediated reasoning on the rational and natural orders. The relationship of these subsequent propositions to the first moral truth is that of coherence and harmony. In addition, revelation points to the grounding of all such moral propositions on the creative divine will.

For Scotus, the moral order, even in its foundation, is revealed in natural and rational reflection.[33] The fact that it is established by the divine will does not entail that this foundation lies beyond the ability of reason to reflect upon the nature of the good. Acts of human moral reasoning are measured by the first principle of *praxis* and by moral relationships in reality. The divine will confirms human conclusions in the commands of the Decalogue.

5.4 The Extent of Divine Willing

At this point, and because the divine will plays such an important foundational role in Scotist thought, a word is needed on the possibility of ethical interference on the part of God's freedom. The problem may be presented in the following manner: if God's will and freedom are so foundational to the moral domain, then in what way does Scotus protect the autonomy of human freedom? Has Scotus set up a framework within which a clash of freedoms is inevitable?

33. Hannes Möhle suggests that Scotus's theory of natural law is that by which he links the will to rationality. See his "Scotus's Theory of Natural Law," in *The Cambridge Companion to Duns Scotus*, 312–31.

Let us lay out the components of the theory to determine more carefully if, indeed, such a clash might be possible, before we consider whether or not Scotus has avoided it. This can be most fruitfully done if we consider an act of choice at the moment of willing. This will be a snapshot, if you will, of the moral moment. In the snapshot we look to see what is present. Consider, then, an act of telling the truth. The moral agent chooses to tell the truth in a given situation, on the basis of deliberate reflection. Let us assume that all the elements are as they should be: the particular truth should be told and for the reasons the agent has decided to do so. The timing is correct, the manner is appropriate; all is in order. The agent chooses freely to perform the moral act. We can call this a perfect moral act on all counts.

What, then, is involved at the moment of telling the truth? At the highest level, the fundamental moral principles are operative: the truth is told because it is a rational good, intrinsically related to the highest good. Moral training is also engaged in this action: the agent has told the truth before and has learned how to do so in an appropriate manner. All aspects of this particular situation conform to the requirements that are developed within the agent, both from past experience and reflection on the goods proper to human life. In addition, the moral agent is fully present: to himself, to the particular situation and to the acquired body of knowledge he brings to that moment. Finally, the choice to tell the truth is not the necessary consequence of rational evidence (such that it is unavoidable), but is freely chosen by the agent following a moment of moral discernment and self-control. Thus far, all elements of the moral moment are intrinsically contained in the situation and in the moral agent who is fully present to that situation.

So much for the human side of things. What is God's freedom doing at this same moment? Scotus offers two ways to understand the role of the divine will, the autonomy of human choice and the relationship of the two wills to the subsequent act.[34] According to the first way, the divine will cooperates in a mediated manner. Here divine freedom creates and conserves the human will as free and autonomous. In every act of human choice, the exercise of free willing is itself sustained and willed by God, while the choice itself belongs to the created will alone. This first way protects human freedom, contingent actions and the possibility for sin, with no blame for the vicious choice (or sin) attributed to the divine will.[35]

A second way of understanding the divine will, however, is preferred by Scotus. This way sees the divine will as immediate to each act of human free choice. Scotus prefers this interpretation, he states, because it protects both divine foreknowledge and omnipotence. Indeed, if divine willing were not immediate, then God would have no foreknowledge of human choices (since God's knowledge depends upon the divine will which cooperates with the created will at the very moment of choice). In addition, were the divine will to concur only in a mediated manner, then divine power would terminate at the existence and exercise of the human will. Divine action could not impede the created will. Consequently, to protect both divine foreknowledge and divine omnipotence, Scotus concludes that the divine will concurs with every act of the human will in an immediate manner. This means that God wills both *that* the human will choose action A, and the *action A* that the human will wills. The act that results comes from both wills.

34. This text, originally as II, d. 37, q. 2 (Vivès 13), appears in the critical edition as II, d. 34–37, q. 5 (ed. Vat. 8:408–22). A. B. Wolter claims that Scotus moved from the position of mediated to immediate concurrence in large part because he was reconciling this solution with the problem of divine foreknowledge and omnipotence. The three related questions were never completely harmonized before his death. See his "Alnwick on Scotus and Divine Concurrence," in *Greek and Medieval Studies in Honor of Leo Sweeney, SJ*, ed. J. Carroll and J. Furlong (New York: Peter Lang, 1994), 255–83.

35. See *Ordinatio* II, d. 34–37, q. 5, n. 96 (ed. Vat. 8:408).

In his explanation of this immediacy, Scotus holds that the divine will sustains the order of free choice at all levels and is therefore immediately present to the human will in this and every act of choice. This presence is an act of concurrence where the divine will exercises a causality that depends upon the free causality of the created will, *de potentia ordinata*. If the human cause does not act, then the divine cause cannot act. As is the case for the four Aristotelian causes, the double causality of divine and human freedoms functions simultaneously, with no priority of nature on either side, in the concrete act of choice. Certainly, there is a priority of perfection on the side of God's will, but this sort of priority does not interfere with the human will's free exercise of its own independent causality. In addition, God could not *de potentia absoluta* interfere with or do violence to the exercise of human willing, by causing it to will a certain act in a certain way. Such an act would involve the divine suppression of the essence of the human will as an autonomous free cause. God could, however, refrain from concurrent willing in the case of a human act, thereby preventing the act from occurring. This restraint would not do violence to the human will. The mere possibility of this sort of preventative action (rather than its actuality) would be sufficient to safeguard both divine omnipotence and the autonomy of human free choice.

Scotus's preference for this more immediate act of divine concurrence suggests, nevertheless, a difficulty where the vicious or sinful act is concerned. The mediated act of divine concurrence (the rejected first way) distances God's will from the human sinful choice. Because of this distance, God is understood to be responsible for human free choice, but not for human sin. Ultimate responsibility for sin falls to the human will alone. This second, more immediate mode of concurrence attributes to the divine will a far greater role in each human choice. Does this mean that God is somehow responsible for sin? Indeed, even if God chose not to refrain from concurrent willing, would this not implicate divine responsibility for the vicious act, at least to some degree?

Scotus will of course deny this as an implication of immediate concurrence. In his discussion of human responsibility, he recalls that sin is the privation of a good that ought to be present. It is the absence of rectitude in an act. In addition, he makes use of the model of partial efficient co-causality,[36] where two independent causes cooperate in the production of a single effect. Since every act has both material and formal components, the material component of a vicious act would be the act itself; the formal component would be the privation of justice or rectitude that ought to be present in the act. There can be no efficient cause of privation; there can only be a deficient cause. In the vicious or sinful act, the human will would be such a deficient cause, since in the vicious act it would fail to do what it had the power to do.[37] The divine will would concur immediately with the virtuous act that ought to emerge from the two wills, giving all support necessary to sustain the good act, yet not supplanting the free choice of the human will. In such an act of antecedent willing, the divine will would be ready to confer righteousness on the human act, should it occur. In the absence of virtuous human willing, the uncreated will would neither force nor impede the free choice of the created will. This latter will already possesses a natural tendency to follow the dictates of right reasoning, and to do the right thing. The created will has everything it needs to act rightly. The divine will, antecedently prepared to bestow righteousness, awaits the act of the created will. When the created will fails to do what it should do, the divine will does not act as it would have.

36. A model of causal interaction key to his explanation of human action. See the discussion of intellect and will in chapter 6.

37. That is, to regulate its own action according to the affection for justice, present and natural to the will. Chapter 6 develops the will's two affections in greater detail. See II, d. 37, q. 2, nn. 124–28 (ed. Vat. 8:420–2).

In this way, the divine will is disposed and acts in the same immediate manner relative to every act of every created will. Desiring the virtuous act, God's will stands ready to cooperate. In the case of a virtuous act, the proper balance of moral affections (in the human will) results in the fullest perfection of the free act. In the case of sin, the deficiency of the resulting act is imputable to the created will alone that had both the knowledge and the power to do otherwise. The sinful act is understood in reference to the divine and human wills, but according to two distinct and important relationships. What is lacking to the sinful act *qua* sinful belongs to the deficient cause (the human will), which could have acted differently. What belongs to the act *qua* act (as potentially righteous) belongs to the divine will, sustaining autonomous free choice and providing all support for the virtuous act. Scotus concludes from this that God is both immediately present to human willing and not responsible for human sin.

Scotus views the moral order as eminently rational and dependent upon the divine will. He holds that natural human reason can conclude to moral certainty based upon its ability to grasp foundational logical moral principles and the order of goods created by God. Because he sets out such a strong rational foundation for moral judgments, Scotus can describe particular moral choices and actions from an aesthetic perspective. This enables him to incorporate insights from the Platonic and Augustinian traditions on love and beauty so important to the monastic understanding of moral wisdom.

Scotus's voluntarism departs from the positions of thinkers like William de la Mare and Henry of Ghent. He does not endow the will with a freedom that is not rational. On the contrary, as the next chapter makes clear, freedom is based upon the will's internal structure as disposed toward right and ordered loving. The rationality of the will enables Scotus to enhance the intellectual objectivity of moral judgments. The certainty of moral judgments that results from such moral objectivity, however, never compromises the will's autonomy and freedom.

Practical science (moral science) can be understood either objectively or subjectively. Objectively, science can refer to a body of moral truths known through reflection upon acts of choice and seen to be in harmony with first principles. It is present to the particular moral agent as acquired knowledge. It can also refer to more general moral propositions that are the result of reflection upon the foundational moral principle of love for the highest good and the requirements of rational perfection. These propositions would be the content of formal moral education. Together, moral truth that has been acquired through experience and moral truths derived from the foundational principle form a coherent body of rational knowledge. This knowledge remains theoretical until it is brought to bear in the moment of choice by the moral agent. Now, at the moment of choice, practical science takes on a second, subjective meaning: it can refer to the personal act of cognition and awareness whereby the moral agent knows both what she is doing, that what she is doing is right and, too, why what she is doing is right. In its fullest articulation, this is the judgment of practical wisdom or prudence that is immediate to *praxis*.

The implications of this discussion of practical science can be seen in three aspects of Scotist ethical thought that subsequent chapters deal with more carefully: the intimate interaction of the orders of cognition and choice, the objective nature of moral goodness, and the central role of moral judgment. Because, according to Scotus, human persons naturally desire an end that surpasses their ability, the moral perspective involves both the natural aspect—(such as human moral aspirations, virtuous behavior, and rational knowledge of the moral law) and aspects that lie beyond the natural (such as human free choice and divine aid in the form of grace) to attain the fullest realization of human excellence. Because of the objective grounding of goodness in the created order and because of the powers of human reasoning, moral truth can be reached with certainty. This certainty never necessitates choice in the will. Like Bonaventure before him, Scotus acknowledges that the world in which philosophers live forms a consistent, coherent whole. Unlike Bonaventure, however, he does not argue that the fault of the philosophical vision lies in a rejection of Plato and the existence of divine, eternal ideas.[38] Rather, the philosophers err when they base their understanding of moral living on the natural order alone and when they center the perfection of human rationality upon the necessity of a teleological, overly intellectualized Aristotelian model. The term *natural* is, for Scotus, synonymous with the necessary. The natural order is the order of causal necessity. The moral order must be the order of freedom. Philosophers overlook the most important characteristics of a practical science when they limit moral discussion to a description of necessary causes and virtuous behavior. What philosophers miss is the central role of rational freedom and creativity as foundations for ethics as a practical science.

38. *Collationes in Hexaemeron*, Vision I, Discussion III.

6. THE RATIONAL WILL AND FREEDOM

M EDIEVAL THINKERS understood both the will and intellect to be powers of the individual, human soul.
Therefore a discussion of the rational will is more
properly understood as a discussion of the person according to the
formality of self-determination and rational desire. The language of
faculty psychology of intellect and will, so common to scholastic vo-
cabulary, should not confuse us into thinking that the two powers of
the human soul operate independently of the single human person
whose soul it is. Indeed, for Scotus the intellect and will are only
formally distinct from one another and from the soul. In this way,
his thought affirms the basic unity of the person behind the multi-
plicity of operations.

Scotus's focus on love as perfective of human rationality completely re-frames the discussion of human moral goodness around
the rational will and, surprisingly, the irrational intellect. From his

perspective, the term rational refers to moral rationality and not at
all, as we shall see, to the activity of speculation or analysis. Rationality involves self-control above all: its perfection is seen in the ability to make the right choices. In this way, Scotus argues, the intellect
is *not* the rational potency. This novel re-casting of what is to us
more familiar, modern modes of understanding human choice requires considerable attention on the part of the reader, for it is too
tempting to see Scotus as one who liberates freedom from reason,
thereby exalting the will's independence from rationality. In truth,
Scotus only liberates the will from the control of the intellect, but
not from reason. As this chapter makes clear, it is precisely insofar as
the will is the sole rational potency that true freedom is discovered
in rational and ordered loving.

Scotus affirms quite clearly throughout his teaching career that
nothing outside the will has the power to determine it. The will is
free with an indetermination that sets it apart from all other causes
that exist. There is no other cause one can use to explain or understand the will's activity because there is no other cause like the will.
The will is *sui generis*. Our present study presents this Scotist affirmation within the context of a moderate voluntarism, that is, according to a moderate understanding of rational freedom belonging
to the will. It considers the Franciscan's position on freedom in the
will to be best understood as a dimension of his presentation of self-
control. Because the will is capable of self-control, it is able to resist
external determinism and to act in a manner that is undetermined by
anything other than itself.

Scotus understands freedom and the causality proper to it as a
subset of contingency and its relationship to possibility. As we saw
earlier, in chapter 4, Scotus clarifies that there are two forms of contingency. One form refers to mutability, and belongs to all corporeal
beings insofar as they are subject to generation and decay. The other
form of contingency refers to events that can be avoided. These

events are not caused necessarily; they are not the result of a cause to which they are related in a necessary, determined or inevitable manner. According to this sense, a contingent event is one that might not have happened at all, or might have happened otherwise than it did. A necessary event, by contrast, could not have *not* happened, given its relationship to the causes that obtained. A necessary event is like a falling stone which, unimpeded, always seeks the center of the earth. For Scotus, it is not the fall of a particular stone that makes the event necessary. Rather, it is the causal relationship of the fall to its antecedent conditions that results in an event occurring of necessity.

Scotus identifies two sorts of causal orders that are operative in reality: the necessary and the free. In the necessary causal order, whenever appropriate conditions obtain, events occur in a predictable and inevitable manner, such as in the order of natural causes. In the free causal order, events occur contingently, because the cause involved is capable of more than one sort of effect at that moment. In this order, the cause (as free) could have "acted otherwise" or "caused differently" than it did. A cause that causes contingently event B at time t, could have caused not-B at the same moment t. Event B, while actual, is not necessary, nor is the truth of its existence a necessary truth. Its existence is contingent as is the truth of that existence.[1]

Scotus's discussion of the will's freedom is based upon this understanding of the nature of contingency and upon his affirmation of the existence of the order of free causality to which the will belongs.[2] As we have seen, the divine will stands at the head of this or-

1. It is clear from this that Scotus departs from the Aristotelian position on the necessity of the present moment.

2. This involves his distinction between *synchronic* and *diachronic* alternatives, discussed in chapter 4 above. See also Simo Knuuttila, "Duns Scotus and the Foundations of Logical Modalities," in *John Duns Scotus: Metaphysics and Ethics*, 127–44;

der. The existence of any causes that are capable of causing contingently depends upon the existence of a first cause that caused contingently.[3] Like the divine will, the human will is a free cause capable of acting differently within identical sets of circumstances. At the moment of choice, Scotus argues, anyone is able to note that he or she could have acted differently. This simple act of self-reflection is sufficient to demonstrate the fact of contingent causality at the heart of rational freedom. It also reveals to the moral agent in an immediate manner how the act of self-control is foundational to rational, voluntary action.

Scotus understands the foundation of freedom in the will as an act of self-control. This is clear, first, from his discussion of the will's two capacities. The first capacity is that for choice between two objects *(velle/nolle)*. Choice for one object *(velle)* implies rejection *(nolle)* of another. By such a capacity, additionally, one might accept *(velle)* or reject *(nolle)* a single object. The second capacity within the power of the will is more basic: it is that of self-restraint, the choice between willing and not willing *(velle/non velle)*. In the presence of a situation involving choice, the person might not choose one of the alternatives at all, but choose not to choose *(non velle)*. For Scotus, the act of *non velle* is an act of the will; it is not the absence of an act. Because the will possesses both capacities, it acts in a manner unlike any other power and alone is rational. Additionally, the capacity for self-restraint *(non velle)* reveals the will's rationality at its most basic level: it shows how the will is a self-moving cause.

In this deeper capacity to choose or not, the will reveals itself as a self-mover in the purest sense. When, in the presence of conditions that appear both necessary and sufficient to move the will to choose, the will does not choose, this can only be because the will is able to

---

and Calvin Normore, "Scotus, Modality, Instants of Nature and the Contingency of the Present," op. cit., 161–74.

3. As Scotus affirms in *A Treatise on God as First Principle,* 4.18, 84.

exercise self-restraint or self-control. Any rational agent who is aware of his own actions, affirms Scotus, can verify with certainty the truth of this. An act is said to be free or contingent (that is, undetermined by factors external to the will) when it is understood that, in the same set of circumstances, the agent might have done otherwise.

There are two textual examples of these capacities and how important they are to Scotus's understanding of free choice in the will. In *Ordinatio* IV, d. 49, qq. 9–10, the Franciscan considers the three acts of willing, nilling, and self-restraint. He states that, when the will is shown happiness, it still chooses freely because no object necessitates it. "Hence, when it is shown happiness, it can refrain from acting at all. In regard to any object, then, the will is able not to will or (nec) nill it, and can suspend itself from eliciting any act in particular with regard to this or that."[4] This act of self-suspension defines the nature of rational human freedom as understood by Scotus. Such freedom remains even in heaven. A second text appears in his *Questions on Aristotle's Metaphysics* IX q. 14, where the Franciscan presents this act of self-suspension and calls the will free insofar as it is capable of just such an act.[5] The act of *non velle* is, for Scotus, both a positive act and, more importantly, the crucial condition for moral willing because it guarantees that the will is undetermined by any cause or series of causes external to its own act of choice.[6] Because of this indetermination at its most basic level, the will is capable of self-

4. *Ordinatio* IV, d. 49, qq. 9–10 (codex A, f. 282va), in *Will and Morality*, 195.

5. "Finally, if it is a free agent, it is able of itself to refrain from acting . . . a sample of [this] sixth is the will, which need not choose what the intellect shows it." *Questions on the Metaphysics*, (II:602).

6. The act of self-restraint as foundational explains both the possibility of conversion, either from a religious or moral point of view. If moral behavior constitutes character, as Aristotle maintains, then at some point, a person's moral character (whether virtuous or vicious) is profoundly unchangeable. Accordingly, if Aristotle's perspective is correct, then no vicious person could ever have a sudden change of heart, nor could a virtuous person fail in a dramatic manner.

regulation and thus, self-determination. Praise and blame (moral responsibility) for an individual's action follow from this foundational freedom for self-control. In this way, the activity of the will (when it wills, rejects, or refrains from either) reveals that the human will is a moral will because it is a rational will. It is a free will insofar as it is rational.

Scotus defends the will's rationality in two key texts: in the *Questions on Aristotle's Metaphysics* IX, q. 15, and in *Ordinatio* II, d. 6. The first text proceeds in an *a posteriori* manner, looking at the will's rationality from its effects. The second text considers Anselm's presentation[7] of the will's two affections (the *affectio iustitiae* and *affectio commodi*) in an *a priori* discussion of the metaphysical constitution of the will as rational. The analysis of *Ordinatio* II, d. 6, builds upon and complements the conclusions of the Aristotelian text. What the Philosopher could only point to by means of a causal inference, verified by introspection, the theologian explains from the nature of any free, rational being. It is the metaphysical constitution of the will that more completely accounts for the causality proper to it as a rational and therefore free potency. For the Subtle Doctor, the will's freedom is defined in terms of its rationality. This freedom is grounded in the ability of the will to control its own acts. The most perfect expression of this freedom is ordered, rational choice.

The current diversity of scholarly opinion on Scotus's view of freedom can be explained in terms of these two texts. Since Scotus presents two very different approaches to the question of the will's freedom, each approach has influenced some scholars. In the Aristotelian text, he points to the existence of a free cause behind contingent events. Aristotle defends the rationality of the will on the basis of its freedom to produce different effects. All this approach can say about the will's freedom is that it is indetermined by causes external

---

7. *De casu diaboli*, chapters 14–26 in *Anselm of Canterbury: The Major Works* ed. B. Davies and G.R. Evans (Oxford: Oxford University Press 1998), 216–231.

to itself. Those scholars who argue for a libertarian reading of Scotus on the will's freedom point to this text as evidence for their interpretation. In the Anselmian text, however, Scotus explains the nature of the will's rationality that lies behind its indetermination. Here, the will's rationality is clearly central to its freedom. Scholars who seek to point out how, for Scotus, rationality and freedom are not antithetical terms use this text as basis for their interpretation.[8]

Clearly, both groups have textual evidence to support their positions. In what follows we shall look at each of the two Scotist arguments. Both texts present the act of self-restraint (identified with *non velle*) as central to their discussion of the will's freedom. They do so differently, however. Taken together, the two texts present an argument in two stages. In stage one, the Aristotelian-based text argues to conclude that self-control is a fact, while, in stage two, the Anselmian-based text explains self-control in terms of the will's constitution as rational potency. The act of self-control (or self-restraint) functions as the concept that bridges the (apparently distinct) domains of freedom and rationality. In his Anselmian argument, Scotus explains the act of self-control in terms of the rational constitution of the will in its two-fold affections. By explaining the act of self-control in terms of its rational constitution, the Anselmian approach also explains, *a fortiori,* the will's freedom in terms of its rationality. Because Scotus admits the insufficiency of the Aristotelian approach to answer all questions about the will's freedom, the Anselmian argument reflects more completely his position on the will and its rational exercise of freedom.

8. An example of the libertarian interpretation can be found in Thomas Williams's "The Libertarian Foundations of Scotus's Moral Philosophy." in *The Thomist* 62 (1998), 193–215. A moderate interpretation can be found in A.B. Wolter's "Native Freedom of the Will as a Key to the Ethics of Scotus" in *The Philosophical Theology,* 148–162.

6.1 The *a posteriori* Argument from Causality

In his *Questions on Aristotle's Metaphysics* IX, q. 15,[9] Scotus calls the will rational because, according to the Stagirite, rational potencies have contrary effects, while irrational potencies admit of only one effect. In his explanation of this, Scotus differentiates between the intellect and the will, identifying the former as natural (and therefore irrational) and the latter as rational.[10] The intellect is a natural potency precisely because, like the eye in the presence of sufficient external conditions (light, the object, etc.), the intellect cannot fail to know, just as the eye cannot fail to see. And, while the intellect can know one thing rather than another, it cannot refuse to know any particular thing at all in the sense that it cannot stop itself from knowing (again, in the presence of sufficient conditions). The intellect is determined in a way that the will is not, for the will (by contrast) can act or not act at all. Thus, on the basis of their effects, the intellect falls within the category of natural causes. It is, therefore, an irrational potency. The will, on the other hand, is self-determining.[11] Accordingly, the will is the sole rational potency.

Because the will is rational in the manner described above, it is a

9. *Opera philosophica* IV (St. Bonaventure, N.Y.: Franciscan Institute 1997), 675–99.

10. "But there is only a twofold generic way an operation proper to a potency can be elicited. For either (1) the potency of itself is determined to act, so that so far as itself is concerned, it cannot fail to act when not impeded from without; or (2) it is not of itself so determined, but can perform either this act or its opposite, or can either act or not act at all. A potency of the first sort is commonly called *nature,* whereas of the second sort is called *will.*" *Questions on the Metaphysics* IX, q. 15, n. 22 (II:608).

11. I take this indetermination to point to self-determination because Scotus gives the will the power not just to perform a certain act or its opposite, but also the power "either to act or not act at all." As I show later, this act of *non velle* can be understood as an act of self-control or self-restraint. Thus, even though Scotus does use the term indetermination, it is reasonable to see in this the self-determination he points to elsewhere.

free (indetermined) potency. Quite simply, this means that no condition external to the will is sufficient to determine its movement.[12] Indeed, if the intellect alone were to exist without the will, then all would occur naturally or in a determined manner.[13] The intellect and will differ, as natural from rational potencies, insofar as the latter is not determined by external conditions (it moves itself) and the former is determined by such factors beyond itself (it is moved by something else).[14] If the will did not exist, all contingent events would occur after the manner of nature. In other words, given sufficient conditions and in the absence of impediments, events would occur in a predictable and determined manner. More importantly, there would be, he clarifies, "no potency sufficient" to resist or counter the cumulative force of factors surrounding any given event. Because the intellect cannot resist or counter the presence of factors surrounding it, because the intellect is moved by the object it knows and cannot prevent itself from being moved (given the presence of sufficient conditions), it gives no evidence of rationality.

12. "As for the second argument, if it is the will one is speaking about, then I say that it is able to do what it does with no conceivable predetermination to act, so that the initial determination, both in the order of nature and in the order of time, occurs in the very placing of its act. And if one claims that at that instant it can do nothing unless first determined [by something other than itself], this is false." IX, q. 15, n. 66 (II:622–23).

13. "But if the argument refers to the intellect knowing opposites, then it is true that the intellect can accomplish nothing externally unless it be determined from some other source, because it knows contraries after the manner of nature, and is unable to determine itself towards any one of these opposites. Hence it will either act towards both or not act at all. And if one concludes from this that the intellect does not suffice to qualify as a rational potency, it follows from what has been said that this is true. Indeed, if—to assume the impossible—the intellect and its subordinate powers alone existed, without a will, everything would occur deterministically after the manner of nature, and there would be no potency sufficient to accomplish anything to the contrary." IX, q. 15, n. 67 (II:623).

14. Scotus rejects the Aristotelian maxim that "everything moved is moved by another." See R. Effler's *John Duns Scotus and the Principle "Omne quod movetur ab alio movetur"* (St. Bonaventure, N.Y.: Franciscan Institute, 1962).

Scotus maintains that the truth of this insight is both certain and readily available. Anyone who is at all self-aware can confirm that sometimes she does not choose, despite factors that would appear to make such choice inevitable.[15] Yet, he admits, this entire argument, while important, is not enough. Such an argument from causality merely establishes (but does not explain) the fact of indetermined choice. The Aristotelian causal analysis does not help us understand why such a cause like the will causes in precisely the way it does. The deeper scientific explanation is still missing.[16]

Because it does not determine itself toward the act of understanding, the intellect falls under the category of natural potencies. Consequently, Scotus hesitates attributing rationality to it in any but a limited sense,[17] and concludes from this that the intellect can only be considered rational insofar as it is related to the will, the only truly rational potency.[18] The Franciscan admits that this is a surprising conclusion and wonders why Aristotle calls the intellect the rational potency when, in fact, it is the will. He suggests that, since the intel-

15. "As for the second objection, the proof here is a posteriori, for the person who wills experiences that he could have nilled or not willed what he did, according to what has been explained more at length elsewhere about the will's liberty." IX, q. 15, n. 30 (II:610). The other texts referred to are I, d. 39, and *Quodlibet* 16, along with IV, d. 49, n. 10.

16. "Suppose someone seeks a further reason for this distinction. Just why does nature have to do with only one sort of action? I.e. if it has to do with this or that, why is it determined of itself to cause just this effect or these effects, whatever they may be, whereas will, by contrast, has alternatives, i.e., it is not intrinsically determined to this action or its opposite, or for that matter to acting or not acting at all? One can reply to such a question that there is no further reason for this. . . . One can give no other reason why it elicits its action in this way except that it is this sort of cause." IX, q. 15, n. 24 (II:608).

17. "Hence, not only as regards its [the intellect's] own acts is it not rational, but it is not fully rational even as regards the external acts it directs. As a matter of fact, speaking precisely, even as regards its intrinsic acts it is irrational. It is rational only in the qualified sense that it is a precondition for the act of a rational potency." IX, q. 15, n. 38 (II:612).

18. "Nevertheless it falls under the other heading [i.e., will] insofar as through its act it is presupposed for acts of the will." IX, q. 15, n. 40 (II:613).

lect is better known to introspection and its acts are more common, the Philosopher has fallen into the obvious trap of identifying it with the rational.[19]

At this point in the argument, it must be noted how central self-control is to the understanding of the will's rationality and, thus, its freedom. According to the Aristotelian approach, all one would be able to conclude about rational freedom is that it is freedom in control of itself. One would not be able to understand freedom in any substantive manner, as having any particular qualitative dimension. Rational freedom here refers solely to the person as an independent moral agent, and not to the person as exhibiting ordered or morally good choices. Indeed, the only ordering of choice is to the moral subject. For this reason, when Scotus raises the question here as to why the will wills in this particular manner, he simply concludes that it is because the will is what it is.

6.2 The *a priori* Consideration from the Will's Constitution

When Scotus turns to the Anselmian approach to explain the will's rationality and freedom in *Ordinatio* II, d. 6, he is more interested in an *a priori* consideration of the nature of the will. In this text, Scotus considers the nature of the will's rationality in order to ground and explain both self-restraint and freedom. In this text, freedom is not used to conclude to rationality; rather, rationality explains moral freedom. Why the will chooses as it does, independently of external influences, is ultimately explainable in terms of the will's metaphysical constitution. This constitution, as we shall see, is itself grounded on the objective order of goods in the world.

19. "But then one might ask, why does he so frequently call the intellect a *rational potency* and not the will, though admittedly, from what has been said, he hints of this? One could say that the act of the intellect is normally prior to and better known to us than the act of the will." IX, q. 15, n. 53 (II:618).

The will possesses a two-fold disposition toward the good: the affection for justice and the affection for possession. These two affections had been presented and explained by Anselm in his *De casu diaboli*. For Scotus, as for Anselm, these affections are two innate inclinations or metaphysical desires that together constitute the rational will. One inclination is deemed natural the other, free. The first, natural, inclination is the *affectio commodi* or the desire for happiness or possession. This desire is ordinarily finalized by the *bonum utile* (or goods of use) as well as *delectabile* (pleasurable goods) and has as its moral intention the good or satisfaction of the agent as realized by the enjoyment and use of external goods. This affection can be identified as a natural inclination toward self-realization within the human moral realm, understood most broadly.[20] The properly moral affection is the *affectio iustitiae,* or affection for justice, finalized by *bonum honestum or bonum in se,* that is, by those goods worthy of love for themselves alone and not necessarily related to any concern for self-preservation or self-actualization. This is the human capacity for disinterested love.

For Scotus, when the affection for happiness (self-regard or possession) is moderated and guided by the affection for justice (awareness of an object's intrinsic worth), the moral agent loves in an orderly manner. Since the moral agent is rational, such ordered loving constitutes the fullest rational perfection. This means that right loving constitutes true human happiness. It does not mean that happiness is disregarded as morally insignificant, nor does it suggest that the good of self must be systematically overlooked in favor of morally right behavior. In fact, in the right and ordered moral action, both metaphysical affections are satisfied. Indeed, they are both finalized in the human choice to act in a perfect manner. When, as a moral agent, I desire that my character be upright, I fulfill both

20. See John Boler's "Transcending the Natural: Duns Scotus on the Two Affections of the Will" *American Catholic Philosophical Quarterly* 57 (1993): 109–26.

affections. On the one hand, I desire my own good (the *affectio commodi*) in the possession of a character that demonstrates integrity. At the same time, I desire to love justly and in an orderly manner (the *affectio iustitiae*), realizing that it is only in this way that my rational nature will be fully perfected and I can be truly happy. This state of perfection and happiness enables me to love God (the highest Good) more perfectly.[21]

These two innate inclinations make the will rational by virtue of their interaction in every moral choice. If, as the *Questions on Aristotle's Metaphysics* made clear, *rational* means to have multiple effects, then the will is rational precisely because it is capable of willing *(velle)*, nilling *(nolle)*, or refraining from either *(non velle)*. This rationality involving choice and self-restraint *(velle/non velle)* is established by the will's internal constitution and by the way the *affectio iustitiae* moderates and directs the *affectio commodi*. The rational and free constitution of the will integrates its natural desire for its own good *(affectio commodi)* in the desire to act well *(affectio iustitiae)*. The affection for justice points to the objective order of created goods and moderates the intensity of loving according to what is appropriate. This affection seeks to give each object what it deserves.

For Scotus, it is precisely in the dynamic interaction of these two affections at the moment of choice that moral rationality finds its source.[22] The interplay of the two inclinations explains self-control, the foundation for moral living. Scotus defines the affection for justice as checkrein on the affection for possession.

Therefore, this affection for justice, which is the first checkrein on the affection for the beneficial, inasmuch as we need not actually seek that toward which the latter affection inclines, nor must we seek it above all else (namely, to the extent to which we are in-

---

21. *Ordinatio* II, d. 6, q. 2, in *Will and Morality*, 477.
22. See Boler, "Transcending the Natural," 114.

clined by this affection for the advantageous)—this affection for what is just, I say, is the liberty innate to the will, since it represents the first checkrein on this affection for the advantageous.[23]

As the higher inclination, the affection for justice moderates the natural desire of the will in its pursuit of its own perfection, experienced as the satisfaction of all desire. Such self-restraint requires the rational capacity for self-reflection, an internal awareness relative not only to an object of choice but also to the self: to the intensity of desire and to the moral requirement for moderation.

In his discussion in *Ordinatio* II, d. 6, Scotus reprises and modifies Anselm's argument to illustrate the importance of the two affections. In the original Anselmian presentation, we are asked to consider a being that possesses only the affection for happiness *(affectio commodi)*. Anselm concludes that such a being would not possess the freedom required for moral choice, since it would love only to the degree that it understood the goodness of the object. It would choose what appeared to satisfy its desire to the fullest extent. With only one affection, the will of such a being could not refrain from willing an external object whose apparent goodness was so great that it necessitated choice.

Scotus takes the basic distinction of the two affections and holds as well that, with only one of the two, the being described would not possess the freedom required for moral choice. He transposes Anselm's discussion in two important respects, however. First, while the original text focused on the desire for the good, Scotus presents the single inclination as an intellectual one. In other words, the being with only one affection who appears in II, d. 6, looks very much like the intellect existing alone without a will (referred to in the text from the *Metaphysics*) and, indeed, like the philosophers Scotus depicted in the *Ordinatio Prologue* whose entire life is devoted to the

23. *Ordinatio* II, d. 6, q. 2, in *Will and Morality,* 469–71.

activity of contemplation understood as the fullest satisfaction of the natural desire to know.[24] The intellectual inclination, were it to exist alone, would move this agent in a manner parallel to the way in which animals are moved by sensible inclinations. Despite the intellectual potential and high level of perfection that this agent could realize through his choices, the perfection would only be natural, and in no sense moral.

A second difference is even more central to a correct understanding of the rational will for Scotus. Unlike Anselm, he does not conclude that the affection for justice was lost through original sin. Its presence in the human will is not, affirms Scotus, the result of grace; rather it is part of the will's innate constitution as a rational potency. Thus, whereas Anselm had argued that the true freedom of ordered loving could only be the result of grace *post lapsum,* Scotus maintains that the human will, despite the consequences of original sin, is still equipped with all that is necessary for the exercise of its rational freedom in moral choice.

Despite these modifications, both Scotus and Anselm insist that the agent with only one of the two affections would be incapable of moral choice. While it seems possible that the agent would indeed have the capacity to move toward one object rather than another *(velle/nolle),* the movement toward the one would be based upon how much better the one object appears to the single-affectioned will, how well it finalizes the desire within the agent, how well it brings the agent to an experience of self-perfection or satisfaction. This sort of action in the will is like that of animals, who experience desire and move toward what satisfies desire. Such a choice could only be moral and free, however, if the agent were to possess another, more foundational, rational capacity for free choice: self-restraint.

24. See *Ordinatio* Prologue, (ed. Vat. 1:1–53). I present and discuss this text as it relates to the question of the rational will in "Duns Scotus, Morality and Happiness: A Reply to Thomas Williams," 173–95.

This is the capacity that could be termed *not-this:* an act of restraint from choosing the one *(non velle),* rather than choice for the other. In the absence of this deeper capacity for self-control, no agent is capable of moral choice.

In his use of Anselm's distinction, Scotus makes it clear that intellectual desire is not enough to explain rational choice. The being with only the intellectual desire is not capable of free, rational choices because (based upon Aristotle's authority) the intellect is incapable of self-restraint. The intellect is determined by external factors in a way that the will is not. Scotus's discussion of the two affections in II, d. 6, provides what is needed to explain the ability of the rational will to suspend choice or execution, to accept all the conditions necessary for action and still not act. This echoes the text from the *Metaphysics* in its affirmation of the will's rationality and clearly goes beyond the Aristotelian discussion. Scotus's *a priori* argument of II, d. 6, reveals the heart of his notion of rational, free choice as foundational to the moral realm. Moral choice depends upon the dynamic capacity of the will for self-restraint and self-control and is measured by the objective order of goodness.

The moral order requires objective conditions that account for the attraction toward the good and toward the goal of self-perfection, along with the power to restrain one's own behavior despite external and internal conditions influencing the choice. The existence of such conditions can be inferred from the Aristotelian discussion of rational potencies and their effects. They can be metaphysically established in the Anselmian analysis of two-fold affections within the will. The causal effect of the will, experienced by anyone in the act of choice, is explained more clearly by the deeper analysis of the natural constitution of the will as it is drawn toward the good. In addition, this text also explains the way in which rational freedom corresponds to ordered choice. The fullest understanding of the will's free choice, then, depends not so much upon my choices insofar as they belong to me, but insofar as they exhibit right and ordered loving.

For Scotus, the moral agent's capacity for self-control is key to her rational freedom and foundation for the moral realm. The possibility for such self-restraint depends upon certain innate types of moral inclinations, namely the two Anselmian affections. Their interaction reveals self-control as the liberty innate to the will. This liberty is expressed in concrete acts of choice where one can choose, reject, or refrain from choice. If in fact it is the act of self-restraint that is crucial to a correct understanding of moral freedom, then that same act finds its metaphysical conditions within the rational will as objectively inclined to goods of use and goods of value. These goods are accessible to the will through the powers of intellectual cognition: abstraction and intuition. The intelligible goodness of external reality informs the deliberation and determination of right reasoning. In the affection for justice, the human will both aspires to and is equipped with the inclination to follow right reasoning. Its natural disposition toward the highest moral act, i.e., loving the good for itself alone, is rooted, as it were, in the very nature of the rational will.[25]

6.3 The Collaboration of Intellect and Will

On the basis of the foregoing discussion, it is clear that Scotus understands freedom in the will to involve rationality and the activity of intellection. In fact, he defines the will's freedom precisely insofar as the will is rational and uses cognition. It is now time to consider more carefully how, exactly, the intellect (or the human person in the modality of knowing) works with the will (or the human per-

25. In the *Reportatio* version of II, d. 6, Scotus states that the *affectio iusti* [sic] is the ultimate specific difference of the human person as rational animal. See Vivès 22, n. 9, 621.

son in the modality of desiring and choosing). Scotus explains the way intellect and will collaborate in the act of choice in his *Sentences* II, d. 25. Unfortunately for the present study, neither the *Ordinatio* nor *Reportatio* versions of this question exist in critical edition. The *Lectura* version (representing Scotus's earliest teaching at Oxford) appeared in 1993 in volume 19 of the Vatican edition. This early text had been erroneously identified by Carlo Balic as part of the *Secundae Additiones*.[26] It was considered by Balic and many scholars to be Scotus's latest and definitive position. As such, it has influenced considerable research on his notion of the will's freedom in light of the act of intellection. At the time of this writing, scholars are debating the possibility of an evolution toward a heavier emphasis on the will's freedom in Scotus's later *Reportatio* version of this question.[27]

Because that debate has not yet been settled, and because the Vatican editors argue that Scotus did not change his teaching on the will even in the later teaching,[28] the *Lectura* version of II, d. 25, will serve the present purposes of this study to illustrate how Scotus understands the way the act of intellection collaborates with the will's native freedom to produce the single act of choice. Following this, we look briefly at the *Reportatio* version to note any significant shifts in his teaching on freedom.

The question of II, d. 25, asks "Regarding the will's freedom, the question is whether the will's act is caused by the object moving it or by the will moving itself."[29] Before he answers, Scotus sets forth the two major positions on this issue: first, the more intellectualist position of Godfrey of Fontaines (the will is moved by the object) and,

26. See his "Une question inédite de Duns Scot sur la volonté," *Recherches de Théologie Ancienne et Médiévale* 3 (1931): 198–208.

27. See Stephen Dumont's "Did Scotus Change His Mind on the Will?" in *After the Condemnation of 1277*, 719–94.

28. In *Opera* (ed. Vat. 19:40*).

29. "Circa libertatem voluntatis queritur, an actus voluntatis causetur in voluntate ab obiecto movente ipsam vel a voluntate movente seipsam."

second, the more extreme voluntarist position of Henry of Ghent (the will's movement is independent of any active causal role on the part of the object). In his own solution, he offers a middle way, where the object as known by the act of intellection is presented to the will and plays an active, but subordinate, causal role. Accordingly, no volition takes place absolutely independently of cognition, but the act of intellection in no way determines the will to choose or not. This moderate solution saves both the need for knowledge and freedom in human action.

Scotus uses an analysis based upon partial efficient co-causality in order to explain how both intellect and will produce the act of free choice. According to this explanation, the object known (presented by the intellect) and the will function in tandem as "partial co-causes," with the will the superior efficient cause and the object known the inferior efficient cause. In this way, the act of willing results from a causal collaboration that involves both natural and free co-causes. Cognition and volition act *ut una causa totalis,* like father and mother in the birth of a child, or pen and stylus in the act of writing. Were no cognition involved with volition, Scotus explains, the act would not be rational. Were there no volition sufficiently independent of cognition, the act would not be free. Since *liberum arbitrium* requires both freedom and rational judgment, both faculties must work together to "give birth" to the act of choice.

The act of choice can be understood as entirely within the power of the will and governed by it. When the object as known is presented by the intellect to the will, cognition enters into the power of volition, and the will directs the act of choice freely and rationally, from a superior causal order. Because he has strengthened the free causality of the will, Scotus is able to strengthen as well the ability of the intellect to know the truth. With its power to know reality both abstractively and intuitively, the intellect can present to the will the results of its own acts of investigation and analysis, acts that may be accompanied by a high level of intellectual and scientific certainty, without compromising the will's independence as a rational potency in control of itself.

Scotus explains this relationship in terms of the differing orders of efficient causality.[30] The intellect operates according to natural causality while the will belongs to a superior, free order. The entire act of choice is a free act because its primary cause is free: the object as known is presented to the will and falls within its power. Once within the will's power, the object known becomes matter for choice. In this way, at the moment of choice, nothing outside the will necessitates its act: the will accepts or rejects the *obiectum cognitum* that is now present to it.

According to Scotus's solution, the will maintains its independence for self-movement in the presence of an object. How might we understand this independence? If we consider the act of the will only in terms of its ability to accept or reject an object (that is, according to the *velle/nolle* disjunction) it is clear that the act of the will is dependent upon the presence of the object and, whatever its choice, is bound to choose some course of action related to the presence of the object. It is difficult to imagine this as completely independent of the object, although one might see it as a weak form of compatibilism. If, however, we consider the act of the will at its deeper level of exercise, that is, in terms of the ability to choose or refrain from choice (the more basic *velle/non velle* disjunction), then there might be a stronger independence one can defend for the will. This is the independence that frees the will from any particular course of action relative to the object. In the will's ability for self-restraint, it separates itself from the object. In this way, the will's nature as a self-moving cause is explained, even in the presence of

---

30. This is the causal framework he used in II, d. 37, to show how divine concurrent willing does not interfere with human freedom. See above, chapter 5.

knowledge that would appear sufficient to determine choice. The will's response to whatever the intellect presents is completely free from anything outside the will's own power.

This *Lectura* text with its explanation based on partial efficient co-causality has been the basis for the standard understanding of Scotus's position on how cognition is involved in choice. It does not contradict anything Scotus maintained about practical cognition and moral science; in fact, it affirms the important role of the intellect at the concrete moment of choice. Nor does it contradict anything Scotus held about the will's capacity to govern its own choices. As the higher cause, the will is always able to restrain itself from a particular choice. In addition, with the object as known within the will's power, Scotus can still maintain that "nothing outside the will is cause of the will's choice." Partial co-causality explains both the collaboration between intellect and will and, more importantly, how no act of intellectual analysis can ever exert more influence on the will than can the will itself.

Indeed, he states, this is the only way to understand free will. Godfrey's intellectualist position fails to defend freedom and Henry's voluntarist position leaves the will blind. Both object as known and free choice in the will are required adequately to explain the foundation for the moral order.[31] The will remains more of a principal cause because it moves freely. The object known is less of a principal cause because it moves naturally, always acting in the same way. It is only relevant to the act of choice when it concurs with the will. Together, the causes act according to their own proper causality (as Scotus explains, like father and mother or pen and stylus) as one total cause in respect to the act of willing.[32]

This text pre-dates both the *Questions on Aristotle's Metaphysics* and *Ordinatio* II, d. 6. Because of this, it does not provide a strong

---

31. See *Lectura* II, d. 25, n. 70 (ed. Vat. 19:253).
32. Ibid., n. 73 (ed. Vat. 19:254).

analysis of the will as sole rational potency. Indeed, in the *Lectura* treatment, the will is the superior cause not because it is rational, but because it is free. One reason that Scotus introduces the "partial co-causal" solution may be the degree to which, in this early text, he may still identify rationality with the intellect. At no point does he refer to the will as the rational potency, or explain the will's freedom in terms of the two Anselmian affections. Indeed, the distinction he used so effectively in his *Questions on Aristotle's Metaphysics,* that of rational vs. natural, is not evident. He claims that the rational potency (in this case the intellect) acts *per modum naturae,* something he will deny in *Questions on Aristotle's Metaphysics* IX, d. 15. In this earliest *Lectura* treatment, the will's superiority is found in its freedom and its ability to direct the intellect, not on its rationality.

The identification of the intellect as rational potency in *Lectura* II, d. 25, is most evident where Scotus addresses the position of extreme voluntarism. In his fifth and final argument against Henry of Ghent's position, Scotus maintains that free will must include cognition. Without cognition, the will as free would be blind. With it, the will is truly free. Therefore, the object as known cannot be mere *sine qua non* (necessary) condition, but must be an active cause included in freedom and the power of free will.[33] Implicit in his argument is the need to safeguard how the will's freedom requires rationality. Here, the object as known (or the act of intellection) saves that rationality required for free will. It is following this argument against Henry that Scotus presents his own middle position between the two extremes.

Scotus's "via media" in *Lectura* II, d. 25, is based on the notion of the will as a free potency, but not as a rational potency. The central difference between intellect and will is the difference between a natural and a free potency, not between an irrational and rational po-

---

33. Ibid., n. 68 (ed. Vat. 19:252).

tency. Because here the will's freedom is not yet the more developed rational freedom (of either the *Questions on Aristotle's Metaphysics* or the more important Anselmian discussion of the will's affections in II, d. 6), Scotus needs partial co-causality to save the blind will from its own arbitrary exercise of freedom. The object as known is a rational guarantee that the highest freedom is not blind, but in accord with reason.

When Scotus comes again to this question in the later *Reportatio* version, he is still intent on defending the rationality of freedom. However, here he appears to have embraced the position that the will, and not the intellect, is the sole rational potency.[34] This text dates from his final years, after he has worked through the *Questions on Aristotle's Metaphysics* and *Ordinatio* II, d. 6. Here we see clearly a stronger defense of the rationality of freedom, not because of partial co-causality, but because the will is the sole rational potency.

The *Reportatio* text is a much shorter treatment of the question of the causality of the will. Yet here, Scotus does indeed affirm what he had denied in the *Lectura* version, i.e., that the object as known can be seen to be *causa sine qua non* (necessary condition) for the act of volition. He affirms here that nothing created other than the will can be total cause of the act of willing. Scotus affirms this, however, on the basis of the will's rationality.

This move to a stronger affirmation of the rational will is clear from the opening arguments that frame the question around the will as a rational potency. Aristotle explains the nature of rational potencies in Book IX of the *Metaphysics*. Such potencies deal with opposites and do nothing unless determined by the will in the act of choice. Indeed, there is a rational potency that can determine itself:

---

34. For an extended treatment of this question and its implications for a possible Scotist alignment with Henry of Ghent, see M.B. Ingham, "Did Scotus Modify His Position on the Relationship of Intellect and Will?" *Recherches de Théologie et Philosophie Médiévales* 69, 1 (2002): 88–116.

this is the will.[35] The body of the question offers some of the arguments seen in the earlier *Lectura* version, but at a critical moment Scotus integrates his conclusions about the will's rationality, taken both from the *Questions on Aristotle's Metaphysics* IX, d. 15, and Anselm's *De casu diaboli*. In addition to everything Aristotle can say about this matter, he argues, one can without contradiction imagine an intellective appetite unable to determine itself. This intellectual appetite would desire *per modum naturae*, as Anselm notes, and *would not be rational*. Because the will alone is capable of self-determination, then nothing created other than it can be the total cause of the act of willing.[36]

There are two significant textual points about this later version of II, d. 25, that are critical to our understanding of Scotus's teaching on the rational will at the end of his career. While the earlier *Lectura* version of this question had a passing reference to Aristotle's discussion of rational potencies, the philosophical text was not mined significantly in support of Scotus's solution. Similarly, Anselm's reference to the two affections had appeared early in the *Lectura* version of this question, but never as part of the discussion of the rational causality proper to willing. But, of course, neither the Philosopher nor the Theologian needed to be present there to support Scotus's moderate position, for the object as known played the important intellectual and rational causal role, partially responsible for the act of the will.

The position Scotus accepts in *Reportatio* clearly enhances the will's role and its rational autonomy regarding its own acts of willing. The object known now becomes *causa sine qua non* (necessary condition). Scotus acknowledges here that the object of intellection is the condition whose existence is necessary but not sufficient for the act of the will. In light of this acknowledgement, clearly a shift

35. *Reportatio* II, d. 25 (Vivès 23:118a).
36. *Reportatio* II, d. 25, n. 20 (Vivès 23:128b).

in his thinking on this matter, we must pay close attention to the textual context. The extended reference to Anselm and minor nod to Aristotle that frame this discussion mitigate the force of the conclusion that this text reveals a significant move away from the moderate *via media* in Oxford, and toward a more radical *voluntarist* position that might be associated with Henry of Ghent. On the basis of the context for his *Reportatio* discussion, a context that clearly adverts to other texts where he analyzes the rational will (a point that he repeats several times in the Parisian text), Scotus's acceptance of the object known as *causa sine qua non* is not more voluntarist, at least not insofar as that term might be understood to mean greater independence of the will from reason. Rather, this text moves in the direction of the integration of intellect and will into the more important rational will. This is why, despite his acceptance of the *causa sine qua non* position, Scotus frames his position within a discussion of the will's constitution as rational in its Anselmian metaphysical components.

A final example from the closing arguments of *Reportatio* confirms this. There is a type of cause, Scotus states, that is an indeterminate cause and also a complete cause. This cause can determine itself to one of two opposites and is a complex rational cause, such as the will with the intellect.[37] When they work together, the intellect and will form a complex rational cause. The rationality of this collaboration is not that of the earlier *Lectura* text (partial efficient co-causality), but clearly that of Anselm's modified *De casu diaboli* analysis. The cause is rational because the will is rational. The cause has a complex nature because of the way in which the rational cause works with the object as known.

The presence and important role of the Anselmian discussion in this text is central to a correct understanding of Scotus's Parisian po-

---

37. *Reportatio* II, d. 25, n. 23 (Vivès 23:129).

sition on the will's freedom. He did not, as the Vatican editors claim, teach in Paris precisely what he had taught at Oxford. Nevertheless, he does not liberate the will from reason when he reduces the object as known to a mere *causa sine qua non*. The similarity of terminology with other, more extreme voluntarists like Henry of Ghent masks a profound difference. While both Scotus and Henry make good use of the Aristotelian distinction of natural and free potencies in their common affirmation of the will's superiority over the intellect as basis for its independence, it is only Scotus who presents the Anselmian affections and their foundational role in making the will a rational will.

This *Reportatio* II, d. 25, text, then, can only be understood to be more voluntarist in the sense that the rational will is understood to be the total cause (and no longer partial co-cause) of its own act. It should not necessarily be seen to be more voluntarist in the sense that the will is increasingly independent of reason. As noted above, reason is here completely identified with the will. This is clear from Scotus's *Questions on Aristotle's Metaphysics* IX, q. 15, and his expanded discussion of the affections in the will in the *Ordinatio* and *Reportatio* versions of II, d. 6. Scotus's voluntarism is a moderate rational voluntarism that becomes increasingly integrated in terms of the rational will. He becomes more of that sort of voluntarist by the time of his *Reportatio* teaching. In his final years, Scotus affirmed the rational will as the specific difference of human nature. He does not, however, liberate the will from reason, nor does he deny that the will is naturally inclined to cooperate with the dictates of right reason.

Throughout his career, whether at Oxford or Paris, Scotus continually argued in favor of the rationality of freedom. He never sought to liberate freedom from reason. His position on the indetermination of the will is based upon his understanding of the three acts of which the will is capable *(velle/nolle/non velle)*. These three acts are possible, given the rational constitution of the will in the two Anselmian affections and its ability to control itself. Additionally, the importance of cognition and deliberation never diminishes the ability of the will to control it own movement. Together, intellect and will, knowledge and desire, cooperate to develop within the moral agent the perfection of moral action: right and ordered choices.

7. PRACTICAL WISDOM AND MORAL GOODNESS

A S THE PRECEDING CHAPTERS MAKE CLEAR, Scotus develops his discussion of the moral domain in terms of the will's rational freedom for self-determination in tandem with the activity of abstractive and intuitive intellection. Together, intellect and will provide the ground for rational action and moral choice for which the agent is accountable and can be praised or blamed. As we look finally at the overall portrait of moral perfection, we recognize the major elements of classical moral thought, yet in a distinct configuration. This configuration is governed by the primacy of the voluntary over the intellectual and reveals how all moral elements serve rational freedom. As we shall see, the centrality of freedom results in a reorganization of the moral domain, where essential elements shift slightly in their relationship to one another.

The first noticeable shift appears in the identification of beauty with moral goodness. There is, according to Scotus, no more appropriate object for the rational will than the beautiful act, where goodness, truth, and unity (the transcendental attributes of being) coincide. The second shift appears in the enhanced scientific dimension accorded to practical reasoning. As if to balance his focus on love and freedom, Scotus strengthens the activity of the intellect relative to moral judgment, and, in this way, safeguards the objectivity of moral reasoning as well as the validity of moral conclusions. This model of moral perfection involves both scientific and aesthetic dimensions. Finally, as a result both of the emphasis on freedom and the heightened scientific character of moral judgment, the virtues no longer take center stage, either to unify or to ground the objective goodness of moral decisions.

Concretely this means that the virtues (which Scotus understands as natural dispositions toward right action) never hold the central place they do for a thinker like Thomas Aquinas. On this point the Franciscan's departure from the Aristotelian approach is most pronounced. Although Scotus uses passages from Aristotle's *Ethics* to explain his moral theory, his placement of virtue in a secondary position sharply distinguishes his approach from that of the Stagirite. The place held by the virtues is, for Scotus, the direct result of his attention to human freedom in the moment of choice, especially as understood within the context of Christian thought. The possibility of repentance and conversion, in their natural foundations, requires that no developed trait of character become a "second nature." As he seeks to ground his philosophical vision on the dignity of nature as created by God, Scotus provides in his moral theory the natural capacity for the profound change of heart experienced when grace perfects nature. Conversion, then, is not the triumph of grace over nature. Rather it is the fullest expression of the perfection of nature, naturally constituted so that it might know and love the good.

If Scotus departs from the Aristotelian affirmation of the centrality of virtue, he also distances himself from the Stoic-Patristic tradition of the four cardinal virtues (prudence, justice, fortitude, temperance). The cardinal virtues, so holds this tradition, when present, are present together: their unity grounds moral character. To possess one of these is to possess them all. Scotus holds that such unity is not necessary nor are the virtues needed to unify moral living. Indeed, the unified moral life is based upon the primacy of prudence alone. Prudence exists in the intellect independently of the other three virtues that are found in the will. Prudence is not one moral virtue among many; it is *the* scientific habit of right reasoning. It is prudence, and not virtue, that governs and unifies the moral domain.

In addition to the scientific presentation of prudence, Scotus presents moral goodness in terms of its aesthetic dimension: the morally good act is a beautiful act. It is an act in which all elements are related in a harmonious whole, both to one another and to the rational judgment that is its norm and measure. In this chapter, we look more carefully at the three-fold dimension of the moral domain: the identification of moral goodness with beauty, the centrality of the judgment of prudence as the rational standard for the act, and the displacement of natural virtue to a minor (rather than essential) role.

7.1 Moral Goodness

Against the background of the foundational moral principle, *Deus diligendus est,* Scotus presents the determination of moral goodness as essentially an act of aesthetic rational judgment in the contingent order. The morally good act is, he states, a beautiful whole comprised of several elements within an appropriate relationship to one another and all under the direction of right reasoning.[1]

---

1. "[Just] as beauty is not some absolute quality in a beautiful body, but a combination of all that is in harmony with such a body . . . so the moral goodness of an act is a kind of decoration it has, including a combination of due proportion to all

Like beauty, moral goodness involves manifold relationships rather than absolute qualities. These relationships can be experienced visually (as in *Ordinatio* I, d. 17) or in an auditory manner (as in the earlier *Lectura* discussion where the example is taken from music). The judgment of moral goodness belongs to right reasoning: the morally good act must be performed in conformity to its dictates. Bringing together the first principle of *praxis,* the conclusions of moral science, and the specific conditions under which the act is considered, the intellect concludes to a moral judgment.

In issuing the dictate *(dictamen)* that follows from this judgment, right reasoning makes a determination about what ought to be done and how it ought to be done. This dictate is then presented to the will. When the dictate is right and all conditions for right execution are fulfilled, the moral act is completely and perfectly good. If, for Scotus, this sort of practical judgment involves a type of seeing or hearing what is there, a moment when the moral agent knows immediately what to do in a present circumstance, there must be something objective in the moral situation that is indeed there to be seen, to be recognized by the moral agent. Whatever the moral agent sees or hears, he is called upon to make the moral decision a source of beauty. In acting morally, the person resembles the artist who, given the raw material, introduces something beautiful into the order of being. In this way, the moral agent imitates divine creative behavior.

As we saw above in chapter 5, the foundational moral principle is not the only objective ground for such a judgment of right reasoning. The world of goods created and established by divine rational freedom has an objective value that human reason can know. Traditionally, the category of goods was explained in a two-fold manner, according to the Augustinian (and ultimately Stoic) tradition: goods

---

to which it should be proportioned (such as potency, object, end, time, place and manner), and this especially as right reason dictates." *Ordinatio* I, d. 17, n. 62 (ed. Vat. 5:163–64), in *Will and Morality,* 207.

of use *(bonum utile)* and goods of value *(bonum honestum)*. Goods of use derive their moral value from the use that is made of them. Goods of value are *per se* or intrinsic goods; they should never be used as a means for any other good. Appropriate loving on the part of the human will follows from the nature of the object loved. Augustine used the objective order to differentiate between the two acts of love in the will: *uti* and *frui*. Goods of value were to be delighted in *(frui)*, never used *(uti)*.

As the discussion of chapter 6 also made clear, the rational will in its two-fold affections is oriented toward these two orders of goods. The affection for justice is directed to goods of value, while the affection for possession is directed toward goods of use. Disordered loving can be understood as the improper relationship of human desire to a particular good in a particular situation. As Augustinian thought informed Franciscan theologians, a marked aesthetic approach framed this tradition's discussion of the human journey of desire and love toward the highest good. For Alexander of Hales, father of the Franciscan intellectual tradition, *bonum honestum* was synonymous with intelligible beauty.[2] Scotus's own rational aesthetic perspective on moral goodness depends upon the foundational and objective order of goods in the world as well as upon the first principle of *praxis,* both as naturally known. When he likens the moral conclusion to an aesthetic judgment, this has little to do with matters of personal taste. Beauty is an objective reality that belongs to the harmonious whole of creation, insofar as it is whole. The judgment of beauty has an objectivity in the same way that judgments of truth and goodness are objective. In the judgment of beauty, one recognizes and loves the whole as an integrated whole, where nothing is lacking.

2. "Cum bonum dicatur dupliciter, honestum et utile. . . . Honestatem autem voco intelligibilem pulchritudinem." *Summa theologica* I, n. 103; t. I:162 (Quarrachi: Ad Claras Aquas 1924). Taken from A. B. Wolter, *The Transcendentals and Their Function in the Metaphysics of Duns Scotus,* 100, n. 1.

In *Ordinatio* I, d. 17, Scotus emphasizes the central and integrating role played by right reasoning in determining the appropriate moral course of action. Reasoning measures the act itself, the suitability of relevant circumstances and the mode of execution. Once concluded, the deliberation of right reasoning issues in a dictate *(dictamen)* that commands what ought to be done. Complete moral goodness consists in the fulfillment of all requirements and conditions deemed necessary by this ordered, rational judgment. These conditions are those listed by Aristotle: the morally perfect act is done for the right reason, at the right time and place, according to the right manner and as the person of moral wisdom would perform it.[3] In this way, moral judgment brings all aspects of a particular situation together in the presence of the moral agent.

Once the moral conclusion is reached, the intellect presents its dictate to the will for choice and execution. This dictate, no matter how compelling or certain, never necessitates the cooperation or consent of the will. When the will acts in full accord with this norm, freely uniting itself to the judgment of right reasoning, it brings to birth an action whose moral goodness is complete and, at the same time, develops moral character within the agent. When something is lacking, either in the judgment of reasoning or in the will's consent and/or execution of the action as commanded, the moral goodness of the act is diminished.

In *Quodlibet* qq. 17 and 18, Scotus takes up the dual questions of moral goodness in the act and moral goodness in the agent. In the first question, he looks at the relationship of natural to meritorious love (corresponding to the relationship between natural love for the good and the theological virtue of charity). At the close of the discussion he situates moral goodness within a four-fold order that begins with the natural dimension and ends with the order of merit.

---

3. *Ordinatio* I, d. 17 n. 62 (ed. Vat. 5:163–64).

The natural order of goodness in a moral agent refers, first, to the "bare act to which blame or praise is imputable." Here is the most basic level of voluntary action that lies naturally within the power of the agent. This basic level grounds the person's moral responsibility as a voluntary agent. In this context, moral means imputable. Upon this basic order is founded a second order, that of the "virtuous act, which stems from moral virtue." This order adds the dimension of habit or virtuous disposition to the voluntary, as well as "to the rule of virtue, i.e., a dictate of right reason." Here natural causes such as developed disposition and, most importantly, right judgment, co-operate with free choice to enhance the perfection of the good act. The third order is that of charity, adding a relationship of love "which inclines the will to such an act." Since love can be either of the neighbor or of God, the order of charity stands at the border between the natural and theological virtues. The theological virtues (faith, hope, and charity) have God as their object. The act of love for God follows logically from the natural virtues governed by right reasoning and ordered toward love for the highest good. Finally, the highest or meritorious order unites the good act in a relationship to the divine will "which accepts the act in a special way" and rewards the agent. Scotus clarifies the importance of the charitable as distinct from the virtuous act: "The third [the order of charity] adds some goodness over and above that conferred by the second [the order of virtue] and is itself required for the fourth [the order of merit], not indeed by the very nature of things, but rather by a disposition of the accepting will."[4]

A simple example may help clarify these four levels of goodness. Suppose one is faced with a situation where the truth should be told. At a primary level, the moral question is whether or not the act (whether to lie, keep silent, or tell the truth) belongs to the power of

---

4. *Quodlibet* 17.34 in *God and Creatures*, 398.

the agent. In other words, is the act voluntary such that, whatever the choice, praise or blame would be appropriate? The second order belongs to the agent's character or natural disposition to tell the truth, as this has developed and now exists under the direction of right reasoning. This refers not simply to natural character traits but to how those traits function in this particular moral decision, how they develop virtuously as determined and directed by right reasoning. Here, it is not simply a question of telling the truth, but of how, when, where, and to what degree the truth should be told. Thirdly, one might ask if the act is informed by love and performed in a loving manner. If so, the act's moral perfection would be further enhanced by the agent's charitable intention. Finally, the fourth order points to the act and agent insofar as both are pleasing to God and worthy of reward. Thus, we can understand the morally good act within an order that lies between the human will (its source) that chooses freely and the divine will (its goal) that freely rewards.

From these four levels, we can also understand how the morally good act is, as it were, suspended between two wills, the human and divine. The act informed by charity (a natural desire to love of which the will is capable) is the horizon for the encounter between the human will that chooses and the divine will that accepts the act and rewards it. Scotus affirms that the divine will, by its liberality, rewards human acts far beyond what they might deserve according to strict justice.[5]

In *Quodlibet* q. 18, Scotus looks more carefully at the second order noted above, i.e., the act as it falls under the judgment of right reasoning and as it is imputable to the moral agent. Here, he considers whether the external act (execution) adds any goodness over and above that of the internal act of the will (consent). This discussion

5. See *Ordinatio* I, d. 17, n. 149 (ed. Vat. 5:210–11). See also the discussion in M.B. Ingham, "Letting Scotus Speak for Himself," *Medieval Philosophy and Theology* 10, 2 (2001): 173–216.

grounds moral goodness in the objective order as understood by right reason in the intellect. The "moral goodness of an act consists in its having all that the agent's right reason declares must pertain to the act or to the agent in acting."[6] This objective order of goodness is based upon both primary (essential) and secondary (accidental) aspects. Primary goodness consists in "the integrity and perfection of the being itself" with nothing lacking. Secondary goodness consists in the suitability or harmony that the being has with something else, "something which ought to have it or which it ought to have."[7] This double suitability of integrity and harmony is commonly connected, as Scotus explains by means of an Augustinian example. Health is good for the person because it suits him. In addition, a healthy person has a cheerful expression and good color. So, the face is called good because it has what is appropriate to it. Only goodness in the primary sense is *per se* good, because it is a good of perfection.

The primary or essential goodness of an act can be determined objectively on the basis of the nature of the terms involved. This means that *per se* goodness of beings in the world is based upon divine judgment in creating this particular world as it is. Human judgments about essential goodness are rational, objective, and based upon the goodness that already exists in the natural world. Moral judgments resemble not only aesthetic assessment, but scientific conclusions as well. For example, Scotus argues, given the physical constitution of the human person, certain objects in reality fall into the category of nutritious food. Eating such food is an act whose goodness is essential, because this sort of food replenishes what the human body has lost through exercise or activity. The judgment of essential goodness, then, is the result of the act of understanding whereby we note first, the nature of the human body and, second, the nutritional value of the food.

6. *Quodlibet* 18.8 in *God and Creatures,* 400.
7. *Quodlibet* 18.9 in *God and Creatures,* 401.

Right reason has access to the objective order of natural goods. In addition, the certainty of moral reflection is founded upon the self-evident, first principle that guides practical reflection. Scotus's assertion of the primacy of the agent's reason is not, therefore, an affirmation of moral subjectivism. On the contrary, it affirms the dignity of objective, moral reflection and autonomy. Right reason's declaration about moral goodness comes as the conclusion to an analysis that makes full use of the intellect's abstractive and intuitive cognitional acts. Because of the powers of natural reasoning, the moral agent has intuitive knowledge of her own actions and is responsible in a way that animals are not. The dictate of right reasoning is therefore a dictate of conscience, which the moral agent is obliged to follow. In fact, Scotus affirms that the determination of *recta ratio* is definitive: someone who erred in judgment, and then acted in accord with the correct judgment on the part of another, would not act rightly, "for by his own knowledge he was meant to regulate his actions and in this case he is not acting in accord with it but against it and hence he does not act rightly."[8]

When making a judgment about the moral goodness of an act, right reasoning bases its deliberation, first, on the object. The object of an act is the primary and fundamental dimension to be considered in coming to the correct moral assessment. The object is the moral matter for choice: it refers to the Aristotelian category of "who the person is and what she is doing," thus it depends on self-awareness in a particular, concrete situation. As such, the object of deliberation frames the objective category "morally good" as identifiable by any rational agent. Every rational agent, explains Scotus, has a foundational awareness about his own nature and those actions appropriate to his well-being. This insight reveals the objective ordering of goods that surround the moral agent and in relationship

8. *Quodlibet* 18.12 in *God and Creatures*, 402.

to which the moral agent can flourish. For example, "knowing what it means to attain knowledge, it would also be clear to [someone] what is not appropriate for his mind to reach."[9] From this perspective, an act such as telling the truth (or at least not lying) belongs to an objective order of moral goodness that can be understood by reflection upon human nature as rational, upon the definition of truth, and upon the requirements for rational perfection.

The objective order of goodness as defined here is, however, only the beginning of the moral determination. In addition to the goodness of an act that belongs to it objectively or by nature, there comes the more specific judgment about the various moral levels of goodness that ought to belong to it. These levels are the parts of the greater whole that further specify the goodness of the act and its relationship to the agent. Here, one considers, first, the end for which the act is performed, that is, the intention of the agent or the moral purpose. Eating food, for example, to remain or become healthy is an appropriate end. This important characteristic belongs to the act, not as actually performed, but as willed and "as related to this end by an act of the will."[10] In fact, the decision to "do something good for a worthy purpose is no less good when the external act that ensues fails to achieve that end than when it succeeds."[11] The morally good act is good even when it involves only an internal act of consent, that is, even when it cannot be successfully executed.

The two-fold determinations of the object and the end constitute the most important criteria for moral specification. Once the object has been further determined by its relationship to the end (its moral intention), the act has an enhanced moral dimension. The appropriate amount of praise or blame due the agent can now be identified. Indeed, it is at the level of moral intention that one differenti-

9. *Quodlibet* 18.13 in *God and Creatures*, 402–403.
10. *Quodlibet* 18.15 in *God and Creatures*, 403.
11. *Quodlibet* 18.15 in *God and Creatures*, 403.

ates a mistake from a vicious act. In a vicious act, the moral intent is to harm. This is quite different from an act that harms someone inadvertently.

Following upon the foundational objective judgment, the agent must now consider the external execution of the act, that is, its manner, timing, and place. These circumstances define the specific moral goodness of a specific act as executed by the agent in a specific set of circumstances. Any evaluative judgment about the goodness of an act or, more importantly, about the amount of praise or blame due the agent, must take all these circumstances into consideration. The most perfect moral act, indeed the most beautiful, according to Scotus, possesses all to the best degree. Any absence or privation of an element that ought to be present diminishes the goodness of the act privatively. For example, one might tell the truth but in a way that does more harm than good. This does not diminish the essential objective goodness of the act of truth telling, nor does it detract from one's intention that might have been noble. Nonetheless, it does affect the overall moral goodness of the performance of the act in a privative manner. By contrast, positive badness (evil) requires the presence of a vicious habit or a positive state of deformity contrary to goodness.[12] One might tell the truth to someone out of a vicious intent, or out of hatred. This is a far more serious act than the mistaken execution of an otherwise correct decision to tell the truth. The hearer might have been hurt in both cases, but in one the harm was intentional; in the other it was not.

Finally, in addition to these levels of distinction, Scotus differentiates between the judgment of moral goodness in an act and the

---

12. "Briefly, then, just as moral goodness is integral suitability, so moral badness is unsuitability. Privative badness is a lack of suitability, i.e., the absence of what ought to be there, whereas badness as the contrary of goodness is unsuitability as a contrary state, i.e., as some condition that is incompatible with suitability." *Quodlibet* 18.21 in *God and Creatures,* 405.

judgment of praise or blame in the agent. The act's moral goodness or rectitude lies in its relationship to the judgment of reason in the intellect. The act must conform to the dictate of right reasoning. The attribution of praise or blame lies in the relationship of the act to the free power of the agent. The agent must choose the act voluntarily. Thus, the moral act lies in a double relationship to rational free choice: there must be knowledge in the intellect and choice in the will. Moral responsibility implies this dual relationship. Like the birth of a child, the act comes from two parents. It "has moral goodness because it conforms to a rule or norm as it should. It is imputable because it lies in the free power of the agent. Praiseworthy and blameworthy presuppose both."[13]

In addition to his discussion of moral action in this text, Scotus discusses the question of the morally indifferent or undifferentiated act. This is an act that is not related to all its causes in the way that morally good acts should be. Something is missing. For example, the act might not be done in the way it ought, as Aristotle explains in the *Ethics*.[14] Such acts fall within the genus of moral, however, they lack the specific difference needed to assign the precise level of goodness or amount of praise. Additionally, since the order of moral goodness points toward the higher order of merit, an act might be undifferentiated at this intermediate level (between moral and meritorious) if it were only habitually referred to its end. An example of this might be an act inspired by love (charity) but not by the conscious act of love for God. Such an act would be ordered (and therefore not sinful), yet not referred intentionally to God and, in such a case, would not be meritorious.

---

13. *Quodlibet* 18.26 in *God and Creatures*, 407.

14. "This is proved first from the Philosopher in *Ethics* II: 'The habit of justice is not produced by doing what the just do, but by doing such things in the way that the just do them.'" Scotus adds: "The first sort of act is not morally good, because it does not proceed from virtue." *Ordinatio* II, d. 41, in *Will and Morality*, 231.

7.2 Practical Reasoning

As the earlier discussion made clear, moral choice requires only two causes: knowledge and the power to choose. Situated in the intellect, prudence (right reasoning) is the proximate norm for moral action. This norm appears as a dictate *(dictamen)* of right reasoning. In the judgment of prudence, the intellect's two cognitional acts (abstraction and intuition) inform moral reflection. In the intellect, truths of moral science are brought to bear on contingent states of affairs.[15]

Prior to the complete reception of Aristotle's text in the thirteenth century, medieval thinkers were not strangers to the discussion of moral wisdom or prudence. Indeed, Stoic and Patristic writers made much of the importance of this central intellectual virtue of moral discernment. Biblical texts also present moral wisdom as a participation in the divine spirit, which orders, measures, and governs all reality. In the earliest interpretations of the *Nicomachean Ethics,* thinkers like Philip the Chancellor and William of Auxerre distinguished two sorts of moral wisdom: prudence-science and prudence-virtue. Prudence-science enjoyed the certainty of scientific knowledge, both regarding principles and deductive conclusions. Prudence-virtue dealt with particular, contingent states of affairs. It was immediate to choice. Philip and William both held that the intermediate level of prudence-science was needed to bridge the gap between the first principles of *praxis* and the command of prudence-virtue.

Scotus's presentation of prudence recalls this distinction of science and virtue. He is familiar with and uses the traditional categories of the cardinal virtues, referring to prudence in tandem with

15. See M.B. Ingham, "Moral Reasoning and Decision-Making: Scotus on Prudence," in *Moral and Political Philosophy in the Middle Ages,* ed. C. Bazán, E. Andújar, L. Sbrocchi, 501–511 (Ottawa: Legas, 1995).

justice, fortitude, and temperance. However, he clearly understands prudence to belong to the higher domain of scientific knowledge, generated both from reflection upon experience and upon the foundational first principles and body of moral knowledge. This broad domain of scientific yet practical moral knowledge forms a coherent body of truths upon which the moral agent reflects in the presence of a situation for choice.

It is possible to trace a progression in Scotist texts from the three-fold distinction of principle, science, and moral dictate in his early texts to a far more unified understanding of prudence as practical reason. This progression mirrors the Franciscan's development toward a more rational will. In other words, as Scotus becomes more convinced that the will alone is the rational potency, he understands the intellectual activity of reasoning about *praxis* to be a unified domain of scientific knowledge, not unlike geometry, that is both directly linked to first principles and immediate to *praxis*. This is the domain of practical reasoning, the source of conclusions about moral matters.

In both his *Lectura* and *Ordinatio* prologues (prior to 1300), Scotus makes it clear that prudence is not scientific knowledge. In both texts he distinguishes prudence from first principles and moral science according to its proximity to *praxis* and its epistemic content. He uses the analogy of the artist to make this distinction clear. An artist's knowledge is "more remotely practical" when it is derived from theoretical knowledge about art than when it is gained "simply from experience." He concludes, "so too one who knows the science of morals is more remotely practical than one who possesses prudence."[16] Moral science is composed of necessary truths that are universal, while prudence is generated from particular acts of moral choice. The content of moral science is more closely related to the

---

16. *Lectura* Prologue, in *Will and Morality,* 141–43.

first principles and to the ends of moral living, understood in a general sense, while prudence is attentive to the order of the contingent and particular.

We find in these early texts a clear distinction between scientific knowledge and acquired knowledge of moral matters. The scientific knowledge is general, related to first principles in an immediate manner, and composed of a body of necessary truths not unlike geometry. Practical knowledge by contrast is specific, related immediately to the contingent order, and learned through experience and reflection. The face of the rational soul, then, looks both upward to principle and downward to action. The entire domain is unified by first principles, to be sure, but it forms an uneasy whole of speculative and inductively acquired knowledge. And, while in the *Questions on Aristotle's Metaphysics* VI, q. 1, Scotus maintains that moral science relates differently to the act of choice than does prudence, he stills calls the scientific dimension less perfect than the practical and never explains precisely how the two domains are related.[17] It is not clear from his presentation how one bridges the gap between certain knowledge of what one ought to do and that knowledge immediate to *praxis* that commands and is followed by execution.

It is only in *Ordinatio* III, d. 36 that Scotus presents the activity of prudence as directive of the entire domain of *praxis*,[18] understood as a distinct and unified domain of human concern. In this later text he offers an explanation of the relationship of knowledge to choice that dispenses entirely with the distinction between moral science and prudence. In other words, and in light of the enhanced rationality he gives the will, toward the close of his career, Scotus identifies prudence with practical reason. As directive of moral matters, pru-

---

17. "But moral science is related in another way to what can be done, namely in general, and is insufficient of itself to direct one in particular matters." *Questions on the Metaphysics* VI, q. 1, n. 68 (II:23).

18. See *Will and Morality*, 411–13.

dence takes over the important role held by moral science in the earlier text and even replaces the first practical principles. In this text, there is no longer the three-fold division between principle, science, and direction. There is only prudence.

Scotus offers this presentation as a second, more probable answer to the question of the unity of moral living. In his first answer he had presented the traditional approach where prudence deals with means leading to the end, and where moral science and principle point to the end in a more general, theoretical manner. In his second answer, however, prudence looks more like moral science because it has access to ends as well as means. Prudence also regulates virtue from a higher scientific standpoint. Here too, Scotus emphasizes the will's freedom where he points out that the act of prudential judgment can indeed take place without necessitating any choice in the will. Finally, knowledge gained from experience and reflection, in light of fundamental principles, replaces the intermediate category held by moral science in the earlier texts. Prudence relates to first principles immediately and not on the basis of the middle level of moral science. Together, principles and prudence form one single mental *habitus* of practical knowledge. Prudence in this solution includes both the immediate access to the particular elements of moral choice (traditionally known as prudence-virtue) and, more importantly, that knowledge of a higher order, involving particular ends as well as means (prudence-science).

This broader solution unifies the domain of practical cognition around the activity of prudence that, as science, deals with the ends as well as the means of moral action. Scotus states that "the practical act that directs one rightly to a particular end is properly speaking prudence *(sit proprie prudentia)*."[19] He concludes that this habit, generated by correct judgments about means or some ends, is prudence

19. *Will and Morality,* 411.

even though correct choice does not follow.[20] Prudence is no longer that habit whose content is generated by experience and whose judgment must conform to the higher demands of moral science. Prudence is now that to which moral action itself conforms. Indeed, it is prudence itself (or better, the prudential agent) who bridges the gap between first principles and concrete situations. At the close of the text, Scotus even extends the name of prudence to the understanding of first principles.[21]

In III, d. 36, Scotus offers a description of the practical domain in which prudence alone functions as sole regulator. Gone is the intermediate level of moral science. Gone is the independent level of first principles. All now is unified under the name of prudence as right reasoning in the domain of *praxis*. Scotus's discussion here must be seen in light of his emphasis on the will's rational freedom and upon the integration of the two cognitive acts of abstraction and intuition as they inform the activity of intellection about the practical domain. The will's rational capacity to refrain from choosing according to the dictates of right reasoning (specifically in the *non velle*) places the locus of moral responsibility in the will, and thus allows greater extension to the discussion of the domain of prudence: not just as judgment of means but as directional knowledge of ends of moral living.

The exercise of practical reasoning requires artisan-like training: attention to particulars, personal creativity, and awareness of moral principles. In the act of moral judgment, all dimensions of the situation converge in the presence of the moral subject. The moral act involving deliberation, judgment, choice, and execution unifies the person in rational self-expression and creativity. It is a moment of giving birth when the moral agent brings forth from within herself the beautiful act in response to the demands of the situation around

20. Ibid.
21. Ibid., 413.

her and in light of moral principles. In the precise moment of moral deliberation and judgment, the fully formed moral agent knows how to identify and pick out the relevant moral elements, sees the situation "as a whole,"[22] and "knows immediately" with a type of discernment what is to be done. The beginner, by contrast, has no such swift grasp of the moral demands—she must reason, slowly and methodically, calculating step by step what must be done. While the non-expert calculates slowly from universal principles, the expert "sees" something in the moral situation.[23] What he sees makes all the difference in what he chooses to do.

7.3 The Role of Moral Virtue

Scotus's presentation of prudence as unifying and integrating habit of practical knowledge effectively removes the need for virtue to ground and unify moral living. His enhanced expansion of intellection to include both abstractive and intuitive acts also removes the need for virtue as objective guarantee for the goodness of the end. In short, it is his reformulation of prudence as right reasoning that removes the need for virtue as a central and essential element in the moral domain. Despite virtue's relegation to the periphery of moral attention, however, Scotus still asserts that an act performed in the presence of moral virtue is more perfect than one that lacks it.

Scotus's position on the role of virtue for moral goodness is perhaps the clearest sign of his response to propositions condemned in 1277 and his rejection of the philosophical model whose completion is described in *Nicomachean Ethics* X, 6–9. Virtue belongs to that category of natural disposition that, for a thinker like Thomas Aquinas,

---

22. In his *Questions on the Metaphysics* VII, q. 15, n. 4 (II:258). See Wolter's "Duns Scotus on Intuition, Memory and our Knowledge of Individuals," in *The Philosophical Theology*, 101.

23. See *Lectura Prologue* IV, qq. 1–2 (ed. Vat. 16:46–59), reproduced in *Will and Morality*, 141–43.

leads logically and necessarily to the experience of *beatitudo.* There cannot be a natural desire or disposition toward human perfection that is frustrated. The human desire for happiness is such a natural desire. Therefore the experience of happiness must be the natural result of a natural disposition. For Scotus, this sort of reasoning does not take adequate account of the importance of freedom in the will, nor does it take seriously the primacy of love over knowledge as the fullest perfection of rationality. An argument such as one finds in Aquinas, Scotus might argue, would reduce morality to natural perfection, both in terms of the natural desire for happiness and of the determination of virtue in light of the fullest understanding of human nature.

Scotus's approach explains how the human person has access to objective moral data and still remains free. The objectivity of moral judgments does not depend on the agent's moral virtue to the same degree as in Aristotle and Aquinas. For these two thinkers, the goodness of moral judgment is assured by the virtuous character of the moral agent. For an act to be right, virtue must relate to the end in an appropriate manner while prudence judges the appropriate means. Moral virtues require the presence of prudence and prudence requires the presence of the virtues. The virtues that finalize the activity of moral reflection on the end constitute the character of the moral agent. Moral judgment depends radically upon personal character to reveal to the agent what it is about the moral situation that is morally relevant. This is why, both for Aristotle and Aquinas, virtue plays such a central role in both of their teleological theories. It is also why the moral agent is morally responsible for his own character and virtue. Moral living is both grounded on and unified by the unity of the virtues.

However, for Scotus, moral judgment is *not* a judgment that necessarily requires a virtuous character. Rather, it depends in a more objective manner, indeed more radically, upon the agent's intellectual access to moral truth as it appears in the present situation. In addition, moral judgments do not emerge as the result of an act of means/end deliberation, where means are chosen on the basis of their relationship to an end. For Scotus, no such teleological reasoning can belong to ethics as a philosophical science. The deliberation of practical reasoning is an objective deliberation in the intellect about what counts as morally relevant in a given situation. This ability for deliberation can never be blinded by the will.[24] It is followed by the moral choice of the will whether or not to consent to the dictates of the moral proposition.

Throughout his texts, Scotus distinguishes the domain of virtue (as natural disposition) from that of freedom and rationality. He states in *Ordinatio* III, d. 33, that both the will and the intellect are capable of performing acts that are morally good (for the will)and correct (for the intellect) without the presence of any practical habit, moral or intellectual.[25] This is the case, quite simply, because virtue is generated from right choice. If virtue itself depends upon right choosing (even logically if not temporally) then no act of virtue is required for moral choice, because no virtue is more basic than rational decision. It is not virtue that grounds moral living, but the science of prudence.

Scotus only displaces virtue, he does not eliminate it from the moral domain. In *Ordinatio* I, d. 17, he considers more carefully how virtue as a practical habit affects moral goodness. While he denies that moral living ever becomes second nature based on virtue, he does not deny the contribution made by the virtues to the overall

---

24. Although the will can distract the intellect or turn its attention to other matters.

25. "One could say to the question that the will on its own without a habit could perform an act that is right and morally good—nor is this true only of the will, for the intellect also could perform a correct judgment without an intellectual habit . . ." in *Will and Morality,* 333.

perfection of the morally good act. In fact, an act performed in the presence of virtue is more perfect than the same act performed by the will alone. When both the will and virtue are present, the choice is the fruit of causes that are both natural and free. The moral act that results from natural and free causes has a greater intensity than a similar act that comes from either cause alone. Accordingly, a freely chosen act of generosity is most intense when accompanied by the practical habit or virtue of generosity. It is more perfect than an act of generosity that is not freely chosen. It is also more perfect than a freely chosen act that is not accompanied by the natural inclination. Scotus explains this causally: two causes working together can produce a more perfect effect than either one alone. The effect would be whole, and *per se* from the two, yet in a diverse causal relationship to each.[26]

While this reference to two causal orders is reminiscent of the partial co-causality of moral choice that involved cognition and volition, there is an important difference here. Moral choice never occurs in the absence of an act of cognition (or the *obiectum cognitum* of II, d. 25). The act of intellection is always present as partial co-cause of the act of volition. By contrast, moral choice can and does take place in the absence of virtue. The virtues contribute to the perfection of the moral act, but not in a manner as necessary as that belonging to the intellect in causing the act of choice. Virtue is not a necessary condition for moral choice, as it is for Aristotle and Aquinas. The perfection of the morally good act coming from the will and virtue is whole because the virtuous inclination, at the moment of choice, is joined to prudence (as rational judgment) and lies within the power of the will.

Even though the perfect moral act is related to both natural and free orders, the relationships are not equal. The free dimension is

26. *Ordinatio* I, d. 17, n. 40 (ed. Vat. 5:154).

obviously the superior order, since free choice in the will defines the moral realm as voluntary and therefore rational. All virtues belong to the will and are subject to the will's freedom. Natural virtue takes on a moral dimension and role when natural dispositions and habits are consciously brought to bear by the will in its acts of deliberation and choice. In other words, *moral virtue* refers to any natural disposition or habit that is within the power of the will in the activity of rational deliberation, choice and execution. In this way, virtues do not ground or define moral action. Nonetheless, they are neither insignificant to moral action, nor left out of moral discussion.

Finally, the centrality of freedom in Scotist thought affects the relationship between prudential judgment and moral virtue. Differing from both Aristotle and Aquinas, Scotus insists that it is indeed possible to have a correct judgment about what ought to be done in the intellect without any moral virtue in the will.[27] This means quite simply that, not only is the person rationally powerful enough to know what to do in the absence of any natural inclination, but she is also free enough to choose what to do in the absence of prior moral habituation. In addition, the rational freedom of the will also allows for there to be a correct moral judgment in the intellect followed by an act of self-restraint *(non velle),* in which case (should consent to the judgment have been the correct moral decision), no virtue would be generated in the will.

As we noted in chapter 6, this strong position on human freedom involves the will's inner constitution and self-determination. The rational will is in control of itself: it can refrain from any action commanded as the result of the moral analysis in the intellect. This self-control is revealed in the interaction of the will's two affections. Under normal circumstances, such self-control is morally appropriate: the mature moral agent thinks twice before acting. However, it

27. See *Ordinatio* III, d. 36, in *Will and Morality,* 413.

is also possible that such self-restraint could impede moral progress. Too much hesitation results in no action at all. In a case where it is better to act, inaction does not generate moral virtue. In a case where not acting is the morally appropriate course, inaction does generate moral virtue.

The person stands in a state of indetermination toward her judgment of prudence. In the presence of the dictate: "Tell the truth" she can choose to do so *(velle)*, choose to lie *(nolle)*, or choose neither *(non velle)*. Ordinarily, the virtuous person would choose to tell the truth and the vicious person would choose to lie. But no person, not even the morally perfect, would lack the ability to exercise the third option and do nothing at all. So if we consider the case of the morally mature or wise person, when Scotus states that the judgment of prudence can take place in the absence of virtue, he can only mean that the expert (who might never reject the moral dictate) could always refrain from acting. This possibility focuses on the act of *velle/non velle* in the will.

When, finally, we consider this act as it might apply to the will's relationship to itself, we understand again that there is more to *non velle* than the absence of choice. The *non velle* involves (or could involve) an act of rational self-restraint, where one might choose to refrain from or postpone a choice. Concretely, this means that the virtuous person never loses the freedom of choice required for moral imputability. In the presence of a command of right reasoning about what ought to be done, this person does not have to reject the command in order to exercise free choice. It is enough for the virtuous to refrain from choice in order to fulfill the conditions set out by Scotus:

1. There is an act of right reasoning or prudence.
2. There is no virtue generated in the will.
3. The will remains free.

Clearly, in the case of the morally weak person, or even the vicious person, one can imagine a dictate of right reason with no virtue generated, especially when the will rejects the dictate outright. But this approach narrows the limits of freedom to either acceptance *(velle)* or rejection *(nolle)*. In such a case, the three conditions could only be fulfilled by the bad choice, made freely and with full knowledge. This reading fails to take adequately into account how the fully developed moral agent also remains undetermined by virtue or any natural inclination. In addition, it fails to explain how even the fully developed vicious person would be free for conversion. If, however, we expand our understanding of the will's act to include the third option *(non velle),* then we can also consider the possibility that one does not have to reject the moral dictate (as a vicious person might) in order to have the judgment of prudence exist without virtue in the will. The ability to restrain oneself *(non velle)* is present to both sinner and saint. Its presence explains in a single act how the saint can fall (by too much restraint), the sinner can convert, and how ordinary people can sin.

In addition to judgments of right reasoning, there is a second way in which prudence can direct moral living in the absence of virtue. We know that, for Scotus, intuition of subjective states is possible and that intuition is an act of the intellect of which prudence is the habit. This means that prudence is capable of reflexive awareness of the activity of knowing as it relates to desire. If practical wisdom involves the intellectual grasp of the activity of the will considered itself as an object, we understand how the act of rational self-restraint might also be an object of choice. Such an act of self-reflexive moral choice could be understood as the choice for a moral orientation of life, and not just individual moral choices as they present themselves. This type of fundamental moral option for free, rational choice can only come in the course of a life of moral goodness and mature self-reflection. Here the object of moral choice is the will itself in its act of moral choice. In such a situation one is able to will "right willing" for itself and as a good in itself. It is an act of right choice about right choice, an act whose object coincides with itself.

There are, then, two ways that practical reasoning directs moral life without depending on the virtues. In a primary and evident sense, prudence determines the best course of action according to right reasoning. It governs the consideration of options, the activity of analysis, and identification of relevant factors within the matter for choice. Even at this immediate level, such prudential judgment never necessitates the will's cooperation; prudence issues a command about what ought to be done. In a secondary and less evident manner, prudence governs and directs the activity of the will insofar as it considers its own act of choice as an object of choice. Here, choosing rightly serves as moral orientation, measured against the highest rational standard. It involves the self-conscious moral orientation on the part of the will. To will rightly right-willing reveals the coincidence of activity and end, the agreement of *praxis* with its object. In such a case, there are no rules external to the act of choice: rational willing defines and directs itself. The act of right willing provides its own rule. In this way, rational desire in the will is self-perfective, and one can understand how Scotus sees ordered loving as the rational perfection of the human person. At this highest level of moral development, human choice in its simplicity and perfection imitates divine freedom and creative generosity.

Scotus's presentation of virtue and practical wisdom (prudence) is clearly more Augustinian and Anselmian than Aristotelian. The centrality of the will as moral ground and the identification of freedom with rationality displace virtue to the periphery. Accordingly, the virtues or natural inclinations can never fully explain why the morally good action is morally good rather than naturally good. The moral goal is not understood as *eudaimonia* or intellectual self-actualization, but rather as the perfection of human willing in the concrete moment of choice, as an end in itself. Right and ordered loving perfects the will, as the rational and free potency. Moral wisdom refers to the perfection of rational insight and judgment in light of the certain truths of moral science and the concrete situation for choice.

We can now see more clearly how all the elements fit together to form the moral order according to Duns Scotus. He maintains that there is an objective order of goodness in reality as created by God. This order involves the natures of beings and their suitability with one another and to certain goods. This suitability of natures constitutes the natural beauty of creation. Human reason is endowed with all the natural powers required to know these natures and to grasp the relationships that found the created order. Because the human intellect enjoys both abstractive and intuitive cognition, human reasoning can understand and deliberate well in making moral judgments. In addition to this judgment of essential goodness, human reason can determine moral suitability in a more specific category of goods: moral judgments determine and dictate what actions are not only essentially good, but suitable and appropriate to the agent at a given time and within a given set of circumstances. Right reasoning issues a dictate about what ought to be done in a particular situation. For its part, the human will retains the freedom to follow the dictates or judgments of reason *(velle)* as well as to reject them *(nolle)* or refrain from action *(non velle)*. In this way, moral imputability is safeguarded, for the person is a responsible moral agent, both in his understanding of what to do and in his free choice whether or not to do it.

In this vision of moral behavior, Scotus does not simply correct Aristotle with the insights of revelation. Scotus uses Aristotle's discussion of voluntary action in Book III of the *Ethics*, as well as the description of the moral expert in Book VI. Aristotle's texts on moral reasoning and choice correct the texts on human fulfillment of Book X. The approach of Book VI of the *Nicomachean Ethics* makes greater use of the moral expert *(phronimos)* as personification of practical wisdom. This reflection upon human freedom for choice and upon the metaphysical requirements for such a freedom (that is, an order which is itself the result of a divine free choice) leads to the Scotist conclusion that true human fulfillment may indeed require openness to accept *qua* gift a perfection of which we are not capable alone, but to which we are naturally disposed. In other words, when Aristotle is read against the background of freedom, one must take seriously the importance of the truths of revelation.

In this way, reflection on the moral domain as the order of freedom, for Scotus, points directly to God and to the God revealed in Scripture. Without such an order, founded metaphysically upon divine creativity, the philosophers would be correct in their assessment of moral progress. Personal human fulfillment would be the necessary result of certain behaviors. The moral goal would be quite simply an autonomous self-deification. In that realm, the caprice of chance or the workings of fate (moral luck) would continually haunt the highest human moral aspirations. There would be no reason to hold that freedom were anything more than wishful thinking.

Both the opening "controversy" of the *Ordinatio Prologue* and the entire discussion of the moral domain affirm the person-centered perspective which grounds and directs Scotus's moral discussion. Happiness, like health, is not a state to be achieved, nor a static goal of an absolute perfection. The person is the moral subject: both as end and as source for moral activity. Moral development involves development of the person, one who is able to respond rationally and freely, morally and creatively, to the demands of a given situation.

8. SCOTUS'S LEGACY

S COTUS IS A BRIDGE THINKER, a transitional figure in the development of thought from the synthesis of the High Middle Ages to the emerging early modern philosophy. He is not, for all that, an *innovator* in the strong sense of the term,[1] if by this one means a thinker who self-consciously re-framed the existing *Weltanshauung* and set a new direction. He stands clearly within the tradition that has gone before him, and artfully restates and affirms its vision of reality, whether this be in the domains of epistemology, metaphysics, or ethics. One can find with little difficulty the same sort of awareness of the relationship between reality, the mind, and God that one finds in Aquinas. When Scotus sets forth a question,

---

1. In *Virtues of the Will: The Transformation of Ethics in the Late Thirteenth Century* (Washington, D.C.: Catholic University of America Press, 1995), Bonnie Kent traces the development of ethical thought after 1260 and shows quite convincingly that Scotus was both faithful to the tradition that had gone before and, in light of that, a moderate voluntarist voice.

all traditional voices are present, from Anselm to Bonaventure, from Aquinas to Henry of Ghent. Nonetheless, in key textual discussions, he also presents a new vision that stands parallel to the tradition. One can discern in Scotist texts an emerging re-formulation of traditional elements into a renewed model of philosophical discourse. To this extent, he mirrors the time in which he lived, at the intellectual turning point of the last quarter of the thirteenth century, after 1277. In this way he prepares, without completely developing, the structural field for thinkers like Ockham and Buridan who follow him.

Among the most important shifts within Scotist thought we find the turn to the contingent as a valid domain for scientific and philosophical reflection. While he is keenly aware of the scientific demands of the *Posterior analytics,* he acknowledges the importance of a science of the contingent. Indeed, the contingent is more noble than the necessary.[2] In this sense, science has less to do with the eternal, absolute, and necessary conclusions derived from syllogistic reasoning. It has more to do with what can be concluded with certainty from the observable phenomena. Science is both a coherent body of propositions deduced from analytic first principles and the certain *habitus* within the knower, based upon inferential judgment and experience.

The contingent order, we have seen, depends upon the freedom of a personal God, and not upon the categories of Aristotelian necessity. For Scotus, this endows the created order with a nobility of preference. The fact that the Creator could have realized any number of other worlds makes the existence of this world an act of divine love and generosity. This world had no intrinsic reason why it should be created over any other, in the same way that a work of art has no intrinsic reason why it should exist, other than the desire of the artist to express herself in this particular way. Thus, the existence

---

2. *Questions on the Metaphysics* IX, q. 15, n. 7 (II:615).

of the created order reveals not divine arbitrary exercise of freedom, but, rather, a glimpse into the divine intent. In other words, if this is the world that was created and, additionally, if its creation owes nothing to itself, it owes everything to the nature of God, benevolent and generous Creator.

Indeed, the theological framework, and specifically what Scripture reveals about the nature of God, is the key to Scotus's philosophical vision.[3] Natural reason can advance to a first being but, in the absence of revelation, can say nothing of significance about this being. Even the term *ens infinitum,* infinite being, the culmination of the philosophical reflection on being and its foundation is a formal definition, an empty term, with no natural referent. As Scotus states in the *De primo principio,* all natural reason can say of this term is that it involves no contradiction. The summit of natural reflection, then, establishes the conditions for the possibility of revelation. Once revealed, the divine nature functions as critical term from which to correct philosophical conclusions. The domain of faith depends on revelation in the same way that all philosophical reasoning depends upon first principles. Revelation establishes those propositions which found the certainty of *sacra doctrina,* the science of theology.

The superiority of faith to reason, indeed the ability of faith to critique reason, depends upon two conditions. The first is the logical relationship between the conclusions of reason and how they establish the formal categories which revelation fills in. From *ens commune* to *ens infinitum,* philosophical reasoning moves from the created to the uncreated order. Once reached, theological conclusions inform philosophical reflection. Theology takes over from *ens infini-*

3. Here we complement the work of Richard Cross who subtitled his *The Physics of John Duns Scotus* the "philosophical background to a theological vision." One can view either philosophy or theology as background. As in a Gestalt figure, what one focuses on as the background changes how one understands the foreground. When theology is the background, then key philosophical terms such as contingency, freedom, and rationality take on a different meaning.

tum and, armed with revelation, fills out the contours of the real. The second condition for the superiority of faith recalls the Scotist emphasis upon contingent, subjective certainty that belongs to the knower as the *habitus* of science. Faith has both objective and subjective superiority over reason. As an objective body of knowledge, faith reasons to conclusions that lie beyond the ken of philosophy. These conclusions are based on the criteria of logic and so, in this way, the domain of rational faith includes and transcends the domain of natural reason. In addition, as a subjective state, the certainty of faith surpasses the domain of philosophical inference. In this way the believer has a higher vantage point from which to view the conclusions of the philosopher. This higher point is the subjective place of cognitive certainty, to which no philosophical conclusions can compare.

In these two points, that is, in the shift to the contingent order and the superiority of faith to reason, we must see the important historical event that was the Condemnation of 1277. Scotus was not alone in his focused attention to these two points. He belonged to a lively dialogue at the end of the thirteenth century in which these points were central. What makes his contribution different from that of someone like Henry of Ghent, however, is the way in which Scotus uses Aristotle and Aristotelian philosophy to critique and correct the errors of the philosophers. Rather than appeal to the Augustinian tradition and to re-instate it within a type of reactionary return to the past, Scotus sees that Aristotle himself admits of other interpretations. He shows how one can successfully correct philosophical conclusions from within the Aristotelian perspective. In this way, natural reason is a self-transcendent activity and Aristotle himself gives way to a different vision of reality, without compromising fundamental philosophical categories.[4]

4. See Ephrem Bettoni, "The Originality of the Scotist Synthesis," in *John*

In the domain of epistemology, as we have seen, Scotus uses the categories of revelation to approach the question of cognition and the use of language. It is the beatific vision, along with its natural conditions, that inform the development of the double cognitive capacity of abstractive and intuitive intellection. Human nature, rather than the human condition, serves as the point of departure for a reflection that argues for the possibility of certain knowledge, the immediate experience of extra-mental reality, and the subjective awareness of internal states. Consideration of the way the mind is present to all that exists reveals the richness of all reality in the formalities. Further reflection unveils the ultimate condition within reality that is required for any knowledge or language about what is real: the univocity of being. Scotus moves by means of a *via resolutionis* (reflective analysis) to affirm the necessary condition for any human knowledge of reality or of God. Language use and the capacity of the mind to express itself to itself in a scientific manner requires the foundational nature of the concept *ens*.

In his discussion of cognition, Scotus balances the objective and subjective fields, with a slight tilt toward the subjective realm. The act of intuitive cognition turns the attention of the philosopher from knowing as a representational act to knowing as an act both immediate and certain. In his "critique" of Aristotelian cognitive theory, Scotus both affirms and transcends Greek philosophy. He accepts the theory of *De anima* and goes beyond it, by endowing natural reason with even more perfection: direct access to reality, if only in the act of existence.

In the domain of metaphysics, Scotus takes what had been a minor element of the metaphysical domain (the transcendentals) and makes of them the primary object of the study of metaphysics. In this way, he opens the tradition to a reflection upon the categories

---

Duns Scotus 1265–1965, ed. J. Ryan and B. Bonansea (Washington, D.C.: Catholic University of America Press, 1965), 28–44.

for thought, categories that transcend and ground the contingent, physical experience. Metaphysics was, for him and those who followed him, understood primarily as a science of the transcendentals. The univocal concept, *ens in quantum ens* (a being insofar as it is), presents metaphysics as ontology, or the science of what exists understood insofar as it exists and is present to the knower. As such, this object of metaphysical reflection is encountered as a concept within consciousness. Thus the domain of metaphysical reflection is truly located, not in extra-mental reality, but in reality as it is known by the mind. Metaphysics, logic, and epistemology are thus intimately connected.

Among those insights that will be important for later philosophical development belongs the Scotist conviction (later advocated most notably by Immanuel Kant) that prior to the elaboration of any metaphysics, one must inquire first as to its possibility. This means, more precisely, an investigation of the possibility of the knowability of its object. While Aristotle had already indicated the problem of knowing the object of metaphysics, Scotus develops a critique of the epistemological grounding for this discipline. In this he points out both the possibilities and boundaries of human cognition. The object of metaphysics can only be derived from the point of departure of cognition of the corporeal world that is possible by means of sense perception. This cognition involves both abstractive and reductive analyses. Such cognition is *a posteriori,* yet it claims necessary validity because its contents are the necessary aspects of contingent being. In this way, metaphysics can rightfully claim a scientific status. By his method of developing a metaphysics that deals with the conceptual realm, Scotus prepares the way for Ockham to develop more fully a universal formal semantics.[5]

5. On this, see L. Honnefelder, "Der zweite Anfang der Metaphysik," in *Philosophie im Mittelalter. Entwicklungslinien und Paradigmen,* ed. J. Beckmann et al. (Hamburg: Felix Meiner, 1987), 165–86.

Scotus's modal doctrine also proves to be fruitful for later philosophical development. His use of logical possibility as an operative methodology for his understanding of creation as contingent and dependent upon the voluntary self-determined act of God, along with his understanding of divine *synchronic* freedom, opens up the possibility for a new interpretation of the world. The contingency of all that exists is radicalized, introducing possibles that were not actually willed into existence by God. Here, of course, we recognize the conception of possible worlds, developed later by Leibniz. In addition, Scotus's presentation of divine freedom replaces the Aristotelian model for causality. Issues arising within the development of this model based upon divine freedom and omnipotence are discernible in the thought of both Ockham and Descartes.

Finally, in the domain of ethics, the rejection of a philosophical teleology in the manner of the *Nicomachean Ethics* X, 6–9, focuses the reflection upon the will and the act of ordered loving as fully perfective of human rationality. The rational will constitutes the horizon within which moral perfection is best considered. Given the rejection of the intellectualist model for human perfection, the criterion for moral goodness was located at a foundational level in first practical principles that are certain. In this way, a rational ethics grounded on *praxis* has an indubitable first principle, *Deus diligendus est,* a moral maxim whose intrinsic goodness is prior to any act of the will and evident to all rational agents.

The moral expert is both capable of correct moral judgment and, at a more foundational level, a self-directed moral orientation. Prudence sees both the external, contingent requirements for right action and, more importantly, the self-perfecting dynamic of right and ordered loving within the will. Prudence unifies the moral life as its source in directing the will's right willing. The ultimate fulfillment of moral life, the order of merit, is left for theological reflection. These ethical elements will continue most directly in Ockham and

Buridan, but are clearly discernable in the philosophy of Immanuel Kant.

Scotus's philosophical legacy, then, can be summarized as an attention to personal, subjective awareness, in light of rational principles. These principles link logic, ontology, and ethics to form a whole whose unifying principle is the person in the act of self-reflection. In his followers, these principles will be developed and enhanced throughout the fourteenth century. The principles will influence the thought of Ockham, as we know, but also thinkers such as Suarez, Molina, Leibniz, Wolff, and Kant. They will echo in the development of the Reformed tradition, in Luther and Calvin. Finally, the tradition of C. S. Peirce and American Pragmatism will find in Scotist thought a fruitful source of philosophical reflection.

As important as the historical significance of Scotus might be, his value for contemporary reflection may prove far greater. In what follows, we trace out what, in our opinion, unifies Scotist thought and represents his significance for our own day.

Scotus is a thinker who is pre-occupied with the act of *presence:* God's presence to the world, the presence of the mind to reality and to itself, the presence of being to cognition, the presence of the moral agent to a given set of circumstances. The act of presence is an act that unites intellect and will. Presence is founded in the intellect, for as Augustine holds, "what is so present to the mind as the mind itself?"[6] Presence is additionally an act of love, for in the act of love the lover is united to the beloved.

Scotus is an incarnational thinker: his philosophical vision is framed by his Christian commitment to the Incarnation as fullest revelation of the divine in time. The God of Judeo-Christian revelation is Emmanuel, God-with-us. The immanent presence of God to all that exists, as creative and sustaining cause, and the presence of

6. *De trinitate* X, 10, in *The Trinity,* 294.

Jesus Christ as incarnate God play an important role in Scotus's philosophical vision. The divine is not to be known or loved outside of time and space, in an eternal now that transcends anything human reason can know. Indeed, the now of eternity is the now of the contingent moment. Human reason enters the domain of the divine by means of attention to the present moment, not by withdrawal from the contingent order. In this act of presence to what is present, human reason imitates divine activity. God is present to each moment in an act of loving immediacy. This presence conserves and sustains all that exists and all that occurs.

Scotus did not have the benefit of a life long enough to complete his thought on the way God knows future contingent events. However, he clearly rejected the model offered by Boethius and Aquinas, a model that depicted God as someone in a tower, looking at all that took place on the ground below. From the vantage point of eternity, and therefore outside of time, God sees all in an "eternal present"; his knowledge is therefore necessary, that is, necessarily true, without influencing the order of human willing that occurs within time. For Scotus, God's knowledge must be a function of his presence to the event, that is, a function of the divine will and not the divine intellect. In this way, for Scotus, God's knowledge of future events must be contingent, not necessary, because the events themselves are contingent and because God is contingently present through the divine will. God is not, then, outside of time, but sempiternally *present* at every moment and to every event as it takes place within time.

Just as God is present to all that exists, so too the human mind experiences presence both to itself and to reality. Scotus corrects the Aristotelian representational cognitive model because it introduces a distance between the mind and reality. While he is willing to attribute such distance to fallen human reason, he is unwilling to conclude that this is the only way the mind relates to reality. When he introduces the act of intuition as a second mode of intellectual presence, he not only corrects the representational act that might separate the mind from the extra-mental world, but also establishes the conditions necessary for the beatific vision. If human reason cannot be present to reality, then it cannot be present to God in eternity without some sort of supernatural transformation. The most perfect act of cognition on the part of the blessed, intuition, lies beyond human capacity not because of a lack of nature, but because its object is the most perfect being whose presence can only be experienced as an *obiectum voluntarium*.

Internal acts of self-presence certify the possibility of intuition as part of the natural constitution of human reason. Even though the most obvious acts of scientific reflection are representational in nature, and therefore reveal the present condition of human cognition (abstraction), human reason is capable of certain and immediate acts of internal, subjective awareness. Self-awareness reveals a non-representational act, immediate and certain. Attention to one's own inner state reveals the highest cognitive act: that which constitutes the beatific vision. In addition, the act of intuitive cognition offers the conditions for the possibility of repentance and conversion. In short, the human mind *pro statu isto* lacks nothing of what it needs for the most important human experience.

Being, all being, reveals itself to consciousness in the act of presence. Scotus's vision reveals the continual epiphany at work in reality. The mind brings forth (births) knowledge from its encounter with its object: all that exists. There are only two requirements for intellection: the mind and the object. Both function equally in the activity of cognition. This activity, as we have noted, admits of two modes: abstraction and intuition. By means of these modes, the intellect is present to the world. Through the double lens, the world is present to the mind. The univocal concept *being* reveals itself as the condition for knowledge, whether in the act of existential awareness (intuition) or in the presence of the object in its essence (abstraction).

This presence of being, a univocal concept, makes possible the use of language to express the experience of what transcends sense knowledge. The univocal concept, *being*, along with its transcendent attributes (true, good, one), frames the horizon of language and cognition. The concept offers the unity required of a science. It is the science of the trans-physical that grounds the physical. It frames both the possibility of metaphysics as a science and, more importantly, theology as meaningful discourse about God.

Finally, Scotus developed a dramatic shift in moral theory. Now, the person as moral agent is present to concrete reality in imitation of the way that God is present to the created order. The person imitates the divine in bringing forth beauty in the contingent. The first principles of practical reasoning are immediately present to the moral agent, and in that immediacy, are certain and indubitable. They frame and unify the domain of *praxis* and the development of the moral agent as rational. The coherent body of knowledge, moral science, whether understood as epistemically separate from first principles and the judgments of prudence (the traditional interpretation) or a unified mental *habitus* of practical reasoning (Scotus's innovative second possibility in *Ordinatio* III, d. 36), is present both to the person and to the contingent state of affairs. The truths of practical reasoning are present in the world because the person is present in that world. The moral expert incarnates moral truth with an immediacy and creativity that mirrors the divine presence to all that exists.

The moral domain is a domain of beauty, pleasing both to human reason and to God. In the perfect moral judgment all elements are present to the mind and to one another, forming a harmonious whole. The moral agent is present to the elements of the moral situation, thanks to abstractive and intuitive cognition. In the fully formed moral expert, such knowledge functions in an immediate manner, leading to a swift judgment about what one should do. But whether one reasons painstakingly, as would the neophyte, or swiftly, as would the expert, it is the person herself who bridges the distance between first practical principles and the moral command. Scotus's depiction of moral perfection is a personification of moral excellence, present to the contingent order of reality with a freedom that imitates divine creativity.

As a Christian philosopher Scotus brings to the fore the conditions required to defend human dignity as created by God. Human nature, as created, lacks nothing for its complete perfection. Even the consequences of sin do not hinder the human ability to know reality, to know God, and to use language and reason in ways that express excellence. The philosophical vision he presents is a personalized vision, based upon the Incarnation as fullest expression both of human nature and of the way in which God is present to the created order. It is a relational vision, to the extent that all things cooperate in the birth of knowledge, the birth of goodness, the birth of grace. It is a realm defined by presence, a rational whole created and sustained by God, who reveals divine nature in the world of beauty that surrounds the human mind and attracts the human heart.

SELECT BIBLIOGRAPHY

Iohannis Duns Scotus. *Opera omnia.* Wadding-Vivès, 1891.

Iohannis Duns Scotus. *Opera.* Civitas Vaticana: Typis polyglottis Vaticanis, 1950–2003.

Ioannis Duns Scoti. *Quaestiones super libros metaphysicorum Aristotelis. (Opera Philosophica* 3–4). St. Bonaventure, NY: Franciscan Institute, 1997.

John Duns Scotus. *Questions on the Metaphysics of Aristotle by John Duns Scotus.* Translated by G. Etzkorn and A. B. Wolter. St. Bonaventure, NY: Franciscan Institute, 1997.

John Duns Scotus. *A Treatise on God as First Principle.* Translated and edited with a commentary by A. B. Wolter. Chicago: Franciscan Herald Press, 1966.

John Duns Scotus. *God and Creatures: The Quodlibetal Questions.* Translated by F. Alluntis and A. B. Wolter. Princeton: Princeton University Press, 1975.

Duns Scotus: Philosophical Writings. Translated and edited by A. B. Wolter. Indianapolis: Hackett Press, 1987.

Duns Scotus on the Will and Morality. Translated by A. B. Wolter. Washington, D.C.: Catholic University of America Press, 1986.

Duns Scotus, Metaphysician. Translated and edited by W. Frank and A. B. Wolter. West Lafayette: Purdue University Press, 1995.

Reportatio IA. Edited with an English translation by O. Bychkov and A.B. Wolter. St. Bonaventure, NY: Franciscan Institute, forthcoming 2004–2005.

Aertsen, Jan. *Medieval Philosophy and the Transcendentals: The Case of Thomas Aquinas.* Studien und Texte zur Geistesgeschichte des Mittelalters 52. Leiden: Brill, 1996.

——. "Beauty in the Middle Ages: A Forgotten Transcendental?" *Medieval Philosophy and Theology* 1 (1991): 68–97.

Alexander of Hales. *Summa theologica.* Quarrachi: Ad Claras Aquas, 1924–.

Anselm. *Monologion and Proslogion.* Translated with an introduction by Thomas Williams. Indianapolis: Hackett, 1995.

——. *De Casu Diaboli. Anselm of Canterbury: The Major Works.* Edited by B. Davies and G.R. Evans. Oxford: Oxford University Press 1998.

Aquinas, Thomas. *Summa Theologiae.* Translated by the Fathers of the English Dominican Province. New York: Benziger 1947.

Aristotle. *The Complete Works of Aristotle.* Edited by J. Barnes. Princeton: Princeton University Press, 1984.

Aubenque, Pierre. "La <<phronésis>> chez les stoiciens." *La prudence chez Aristote,* 184–5. Paris: Presses Universitaires de France, 1986.

Augustine. *The Trinity.* Introduction, translation, and notes by Edmund Hill, O.P. Brooklyn: New City Press, 1991.

Avicenna (Ibn Sina). *Liber De Philosophia Prima sive scientia divina,* I–IV, edited by S. Van Riet. Leiden: E.Peeters 1977.

Balic, Carlo. "Une question inédite de Duns Scot sur la volonté." *Recherches de Théologie Ancienne et Médiévale* 3 (1931): 198–208.

Barth, Timothy. "Being, Univocity and Analogy According to Duns Scotus." In *John Duns Scotus, 1265–1965.* Edited by J. Ryan and B. Bonansea, 210–62. Washington, D.C.: Catholic University of America Press, 1965.

Beckmann, J. P. "Entdecken oder Setzen? Die Besonderheit der Relationstheorie des Duns Scotus und ihre Bedeutung für die Metaphysik." In *John Duns Scotus: Metaphysics and Ethics.* Edited by L. Honnefelder, R. Wood, and M. Dreyer, 367–84. Studien und Texte zur Geistesgeschichte des Mittelalters 53. Leiden: Brill, 1996.

Bérubé, Camille. *La connaissance de l'individu au Moyen Age.* Paris: Presses Universitaires de France, 1964.

Bettoni, Ephrem. *Duns Scotus: Basic Principles of His Philosophy.* Washington, D.C.: Catholic University of America Press, 1961.

——. "The Originality of the Scotist Synthesis." In *John Duns Scotus, 1265–1965.* Edited by J. Ryan and B. Bonansea, 28–44. Washington, D.C.: Catholic University of America Press, 1965.

Bianchi, L., and Randi, E. *Vérités Dissonantes: Aristote à la fin du Moyen Age*. Fribourg/Paris: Cerf, 1993.

Boler, John. "Transcending the Natural: Duns Scotus on the Two Affections in the Will." *American Catholic Philosophical Quarterly* 57 (1993): 109–26.

Bonaventure. *Collationes in Hexaemeron*. Edited by F. Delorme. Quarrachi: Ad Claras Aquas, 1934.

Boulnois, Olivier. *Jean Duns Scot: Sur la connaissance de Dieu et l'univocité de l'étant. Introduction, traduction et commentaire*. Paris: Presses Universitaires de France, 1988.

———. "La présence chez Duns Scot." In *Via Scoti: Methodologica ad mentem Joannis Duns Scoti*. Edited by L. Sileo, I:95–119. Rome: Edizione Antonianum, 1995.

———. "Duns Scot, théoricien de l'analogie de l'être." In *John Duns Scotus: Metaphysics and Ethics*. Edited by L. Honnefelder, R. Wood, and M. Dreyer, 293–315. Studien und Texte zur Geistesgeschichte des Mittelalters 53. Leiden: Brill, 1996.

———. *Duns Scot: La rigueur de la charité*. Paris: Cerf, 1998.

Courtenay, William. *Schools and Scholars in Fourteenth-Century England*. Princeton: Princeton University Press, 1987.

———. "The Parisian Franciscan Community in 1303." *Franciscan Studies* 53 (1993): 155–73.

———. "The Instructional Programme of the Mendicant Convents at Paris in the Early Fourteenth Century." In *The Medieval Church: Universities, Heresy and the Religious Life (Essays in Honour of Gordon Leff)*. Edited by P. Biller and B. Dobson, 77–92. The Boydell Press, 1999.

———. "The Parisian Faculty of Theology in the Late Thirteenth and Early Fourteenth Centuries." In *After the Condemnation of 1277: Philosophy and Theology at the University of Paris in the Last Quarter of the Thirteenth Century*. Edited by J. Aertsen, K. Emery, and A. Speer, 235–47. Berlin: Walter de Gruyter, 2001.

Cross, Richard. *The Physics of Duns Scotus*. Oxford: Clarendon Press, 1998.

———. *John Duns Scotus*. Oxford: Great Medieval Thinkers Series, 1999.

Day, Sebastian. *Intuitive Cognition: A Key to the Later Scholastics*. St. Bonaventure, NY: Franciscan Institute, 1947.

Dod, Bernard G. "Aristoteles latinus." In *The Cambridge History of Later Medieval Philosophy*. Edited by N. Kretzmann, A. Kenny, and J. Pinborg, 45–79. Cambridge: Cambridge University Press, 1982.

Dreyer, Mechthild. "Wissenschaft als Satzsystem: Die *Theoremata* des Johannes Duns Scotus und die Entwicklung des Kategorisch-Deduktiven Wissenschaftsbegriffs." In *John Duns Scotus: Metaphysics and Ethics*. Edited by L. Honnefelder, R. Wood, and M. Dreyer, 87–105. Studien und Texte zur Geistesgeschichte des Mittelalters 53. Leiden: Brill, 1996.

Dumont, Richard. "Intuition: Prescript or Postscript to Scotus' Demonstration of God's Existence." In *Deus et homo ad mentem I. Duns Scoti.* Edited by C. Bérubé, 81–87. Rome: Cura Commissionis Scotisticae, 1972.

Dumont, Stephen. "Theology as a Science and Duns Scotus's Distinction between Intuitive and Abstractive Cognition." *Speculum* 64 (1989): 579–99.

——. "The Question on Individuation in Scotus's *Quaestiones super metaphysicam.*" In *Via Scoti: Methodologica ad mentem Joannis Duns Scoti*. Edited by L. Sileo, I:193–228. Rome: Edizione Antonianum, 1995.

——. "William of Ware, Richard of Conington and the *Collationes Oxonienses* of John Duns Scotus." In *John Duns Scotus: Metaphysics and Ethics*. Edited by L. Honnefelder, R. Wood, and M. Dreyer, 59–85. Studien und Texte zur Geistesgeschichte des Mittelalters 53. Leiden: Brill, 1996.

——. "Did Scotus Change His Mind on the Will?" In *After the Condemnation of 1277: The University of Paris in the Last Quarter of the Thirteenth Century.* Edited by J. Aertsen, K. Emery, and A. Speer, 719–94. *Miscellanea medievalia* 28. Berlin: Walter de Gruyter, 2001.

Effler, R. *John Duns Scotus and the Principle "Omne quod movetur ab alio movetur."* St. Bonaventure, NY: Franciscan Institute, 1962.

Frank, William. "Duns Scotus' Concept of Willing Freely: What Divine Freedom Beyond Choice Teaches Us." *Franciscan Studies* 42 (1982): 68–89.

Ghisalberti, A. "Ens infinitum e dimonstrazione dell'esistenza di Dio in Duns Scoto." In *John Duns Scotus: Metaphysics and Ethics*. Edited by L. Honnefelder, R. Wood, and M. Dreyer, 415–34. Studien und Texte zur Geistesgeschichte des Mittelalters 53. Leiden: Brill, 1996.

Gilson, Etienne. "Avicenne et le point de départ de Duns Scot." *Archives d'histoire doctrinale et littéraire du moyen age* (1927): 89–149.

Grajewski, M. *The Formal Distinction of Duns Scotus: A Study in Metaphysics.* Washington, D.C.: Catholic University of America Press, 1944.

Hissette, Roland. *Enquête sur les 219 articles condamnés à Paris le 7 mars 1277.* Louvain-Paris, 1977.

Hoeres, W. *Der Wille als reine Vollkommenheit nach Duns Scotus.* Salzburger Studien zur Philosophie 1. Munich: Pustet, 1962.

Hoffmann, Tobias. "The Distinction between Nature and Will in Duns Scotus." *Archives d'histoire doctrinale et littéraire du Moyen Age* 66 (1999): 189–224.

Honnefelder, Ludger. *Ens Inquantum Ens. Der Begriff des Seienden als solchen als Gegenstand der Metaphysik nach der Lehre des Johannes Duns Scotus.* In *Beiträge zur Geschichte der Philosophie und Theologie des Mittelalters* N.F. 16. Münster: Aschendorff, 1979.

———. "Der zweite Anfang der Metaphysik," in *Philosophie im Mittelalter. Entwicklungslinien und Paradigmen.* Edited by J. Beckmann et al, 165–186. Hamburg: Felix Meiner, 1987.

———. *Scientia Transcendens. Die formale Bestimmung der Seiendheit und Realität in der Metaphysik des Mittelalters und der Neuzeit (Duns Scotus— Suárez—Wolff—Kant—Peirce).* Hamburg: Felix Meiner, 1990.

———. "Die Kritik des Johannes Duns Scotus am kosmologischen Nezessitarismus der Araber: Ansätze zu einem neuen Freiheitsbegriff." In *Die abendländische Freiheit vom 10. zum 14. Jahrhundert. Der Wirkungszusammenhang von Idee und Wirklichkeit in europäischen Vergleich.* Edited by J. Fried, 249–263. Sigmaringen 1991.

———. "Metaphysik und Transzendenz. Ueberlegungen zu Johannes Duns Scotus im Blick auf Thomas von Aquin und Anselm von Canterbury." In *Transzendenz: Zu einem Grundwort der klassischen Metaphysik.* Edited by L. Honnefelder and W. Schüßler, 137–61. Paderborn, 1992.

———. "Scientia in se—Scientia in nobis. Zur philosophischen Bedeutung einer wissenschaftstheoretischen Unterscheidung." In *Scientia und ars im Hoch- und Spätmittelalter.* Edited by A. Speer, 204–14. Miscellanea Mediaevalia 22. Berlin: Walter de Gruyter, 1994.

Ingham, Mary Elizabeth. "The Condemnation of 1277: Another Light on Scotist Ethics." *Freiburger Zeitschrift für Philosophie und Theologie* 37 (1990): 91–103.

———. *"Ea Quae Sunt ad Finem:* Reflections on Virtue as Means to Moral Excellence in Scotist Thought." *Franciscan Studies* 50 (1990): 177–95.

———. "Scotus and the Moral Order." *American Catholic Philosophical Quarterly* 47 (1993): 127–50.

———. "John Duns Scotus: An Integrated Vision." In *The History of Franciscan Theology.* Edited by Kenan Osborne, OFM, 185–230. St. Bonaventure: Franciscan Institute, 1994.

———. "Duns Scotus: Moral Reasoning and the Artistic Paradigm." In *Via*

Scoti: Methodologica ad mentem Joannis Duns Scoti. Edited by L. Sileo, II:825–37. Rome: Edizioni Antonianum, 1995.

———. "Moral Reasoning and Decision-Making: Scotus on Prudence." In *Moral and Political Philosophy in the Middle Ages.* Edited by C. Bazán, E. Andújar, L. Sbrocchi. 501–511. Ottawa: Legas, 1995.

———. *The Harmony of Goodness: Mutuality and Moral Living According to John Duns Scotus.* Quincy: The Franciscan Press, 1996.

———. "Practical Wisdom: Scotus's Presentation of Prudence." In *John Duns Scotus: Metaphysics and Ethics.* Edited by L. Honnefelder, R. Wood, and M. Dreyer, 551–71. Studien und Texte zur Geistesgeschichte des Mittelalters 53. Leiden: Brill, 1996.

———. "Duns Scotus, Morality and Happiness: A Reply to Thomas Williams." *American Catholic Philosophical Quarterly* 74 (2000): 173–95.

———. "Letting Scotus Speak for Himself." *Medieval Philosophy and Theology* 10, 2 (2001): 173–216.

———. "Did Scotus Modify His Position on the Relationship of Intellect and Will?" *Recherches de Théologie et Philosophie Médiévales* 69, 1 (2002): 88–116.

Kent, Bonnie. *Virtues of the Will: The Transformation of Ethics in the Late Thirteenth Century.* Washington, D.C.: Catholic University of America Press, 1995.

Kluxen, Wolfgang. "Welterfahrung und Gottesbeweis: eine Studie zum 'Tractatus de Primo Principio' des Johannes Duns Scotus." In *Deus et Homo ad Mentem I. Duns Scoti.* Edited by C. Bérubé, 47–59. Rome: Cura Commissionis Scotisticae, 1972.

Knuuttila, Simo. "Duns Scotus and the Foundations of Logical Modalities." In *John Duns Scotus: Metaphysics and Ethics.* Edited by L. Honnefelder, R. Wood, and M. Dreyer, 127–44. Studien une Texte zur Geistesgeschichte des Mittelalters 53. Leiden: Brill, 1996.

Kovach, Francis. "Divine and Human Beauty in Duns Scotus' Philosophy and Theology." In *Deus et Homo ad Mentem I. Duns Scoti.* Edited by C. Bérubé, 445–59. Rome: Cura Commissionis Scotisticae, 1972.

Libera, Alain de. *Penser au Moyen Age.* Paris: Seuil, 1991.

Lottin, O. *Psychologie et morale aux XIIe et XIIIe siècles.* Gembloux, 1957.

Marrone, Steven. "Henry of Ghent and Duns Scotus on the Knowledge of Being." *Speculum* 63, 1 (1988): 22–57.

———. "Aristotle, Augustine and the Identity of Philosophy in Late Thirteenth-Century Paris: The Case of Some Theologians." In *After the Con-*

demnation of 1277: Philosophy and Theology at the University of Paris in the Last Quarter of the Thirteenth Century. Edited by J. Aertsen, K. Emery, and A. Speer, 276–98. Berlin: Walter de Gruyter, 2001.

Möhle, Hannes. "Scotus's Theory of Natural Law." In *The Cambridge Companion to Duns Scotus.* Edited by Thomas Williams, 312–31. Cambridge: Cambridge University Press, 2003.

Noone, T. "Scotus's Critique of the Thomistic Theory of Individuation and the Dating of the *Quaestiones Super Libros Metaphysicorum, VII, q.13.*" In *Via Scoti: Methodologica ad mentem Joannis Duns Scoti.* Edited by L. Sileo, I:391–406. Rome: Edizione Antonianum, 1995.

———. "Universals and Individuation." In *The Cambridge Companion to Duns Scotus.* Edited by Thomas Williams, 100–28. Cambridge: Cambridge University Press, 2003.

Normore, C. "Scotus, Modality, Instants of Nature and the Contingency of the Present." In *John Duns Scotus: Metaphysics and Ethics.* Edited by L. Honnefelder, R. Wood, and M. Dreyer, 161–74. Studien und Texte zur Geistesgeschichte des Mittelalters 53. Leiden: Brill, 1996.

O'Connor, T. "From First Efficient Cause to God: Scotus on the Identification Stage of the Cosmological Argument." In *John Duns Scotus: Metaphysics and Ethics.* Edited by L. Honnefelder, R. Wood, and M. Dreyer, 435–54. Studien und Texte zur Geistesgeschichte des Mittelalters 53. Leiden: Brill, 1996.

Piché, D. *La Condamnation Parisienne de 1277.* Paris: Vrin, 1999.

Pini, G. "Notabilia Scoti super Metaphysicam: Una testimonianza ritrovata dell'insegnamentio di Duns Scoto sulla *Metaphysica.*" *Archivum Franciscanum Historicum* 89 (1996): 137–80.

Prentice, Robert. "The Contingent Element Governing the Natural Law on the Last Seven Precepts of the Decalogue, According to Duns Scotus." *Antonianum* 42 (1967): 259–92.

Putallaz, F. X. *Figures Franciscains: De Bonaventure à Duns Scot.* Paris: Cerf, 1997.

Roest, Bert. *A History of Franciscan Education (c. 1210–1517).* Leiden: Brill, 2000.

Rudavsky, T. M. "The doctrine of individuation in Duns Scotus." *Franziskanische Studien* 59 (1977): 320–77, 62 (1980): 62–83.

Söder, J. R. *Kontingenz und Wissen. Die Lehre von den futura contingentia bei Johannes Duns Scotus.* Beiträge zur Geschichte der Philosophie und Theologie des Mittelalters NF 49. Münster: Aschendorff, 1998.

Spade, P. V. *Five Texts on the Mediaeval Problem of Universals: Porphyry, Boethius, Abelard, Duns Scotus, and Ockham*. Indianapolis: Hackett, 1994.

Steenberghen, Fernand Van. "La philosophie à la veille de l'entrée en scène de Jean Duns Scot." In *De Doctrina I. Duns Scoti*. Edited by C. Bérubé, I:65–74. Rome: Cura Commissionis Scotisticae, 1968.

Sylwanowicz, M. *Contingent Causality and the Foundations of Duns Scotus's Metaphysics*. Studien und Texte zur Geistesgeschichte des Mittelalters 51. Leiden: Brill, 1996.

Teske R., S.J., ed. *Henry of Ghent: Quodlibetal Questions on Free Will*. Milwaukee, WI: Marquette University Press, 1993.

Verbeke, Gérard. *The Presence of Stoicism in Medieval Thought*. Washington, D.C.: Catholic University of America Press, 1983.

Vignaux, Paul. "Lire Duns Scot aujourd'hui." In *Regnum hominis et regnum Dei*. Edited by C. Bérubé, 33–46. Rome: Cura Commissionis Scotisticae, 1976.

———. "Métaphysique de l'exode, philosophie de la religion (A partir du *De primo principio* selon Duns Scot)." *Rivista di filosofia neo-scolastica* 70 (1978): 135–48.

———. "Valeur morale et valeur de salut." In *Homo et mundus*. Edited by C. Bérubé, 53–67. Rome: Cura Commissionis Scotisticae, 1984.

Vos Jaczn, A. *John Duns Scotus: Contingency and Freedom. Lectura I, 39. Introduction, Translation and Commentary*. Dordrecht, 1994.

Werner, H. J. "Die Erfassung des Schönen in seiner personalen und ethischen Bedeutung bei Duns Scotus." In *John Duns Scotus: Metaphysics and Ethics*. Edited by L. Honnefelder, R. Wood, and M. Dreyer, 535–50. Studien und Texte zur Geistesgeschichte des Mittelalters 53. Leiden: Brill, 1996.

Wieland, Georg. *Ethica: Scientia Practica*. Münster: Aschendorff, 1981.

———. "The Reception and Interpretation of Aristotle's Ethics." In *The Cambridge History of Later Medieval Philosophy*. Edited by A. Kenny, N. Kretzmann, and J. Pinborg, 657–72. Cambridge: Cambridge University Press, 1982.

———. "Happiness: The Perfection of Man." In *The Cambridge History of Later Medieval Philosophy*. Edited by A. Kenny, N. Kretzmann, and J. Pinborg, 673–86. Cambridge: Cambridge University Press, 1982.

Williams, Thomas. "The Libertarian Foundations of Scotus's Moral Philosophy." *The Thomist* 62 (1998): 193–215.

———. "From Metaethics to Action Theory." In *The Cambridge Companion to*

Duns Scotus. Edited by Thomas Williams, 332–51. Cambridge: Cambridge University Press, 2003.

Wippel, John. *The Metaphysical Thought of Godfrey of Fontaines.* Washington, D.C.: Catholic University of America Press, 1981.

Wolter, Allan B. *The Transcendentals and Their Function in the Metaphysics of Duns Scotus.* St. Bonaventure, NY: Franciscan Institute, 1946.

———. "Duns Scotus on the Necessity of Revealed Knowledge." *Franciscan Studies* 11, 3–4 (1951): 231–72.

———, and Adams, M. McCord. "Duns Scotus' Parisian Proof for the Existence of God." *Franciscan Studies* 42 (1982): 248–321.

———. *The Philosophical Theology of John Duns Scotus.* Edited by Marilyn McCord Adams. Ithaca: Cornell University Press, 1990.

———. *Duns Scotus' Early Oxford Lecture on Individuation.* Santa Barbara, CA: Old Mission, 1992.

———, and Blaine O'Neill. *Duns Scotus: Mary's Architect.* Quincy: Franciscan Press. 1992.

———. "Reflections on the Life and Works of Scotus." *American Catholic Philosophical Quarterly* 67 (1993): 1–36.

———. "John Duns Scotus." In *Individuation in Scholasticism: The Later Middle Ages and the Counter Reformation 1150–1650.* Edited by J. Gracia, 271–98. Albany: State University of New York Press, 1994.

———. "Alnwick on Scotus and Divine Concurrence." In *Greek and Medieval Studies in Honor of Leo Sweeney, SJ.* Edited by J. Carroll and J. Furlong, 255–83. New York: Peter Lang, 1994.

———. "Reflections about Scotus's Early Works." In *John Duns Scotus: Metaphysics and Ethics.* Edited by L. Honnefelder, R. Wood, and M. Dreyer, 37–58. Studien und Texte zur Geistesgeschichte des Mittelalters 53. Leiden: Brill, 1996.

INDEX

Absolute vs. ordained power. *See Potentia absoluta/ordinata*

Abstractive cognition, 9, 22–24, 25–33, 39, 123–24, 129–30, 205, 211; and common nature, 106 (*see also* Common nature); and ethics, 164, 173, 182, 191, 199; and knowledge of God, 44–46, 74–75

Adams, Marilyn M., 74

Aesthetic, 120, 143–44, 175, 177; artisan, 130; artistic judgment, 132–34, 175, 177, 181, 190; a category of moral goodness, 173–74, 176–77, 184, 211–12; and prudence, 187–88, 190

Affectio commodi. See Moral affections; Happiness

Affectio iustitia. See Moral affections

Agent intellect (*intellectus agens*), 18, 22, 25, 123; and phantasms, 107–8; and possible intellect, 47; and *quidditas*, 26–27, 41

Albert the Great, 3

Alexander of Hales, 177

Anselm of Canterbury, 8, 12, 119; ethical influence, 198, 202; moral affections in *De casu diaboli*, 151–52, 171–72; ontological argument for God's existence, 84–86; will's rational freedom, 156–62, 169–71

Aquinas, Thomas, 3, 12–13, 19, 21, 31, 125, 136, 174, 201–2, 209; and beatitude, 191–94; and virtue, 174

Aristotle, 2–4, 9, 17, 22, 25, 41, 58, 62, 78–79, 87–88, 174, 178, 182, 185, 191–94, 198–99, 200, 204, 206; and cognitional theory, 27, 31, 41, 42–48, 50, 73–74, 125, 209; and ethics, 122–23, 128–30, 151–56, 168–69, 171; and metaphysics, 53, 103–4, 107; and individuation, 109–10

Augustine: and ethics, 117–19, 143, 177, 198; illumination, 16–17, 19, 22, 25, 41, 45, 50, 79, 204, 208

Averroes, 3, 20; and metaphysics, 39, 59, 63, 67–68, 122

Avicenna, 3, 20, 55; and cognition, 36;

❈

The Philosophical Vision of John Duns Scotus was designed and composed in
Galliard with Charlemagne display type by Kachergis Book Design, Pittsboro,
North Carolina; and printed on 60-pound Glatfelter Natural and bound by
Edwards Brothers, Inc., Lillington, North Carolina.